L

Sotirios Christou

Books by Sotirios Christou

The Priest & The People Of God – 2003
revised as Images Of Formation – 2009
Evangelism & Collaborative Ministry – 2004
The Unsearchable Riches Of Christ – & Paul 2006
Informed Worship – 2007, revised 2010, 2014
The Psalms – 2010
Messianic & Intimate Psalms – 2010
The Psalms, Intimacy, doxology & Theology – 2011
Breathtaking Authority – 2013
Esther – 2013
Ruth & Esther – 2014
David, Jonathan & Saul – 2016

First published in Great Britain by Phoenix Books.
18 Bullen Close, Cambridge, CB1 8YU

ACKNOWLEDGEMENTS

I am pleased to give permission to Sotirios to use my late husband's painting *Let There Be Light* for the cover of his book.

My husband always believed that his paintings, although based on Bible stories, were nevertheless universal in their truth.

He said of his work: *'My paintings are not concerned with the surface appearance of people or things, but try to express something of the fundamental spiritual reality behind this surface appearance. I try to express in visible form the oneness and unity of this invisible power binding all things into one whole.*

I do not illustrate stories literally as I am not interested in the place or the people, but try to express what I feel is the deeper significance of each story for every individual throughout all time.'

Not long before John passed on, a book was published of fifty of his recent paintings entitled, ***'The Painted Word – Paintings of John Reilly'*** – which also includes the Bible passage that inspired each painting. John's book, also prints can be obtained from the theJohnreillygallery.co.uk or from the Amazon website.

CONTENTS

CHAPTER FOUR
DAVID

CHAPTER FIVE
DAVID, JONATHAN & SAUL

CHAPTER SIX
DAVID'S REIGN

PREFACE

Interpreting the narrative about Samuel and Saul is difficult because Samuel is conflicted, as he did not support the idea of a king, but had to go along with it because God agreed to his peoples' request. Saul, the Lord's choice as the first king of Israel, ends up a conflicted king after he is rejected by Samuel, and descends into paranoia. Samuel the last of the judges has to oversee the transition from judgeship to kingship, and 1 Samuel offers the continuity between the two systems. For Samuel this means stepping out of character and contradicting everything he has stood for and will stand.[1]The narrative about Samuel and Saul can be interpreted ambiguously, and Saul is not portrayed in a very positive manner. There may be a sense of injustice at his rejection, as David's sins are far, far more serious. When Samuel announces that Saul has been rejected as king, although he protests his innocence he does not contest it, as Saul cannot contend with Samuel, 'who articulates the most rigorous and demanding claims of covenantal theology.'[2]

One of the main themes of 1 Samuel is Israel's transition to the monarchy. 1 Samuel is not to be interpreted in isolation, as it is part of a much larger narrative. David Jobling believes, that 1 Samuel is a national autobiography about how Israel's present is related to its past. 1 Samuel and the surrounding narrative can be seen as national autobiography, forged out of long wrestling with the memory of the past and subject to constant revision up to a late date. He believes 'Samuel is more unstable and fragmented than the books around it because it is the book that deals with this transition head on. Judgeship and kingship meet in Samuel like two continental plates that as they distort each other leave a narrative landscape marked by every kind of thinly covered geological irregularity.'[3] We may well discern some theological irregularity in 1 Samuel and be conflicted at God's instructions to annihilate Israel's enemies, and also struggle to reconcile David the warrior with David the sweet psalmist of Israel.

The life of David is clearly inextricably linked to Jonathan and Saul. Fate and fortune, triumph and tragedy, honour and shame, dominate the landscape of their lives. We are not kings or heirs, nor warriors: and while the 21st century we live in is incomparably different, spiritual truths can be learned from these great men. When I was younger and lived in London and travelled on the underground, there was a poster advertising shoes. '*Start rite and you'll walk happily ever after.*' Sadly, that did not prove to be true for David or Saul, nor for Jonathan who was loyal to Saul unto death. It may also prove not to be true for us, as in time the misuse of authority, power, and sin, may gradually erode our faith in the Lord. This can happen insidiously and the issue at stake is, 'In whom do we trust – ourselves or the Lord?' Another major theme that recurs in 1 Samuel is 'Inquiring what the Lord's will is.'

David's courage in challenging Goliath, a sign of his faith in the Lord after being anointed with the Holy Spirit, his spirituality in The Psalms that reveal his relationship with the Lord, and his refusal to kill Saul – portray David at his best. But, there are also major flaws. Dark stains on his soul – his adultery with Bathsheba and the murder of Uriah – 2 Sam. Ch. 11, along with taking many wives, forbidden to the king in Deut. 17: 17. David, a charismatic and gifted young man, turns out to be a complex character. The spontaneous innocence of his youth, and his youthful precociousness in challenging Goliath, in time were eroded by the self-indulgence of Saul's political envy, his fear and jealous paranoia because of David's success as the Lord was with him: and also by David's serious sins that despised the Lord. Paul Borgman captures David's complexity: 'self-interested politician and pious worshipper: fierce warrior and accomplished musician: a king of justice and an adulterous murderer: an admitted sinner: terrible father. He is capable of simultaneous piety and political manoeuvering.'[4]

Sotirios Christou Cambridge January 2016

CHAPTER ONE

INTRODUCTION

ADONIS

David is a familiar and well known Bible character. He is the Old testament Adonis, the subject of the most celebrated Renaissance artists, from Donatello and Michelangelo to Caravaggio and Rembrandt. The statue of David is a masterpiece of Renaissance sculpture created between 1501 and 1504, by Michelangelo. It is a 14ft by 17ft with the base marble statue of a standing male nude. The statue represents the biblical hero David, a favoured subject in the art of Florence. Originally commissioned as one of a series of statues of prophets to be positioned along the roofline of the east end of Florence Cathedral, the statue was placed instead in a public square, outside the Palazzo della Signoria, the seat of civic government in Florence, where it was unveiled on 8 September 1504. The history of the statue begins before Michelangelo's work on it from 1501 to 1504. Prior to Michelangelo's involvement, the Overseers of the Office of Works of Florence Cathedral, consisting mostly of members of the influential woolen cloth guild, the Arte della Lana, had plans to commission a series of twelve large Old Testament statues for the buttresses of the cathedral. In 1410, Donatello made the first of these statues, a figure of Joshua in terracotta. A figure of Hercules, also in terracotta, was commissioned from the Florentine sculptor Agostino di Duccio in 1463 and was made perhaps under Donatello's direction. Eager to continue their project, in 1464, the *Operai* contracted Agostino to create a sculpture of David. A block of marble was provided from a quarry in Carrara, a town in the Apuan Alps in northern Tuscany. Agostino only got as far as beginning to shape the legs, feet and the torso, roughing out some drapery and probably gouging a hole between the legs. His association with the project ceased, for reasons unknown, with the death of Donatello in 1466, and ten years later Antonio Rossellino was commissioned to take up where Agostino had left off.

Rossellino's contract was soon terminated soon and the block of marble remained neglected for 25 years, all the while exposed to the elements in the yard of the cathedral workshop. This was of great concern to the Opera authorities as such a large piece of marble was not only costly but represented a large amount of labour and difficulty in its transportation to Florence. In 1500, an inventory of the cathedral workshops described the piece as 'a certain figure of marble called David, badly blocked out and supine.' A year later, documents showed that the Operai were determined to find an artist who could take this large piece of marble and turn it into a finished work of art. They ordered the block of stone, which they called The Giant, to be raised on its feet so that a master experienced in this kind of work might examine it and express an opinion. Though Leonardo da Vinci and others were consulted, it was Michelangelo only 26 years old, who convinced the Operai he deserved the commission. On 16 August 1501 Michelangelo was given the official contract to undertake this challenging new task. He began carving the statue on the 13th September, a month after he was awarded the contract. He would work on the massive statue for more than two years

Rembrandt's painting of Saul and David carries the complex dating 'circa 1651–1654 and circa 1655–1658.' His painting was bought in 1898 by the Director of Mauritshuis, Abraham Bredius who left it to the museum when he died in 1946. Bredius never doubted this was a Rembrandt painting but when the painter's works were reassessed in the 1960s and 1970s, Saul and David was rejected as a genuine Rembrandt by Rembrandt specialist Horst Gerson. Since then opinions about its provenance have been divided. Was it a Rembrandt done by one of his pupils or perhaps a joint work? In order to answer the question once and for all, the Mauritshuis brought together an international team of experts to research and restore Saul and David.

In modern day Israel, the concept of Zionism is inextricably linked with David. In every city, a major road or square is dedicated to his memory. Famous hotels and institutions bear the name of the son of Jesse. Patriotic songs, poems and books sing his praises and extol his virtues. For pious men and women, he is a role model and an ideal whose deeds of courage and honour act as a guiding light and an eternal inspiration, and whose admitted barbarities are indulgently swept aside as understandable human frailties. Since the 13th century, the very emblem of Judaism itself, the six pointed star, has borne David's name.

Tony Cartledge says 'The narratives in the books of Samuel have proved to be 'classics' in the sense that they frame the human condition in such a profound way, that generations of listeners and readers have found their own foibles, questions and aspirations mirrored in the story…The David story in particular, with its themes of greatness and tragedy, of virtue and shame, of war and peace, of family scandal and political intrigue, has inspired numerous retellings…Novelists, poets and playwrights have exploited a rich variety of themes from the Samuel narratives…In the pre-Renaissance period, David appeared in literature as a type – a pattern or prototype that foreshadows a later reality. David most often appears as a type of Christ, as the archetypal penitent, and as the model king.'[1]

SAMUEL

Samuel is one of the children in Scripture who grew up to be powerfully used by the Lord. He was a much longed for child by Hannah, his mother, who was childless. We do not know what made her offer in prayer her most precious desire to the Lord, a child, whom she would give back to the Lord all the days of his life – 1 Sam. 1:11. We can but speculate it was the Holy Spirit. Presumably, his mother must have told Samuel the story that led to his birth and why he lived with Eli the priest and his family, as she visited him at Shiloh each year. Exactly what he must have made of this we do not know. But it must have seemed a very strange thing to him as a young child, especially as he had no say in the matter. Nevertheless, we learn he grew up in the presence of the Lord – 2:21.

As in the Gospels, we only have one account about Jesus when he was a young boy, so too we only have one account about Samuel as a young lad – 3:1-41. As a young boy, Samuel is helping Eli in the sanctuary at Shiloh when the Lord appears to him and speaks to him with a severe message for Eli and his sons. This is the first time the Lord has spoken to him in this way and it was only on the third occasion at the prompting of Eli that he recognised it was the Lord. Samuel is destined to become a priest and a prophet whose reputation is established as he grows up, as the Lord spoke to him and 'revealed himself to him at Shiloh, by the word of the Lord' – 4:1, although after this the next mention of Samuel is an old man in 8:5. Samuel established the school for prophets, men who trained in the law of God who would interpret God's word to his people and tell the people what the Lord instructed them to. These schools flourished in the days of Elijah and Elisha, some apparently on the same sites where they had been instituted by Samuel. These prophets make an appearance in 1 Sam. 10:3-5, 19:18-24, and 2 Kings 2.[2]

The ark of the Lord had been captured by the Philistines – Ch. 4-5, and after its return to Israel, Samuel appeared and inaugurated a reformation that was almost a revolution in its far-reaching effects. All Israel assembled at Mizpah, and they drew water and poured it out before the Lord, fasted, acknowledged their sins, and Samuel judged the people – 7: 3-6. When the Philistines heard they were gathered at Mizpah, they went up to make war against them, and the people greatly feared and asked Samuel to pray continuously for them – 7:6-8. He presented a burnt offering unto the Lord and cried unto him for Israel, and the Lord answered by sending a terrific thunder storm which frightened the Philistines, and they were routed by Israel – 7:9-11. Samuel set up a monument to mark the victory between Mizpah and Shen, and called it Ebenezer, declaring that the Lord had been their helper – 7:12 After the defeat of the Philistines, Samuel judged Israel and went on a circuit from year to year to Bethel, Gilgal, Mizpah and Ramah his home, where he built an altar unto the Lord – 7:13-17.

John Goldingay's description of Samuel is as an impressive young man with clear potential for giving the sanctuary at Shiloh a new start. He perceives an austere side to Samuel that perhaps reflects the tough side of his early experiences.[3]

He certainly displayed an uncompromising tough response to Saul's failures. Like the time he slew Agag king of the Amalekites after Saul spared him – 15:32-33. Robert Alter has a much harsher view of Samuel who he describes as a densely imagined character and in many respects a rather unattractive one. He says, 'The prophet Samuel may have God on his side, but he is also an implacable, irascible man, and often a palpably self-interested one as well. His resistance to the establishment of the monarchy may express a commitment to the noble ideal of the direct kingship of God over Israel, but it is also motivated by resentment that he must surrender authority: and the second of his two antimonarchic speeches is informed by belligerent self-defensiveness about his own career as a national leader. When he chooses Saul, he wants to play him as his own puppet, dictating elaborate scenarios to the neophyte king, even setting him up for failure by arriving at an arranged rendezvous at the last possible moment. He is proud, imperious, histrionic – until the very end, when he is conjured up by Saul as a ghost on the eve of the fatal battle at Mount Gilboa.

It would be misleading, I think, to imagine any of this is intended to discredit the idea of prophetic authority. Samuel is invested with prophetic authority by an act of God. But the writer understands that he is also a man, all too human, and that any kind of power, including spiritual power, can lead to abuse. Samuel toys with the idea of creating a kind of prophetic dynasty through his two sons even though they are just as corrupt as the sons of Eli.'[4] Samuel is doctrinally very orthodox and always seems to be on a different spiritual plane than Saul. The narrator never gives the impression that Samuel is pro-Saul and one wonders whether the way he relates to him, is due to some transference because of his son's failures and his own failure as a father, and the fact that Saul as king means the end of his family's dynastic future, even though his sons are scoundrels. Samuel comes across as a prophet of doom, unlike, for example, Jeremiah, the prophet of tears, who keenly felt the impending judgment of the Lord on his people, and tried to avert it. One does not sense that Samuel has any empathy with Saul nor any sympathy for him.

Samuel represents the old tradition and as the last of the judges, he is reluctant to make the transition to kingship. *(To appreciate Samuel's difficulty a contemporary issue may be women as priests and bishops in the Church).*As the last of the judges, he also has to oversee the transition from judgeship to kingship, which involves contradicting everything he has stood for. Consequently, he is conflicted because he did not support the idea of a king, but had to go along with it because God agreed to his peoples' request. In his relationship with Israel and Saul, he continues to represent the old tradition that is passing and we may discern an undercurrent of subconscious opposition to Saul. Therefore, Samuel as the kingmaker is also the king-breaker. On the one hand, he anoints Saul and on the other, he appears to set him up to fail. Biblical commentators see an ambiguity and contradiction between 1 Sam. 10:7-8. Whereas in v. 7 Samuel appears to give Saul the authority to act independently as king, in v. 8 he instructs him to wait for him to arrive at Gilgal to offer sacrifices, after which he will show Saul what to do. The text is silent about the matter, so we don't know if Samuel's instructions were the Lord's. When we arrive at 13:8-15, Saul does not wait for Samuel and offers the burnt sacrifice himself. So Samuel announces Saul's rejection, but as we shall see, the text does not state this was on the Lord's authority. Saul is not allowed to break free of Samuel who represents the old order of judges, as he will not let him.

DAVID

David is one of the most colourful, familiar and popular Bible characters, and over the years he has attracted a great deal of scholarly attention. David is a courageous, handsome young man, charismatic, and as we shall see complex. He is also full of faith, powerfully anointed by the Holy Spirit, who after killing Goliath won the admiration of Saul, Michal his daughter, Jonathan, and all Israel who loved him – 1 Sam. Ch. 17-18. John Goldingay captures his complex nature when he says, 'We have David in all his ambiguity in 1 & 2 Samuel and David in 1 & 2 Kings that focuses on his faithfulness to Yahweh. There is David of The Psalms, ancient worship leader. There is David of 1 & 2 Chronicles. The Thomas Cranmer of the Old Testament, the man whose significance lay in the way he set up the worship of the Temple. There is David of the Prophets, whose far reaching promises from Yahweh constituted part of his guarantee of his future commitment to Israel…It seems that David was so important to Israel that his story needed repeated telling in different connections.'[5] Walter Brueggeman sees Kings & Samuel as being 'endlessly fascinated with David…before whom Israel pauses with a sense of awe.[6] Yet his life and exploits, his successes as a warrior, his sins, his marriages, his failure as a father, his adultery and murder of Uriah, his family tragedies of incest by Amnon with Tamar, the murder of Amnon by Absalom, the revolt of Absalom and his death by Joab, his Mafia like instructions to Solomon in 1 Kings 2: 5-8 on his deathbed to kill Joab and Shimei, resemble an ancient biblical soap opera.

In comparing David's failures and sins with those of Saul, their seriousness far outweigh Saul's. Despite God's severe judgment on David's family as punishment for his adultery with Bathsheba and the murder of Uriah, we are confronted by God's inscrutable ways through the birth of Solomon, and his salvation in a covenant with David. The Lord saw that kings to rule his people was a failure so through his covenant with David he would establish his kingly rule and kingdom through Christ. Isaiah Ch. 11:1-5 points to Jesus as a descendent of David, being a shoot from the stump of Jesse. Although the Lord forgave David for his adultery and murder, he declared his punishment on his family. David's self-indulgence leading to sin and disobedience to God's laws was the catalyst for tragedy that resulted in God's retribution. His sins of adultery and murder were replicated by members in his own family. In an act of self-indulgence, Amnon raped his sister by another mother and David did nothing about this, as he knew he was guilty of the sin of adultery. In turn, two years later, in an act of revenge, Absalom murdered Amnon, again David did nothing about this as he knew he was also guilty of murder. Absalom then fled from David, but after three years, he allowed him to return although he never spoke to him. When Absalom revolted against David in an attempt to seize the throne, against his father's wish he was murdered by Joab, who replicated the murder of Uriah David planned. There is a great sense of sadness and tragedy in David's family resulting from his sins of self-indulgence, the Lord described as 'despising the word of the Lord, to do what is evil in his sight' – 2 Sam. 12: 9 – which as a young man would have been unthinkable to David.

David's story in 1 & 11 Samuel is a powerful narrative, 'A masterpiece, unsurpassed in…psychological insight, literary style and dramatic power.'[7] In Israel's history as a united kingdom, the story of David is the longest and most important. A history that is recounted in the books of Samuel and Kings and retold in Chronicles. We also have around 73 Psalms that are attributed to David, some of which we identify with periods in his life, and allow us a glimpse into his faith and relationship with the Lord, and some of which prophetically point to Christ. David was a flawed hero whose successes were punctuated by serious sins. Sins that brought catastrophe on his family and threatened the nation. Yet despite his failures, the Lord committed himself in an unconditional covenant with David and Christ descended from his family line.

We may well have an idealistic or romantic image of David, a shepherd, a hero defeating Goliath, an attractive, charismatic, courageous young man with a remarkable faith in the Lord. 'Everyone seems to love him. He is beautiful. He is musical and he is brave…He is also from the start quite calculating.'[8] But as we probe deeper into the stories about him from the narrative biblical texts we discover that David is an intriguing character. 'The characterisation of David suggests a unique and complex individual, a most unusual king…His story is filled with suspenseful and surprising action, but the questions of character loom, driving much of what we think as plot.'[9] Paul Borgman captures David's complexity:

> '…self-interested politician and pious worshipper: fierce warrior and accomplished musician: a king of justice and an adulterous murderer: an admitted sinner and self proclaimed blameless one: brash, smooth-

> tongued talker and extraordinary listener: ruthless executioner and great weeper: fine administrator of people and terrible father...He is capable of simultaneous piety and political manoeuvering.[10]

More chapters in the Old Testament have been written about David than any other biblical character. Abraham and Joseph have eleven chapters each about their lives, Jacob has eleven chapters and Elijah ten. But in the books of Samuel, Kings and Chronicles, there are around sixty-six chapters about David, with fifty-nine references to his life in the New Testament.[11] It is no surprise if he is seen to be a complex and intriguing Bible character, chosen by God from the obscurity of looking after sheep to becoming king, and a national hero having defeated Goliath. From the anonymity as a shepherd after his victory over Goliath, David's life will never be the same again. After David's victory, his role as a soldier killing his enemies is alien to our experience. It is not surprising if we find it difficult to reconcile this with the spiritual dimension of his life from the psalms that he wrote. After killing Goliath, the early years of David's life are inextricably bound up with Jonathan and Saul. Saul in his awe of David and because of his insecurity was his relentless enemy, consumed with jealousy at his success as a warrior and by his popularity. If anyone had reason to be jealous of David, it was his son Jonathan who would have become king after his father's death. But Jonathan is a noble guileless character, filled with overwhelming admiration for David because of his courage in killing Goliath, and his remarkable faith in the Lord. His instant attachment and love for David led to Jonathan becoming his closest friend and advocate. Everyone loved David including Saul initially, his daughter Michal along with Jonathan, and all Israel and Judah and Saul's servants, as David was an attractive and charismatic figure who captured their imagination and adulation.

It is striking to reflect that David was on the edge of family life and naturally excluded when Samuel came to his household to anoint God's choice of a new king. As the youngest of eight brothers, his natural prospects were virtually non existent. Perhaps the isolation of looking after sheep, cultivated his imagination and contemplative spirit. In the outdoor panorama of God's creation, we perceive the Lord spoke to him through the natural revelation of creation and drew him into a relationship with himself. Equally, in his imagination, David may well have been a precocious young man with ambition. Perhaps he dreamed of joining Saul's army to make a name for himself.

IMAGES

The first image of David introduces us to him from God's perspective in 1 Sam 16, when Samuel was instructed by the Lord to go to Jesse's household to anoint the man after God's own heart as the future king – 1 Sam. 13: 14. When David is called to meet Samuel and then anointed king, he is 'quietly responsive'[12] and says nothing. In fact, the entire drama is played out in silence with no inquisitiveness from any family member recorded by the narrator, perhaps because Samuel did not tell them the purpose of the anointing. The second image of David's is introduced when Saul's servants suggest they find a man who is skillful in playing the lyre to alleviate his dark moods due to an evil spirit. They recommend David who they describe as: 'a son of Jesse the Bethlehemite who is skillful in playing, a man of valour, a warrior, prudent in speech, and a man of good presence and the Lord is with him' – 16:15-18. Although the narrator does not inform us how David's reputation has preceded him, Saul asks Jesse, David's father, to send him to his household. At this request, David complies and says nothing. He is, 'quiet, responsive and musical, a servant responding to solicitation, not a person initiating action or conversation. The quiescence here is almost a passivity. This quiescent, receptive and lyrical David resurfaces often in the story to come – for better or worse.'[13] When his father sends him with provisions for his brothers in Saul's army again he obeys and says nothing – 1 Sam 16:17. David comes across as self-contained, almost passive. But once he arrives at Saul's camp, he is assertive and confident. He takes the initiative and speaks out to challenge Goliath. He asks questions that indicate an extraordinary faith in the Lord and a fearless courage that point to future greatness. He is a precocious young man with a sharp mind, aware of a reward for slaying Goliath. The public figure that has stepped out onto Israel's political arena in challenging Goliath, contrasts with the private David looking after sheep. Robert Alter captures how his character evolves, as neither God nor Samuel give David any details or plan about how he will become king.

> The story of David is probably the greatest single narrative representation in antiquity of a human life evolving by slow stages through time, shaped and altered by the pressures of political life, public institutions, family and the impulses of body and spirit, the eventual sad decay of the flesh.[14]

After David has arrived at the battle scene with food for his brothers, he speaks to the men in the vicinity and says, 'What shall be done for the man who kills this Philistine and takes away the reproach form Israel? For who is this uncircumcised Philistine that he should defy the armies of the living God' – 1 Sam. 16:26-27. The third image of David is introduced when the soldiers who heard what he said, repeated his words to Saul, who sent for him. When David came before Saul he said, 'Let no one's heart fail because of him, your servant will go and fight with this Philistine. David is precocious, has a lot to say for himself, and also shows extraordinary confidence and courage that belies his youth. He tells Saul about his successful encounters with wild animals 'and that it was the Lord who saved me from the claw of the lion and the bear, who will save me from the hand of this Philistine' – 1 Sam. 17:37. Borgman says, 'This particular David displays initiative of word and daring-do, and will do so throughout the story ahead, for better or worse. The two David's Saul has met couldn't be more different, to be sure. The one David is silent, the other talks: one waits dutifully for a call to action like carrying lunch to his brothers or playing music for the king, the other talks without waiting and acts as if impulsively. The one David is musically gifted, the other militaristically brilliant: one exercises receptivity, the other initiative. What the text ahead will reveal, in fact, is not the superiority of one David over the other…

Rather, we will find an integrity of both Davids, in a coherent character whose greatness and wretchedness are spread evenly through all of his person, quiescent and active.'[15]

The fourth image of David is in fact his third introduction to Saul. In Ch. 17:55 after David has gone to fight Goliath, Saul asks Abner whose son 'the stripling is?' When David comes to Saul with Goliath's head, he asks him whose son he is – 17: 58. It does seem strange the narrator should portray Saul as being ignorant that David has been welcomed by him into the royal court as a musician. It is also a mystery that he did not recognise who David was when he came to Saul before he went to challenge Goliath. There is clearly confusion in Saul's mind about David's identity. Here biblical scholars note that there is an inconsistency in the sources about this issue, and question why the narrator – the final redactor tells the story in this way, and presents it in such a confusing manner. Perhaps Saul's mind has been numbed and paralysed by the fear Goliath has engendered and his impotence in dealing with it as the king. Or perhaps we can forgive Saul for not being able to reconcile David the quiet musician with this hero. Or Perhaps the narrator is introducing an element of mystery about who David is – simultaneously a shepherd, a musician in the royal court soothing Saul's dark moods, and now a national hero. 'David learned more than songs playing in the court of Saul. Harping and political intrigue, often with deadly outcomes, are part of a representation of court scenes.'[16] As a consequence of David's momentous victory over Goliath, we have the fifth and final image of David, when Saul promoted him as the general of his men and would not let him return to his father's house. He has gone from being an anonymous youth to a cult hero of charismatic proportion. He is established in Saul's royal court. Life will never again be the same for him

JONATHAN

After slaying Goliath, David's life was touched by the selfless friendship of Jonathan, which is compatible with the classical ideals of friendship. Most ancient authorities believed that friends had to be of equal rank with complete trust and be in total agreement in aims, ambitions and attitudes. They denigrated a friendship entered with the hope of selfish gain, and that a friend should be willing to sacrifice himself and all he possessed for his companion. Aristotle believed that for the sake of a friend, one should be willing, if necessary, to 'throw away both wealth and honours and in general the goods that are objects of competition.' Because of his love for David Jonathan willingly gives up any hereditary rights to the throne of Israel, while Saul finds such devotion to a friend incomprehensible and even traitorous. In the classical tradition, the ultimate goal of friends should be the rise of 'one's souls in bodies twain.' Such a merger of souls is also a step in the kind of love envisioned during the Renaissance. It was believed that a spiritual union was possible in such friendship, where the union of two souls was seen as the penultimate state, followed – if the love was pure and strong – by a merger with the Godhead.[17]

In the 17th Century Abraham Cowley raises to preeminent importance the relationship of David and Jonathan, seeing their love within the context of divine love, and who realise the Renaissance ideal of friendship – the duplication of divine love. As early as the 13th Century Thomas Aquinas notes, 'In the love of friendship, a man's affection goes out from itself...because he wishes and does good to a friend...caring and providing for him, for his sake.'[18]

One of the outstanding qualities of Jonathan was his devotion and loyalty – to David, to Saul and to his own family, couples with a spirit of sacrifice. Jonathan found himself torn between being loyal to his father and David. His love for them enabled him to be faithful to both. As a brave soldier himself, he was attracted by David's fearless courage in defeating Goliath with only a sling and stone, and full of admiration for his adventurous spirit. After David's victory over Goliath Jonathan displayed great generosity in making a covenant with him, giving him his robe, his armour, his sword and even his bow and girdle. As the king's son and heir, Jonathan's commitment in a covenant relationship to David was an unequivocal sign of his acceptance. This reflected the covenant between a powerful nation protecting a weaker ally. Although Jonathan made a covenant with David, he also chose to remain loyal to his father Saul. And while he stood up for David against his father who was determined to kill him, ultimately he was devoted to being at his father's side and died alongside him. Such was the noble character of Jonathan as he could have chosen to follow David in preference to his father. His death was a great tragedy and loss to Israel, to David and Jonathan himself. Had he lived, as a devoted colleague to David, we can imagine him being an invaluable commander of his army and closest companion and unselfish friend. Jonathan was equally devoted to his family and made David promise that he would be loyal him to and protect his family for ever, not letting the name of Jonathan be cut off from the house of David – 1 Sam. 20:14-17.

We also glimpse Jonathan's adventurous spirit and courage when with his armour bearer he stealthily seeks to attack the Philistines. In 1 Sam. Ch. 14 he goes to spy on the Philistine garrison, without informing his father. From this event in v. 6-15, we also see his faith in the Lord when he says, '…it may be that the Lord will work for us: for nothing can hinder the Lord from saving by many or by few. Behold we will cross over to the men and we will show ourselves to them. If they say to us, 'Wait until we come to you' then we will standstill in one place and we will not go up to them. But if they say, 'Come up to us' then we will go up, for the Lord has given them into our hand. And this shall be the sign to us…And the men of the garrison saw Jonathan and his armour bearer and said, 'Come up to us, we will show you a thing.' And Jonathan said to his armour bearer, 'Come up after me, for the Lord has given them into the hand of Israel. And they fell before Jonathan, and his armour bearer killed them after him: and that first slaughter…was of about twenty men within at it were half a furrow's length in an acre of land. And there was panic in the camp, in the field and among all the people: the garrison and even the raiders trembled, the earth quaked and it became a very great panic.'

What we also glimpse about Jonathan's character is the love that he inspires in the soldiers in Saul's army. In 14:24, Saul announces a curse if anyone ate food before his victory over his enemies that evening. However, Jonathan was not present and did not know about this and he ate some honey – 14:27. When Saul discovers this he intends to kill his son, but the people would not let him and they said to Saul, 'Shall Jonathan die who has brought about this great victory in Israel? Far be it from it! As the Lord lives not one hair of his head shall fall to the ground, for he did this today with God's help. So the people rescued Jonathan and he did not die' – 14: 45. Power meant nothing to Jonathan. He carried authority comfortably within himself. Jonathan had an air of nobility about him. He commanded respect and he was generous and big-hearted.[19]

Jonathan is an exceptional and a remarkable character as he aligns and identifies himself with David and sacrifices himself as the heir to Saul for David. Saul is not going to abdicate his kingdom for David, but Jonathan in some intuitive way knows that David is going to be king after Saul, and symbolically abdicates when he gives David his royal armour after he kills Goliath. In some mysterious way, 'Jonathan knows the divine plan and acts in accordance with it…Jonathan receives no revelations yet he knows…It is hopeless to try to explain Jonathan through standard categories of narrative…Without his mysterious knowledge he could not fulfill his role.'[20] Jobling also suggests that there is an, 'identification pattern between Jonathan and David. Jonathan oscillates between close identification with David and an emptying of himself into David, a readiness to be replaced by David as Saul's heir…The kingship has in effect already passed from Saul to David by the mediation of Jonathan…In 1 Sam. 23:17, Jonathan goes to David as a king – 'you shall be king over Israel, and I shall be next to you'[21] Jonathan's self-sacrifice can be compared with John The Baptist, who said about Jesus, 'He must increase and I must decrease' – John 3: 30.

SAUL

Saul was the leader the Lord chose when Israel wanted a king. His introduction in 1 Samuel 9 is as an impressive, tall and handsome young man. In Ch. 11 Saul is publically elected leader after the Lord acceded to the peoples' request for a king. Their expectation was that he would be a hero like the men in

Judges who delivered Israel from her enemies. However, when the public elections to choose the king are taking place, Saul hides himself. It is difficult to escape the impression that he did not want to be chosen and is a somewhat reluctant hero. In 1 Samuel the narrator portrays Saul in a negative light, and so there is a certain complexity and opaqueness in understanding his character between chapters 9-15. He is almost presented as an apology and foil for the introduction of David. Saul's apparent failure of disobedience to the Lord can be ambiguously interpreted when assessing his character and life. In the early chapters, there is almost a naïve youthful innocence about Saul. He does not seem to know anything and by contrast, his servant knows everything. Shaul Bar believes, 'The book of Samuel portrays Saul as a colourful personality with excesses …Evidently. there is a contradiction between his physical appearance and his behaviour, which points to his irreconcilable character.'[22]

As the story of Saul progresses, due to circumstances and the choices he makes, he is a tragic hero as he is rejected by the Lord. Samuel who anointed and elected Saul is a reluctant messenger, as he did not really endorse the idea of a king. Unfortunately, for Saul, Samuel will become his nemesis. He did not take into account that as a boy in the temple Eli the priest taught him the ways of the Lord and that he had a long apprenticeship learning to hear God's voice. But Saul was wrenched out of his rural life as a land owner and farmer and cast into the furnace of the peoples' heroic expectations under the vengeful eye of Samuel. No allowance was made for a young man, naïve and inexperienced in the ways of politics and prophetic intransigence, unschooled in hearing the voice of the Lord, as well as the expectations placed on him. What he needed was a sympathetic mentor – but in Samuel he encountered the reluctant emissary. It is not surprising if we discern Saul was conflicted and compromised as the first king of Israel.

Emil Bock describes the spirit of Saul he perceives in 1 Samuel, when he says, 'Saul was not a person of intellectual insight. The soul forces in his nature resembled the unpredictability of the weather and the raging of the elements…The ecstatic experiences *(due to being gripped by the prophets)* resembling intoxication that is not directed by the self, need not always bear a person upwards into pure, spiritual heights. Herein lies its ambiguity…Saul was not a sanguine person who responds to joy, he was a choleric. The key to his soul was rage: either the noble anger in which, enkindled by opposition, the stormy will to do good flamed up, or the sinister fury fed by selfishness…In the battles that he had to lead, it soon came about that Saul inwardly forfeited the kingship because of the ambiguity of his nature…Prior to the war against the Amalekites, Saul's soul could blaze in holy wrath and fervid activity. Afterwards, we see it erupt in demonic fury that is mixed with egotistical fear.'[23] Although I think it fair to say, Saul as king was not like this at the outset.

Saul was a young man when he became king and defeated many of Israel's enemies including the Ammonites, Philistines, Moabites and Amalekites, uniting the scattered tribes, giving them greater strength. The introduction to Saul in 1 Samuel 9:2-3, where he is described as handsome, taller than any of his contemporaries is inauspicious, as his father's she asses are lost and he is going with his servant to find them. In this incident, we have a striking contrast between Saul and his servant, where the latter takes the initiative. After several days, looking for the asses without success Saul suggests they return to his father, but his servant encourages him to find the man of God in the city who will help them in their quest – 9:5-6. Saul is reluctant as they have no gift to give him, but the servant says he has some silver, so he is persuaded to go – 9:7-10. Philips Long suggest there is a growing impression throughout these early verses the servant is taking the lead, as he is the one who mentions the existence of the man of God, and persists in finding him to a reluctant Saul. It is the servant who initiates and facilitates movement towards Samuel. By contrast, Saul appears hesitant, passive, tending to impede rather than further the action. He eventually concedes to his servant's initiative, and there is a certain misguidedness about Saul's action, compared to his servant's that leads to the providential encounter with Samuel. 'Perhaps the most disconcerting aspect of the portrayal of Saul in this first episode is his rather conspicuous ignorance of the 'man of God…In this regard, Saul again stands in contrast to his servant, who not only knows of the man of God's existence and whereabouts but also regards him as a respected individual whose every word comes true.'[24]

Long also perceives there is a contrast between the activity of the servant and the passivity of Saul that suggests a similar contrast between Saul and Jonathan in Ch. 14, as Jonathan takes the initiative and is the primary agent of deliverance with his armour bearer against the Philistines. These early incidents hint at a deficiency in Saul that becomes increasingly apparent as the narrative progresses.[25] Long points out that we can also detect a narrative analogy between Saul and Jonathan that enables a contrast between them which reveals how they act in similar situations. 'There is Saul's general passivity (14:2) that contrasts with Jonathan's activity: he initiates the action (13:3, 14:1, 6), while Saul simply responds to it (13: 3b, 14: 16-18). Jonathan succeeds in discovering Yahweh's will, even without access to oracular devices (14:9-10), while Saul is singularly unsuccessful on three occasions, and his commitment to the divine inquiry seems to deteriorate as the narrative progresses – in 13:8-9…14:18-19,14:36.'[26]

Barbara Green points out, 'The narrator's style often gives us access to Saul's private thoughts, so that we know what he is planning to do but often fails to accomplish. Whereas we rarely have any inside information about David, who comes across as enigmatic and holds his cards close to his chest.'[27] 'Saul's major characteristic is his refusal of responsibility, an incapacity for answerability. As we engage the story of this very human character, we see his struggles with so many difficulties, even those he himself invites. Saul's story involves him dealing with a silent deity, with minimal self-knowledge and with paltry social skills.'[28] Saul begins his reign at the start of 1 Sam. 13 and by the end of Ch. 15 he is rejected, yet he is still the king until the end of Ch. 31. 'His monarchy is short and long, its apparent end deferred past the moment of its actual demise…It is the story of a monarch(y) whose asking is shown deficient from its roots.'[29]

One of the characteristics that Saul displays in his reign as king is his reticence. A hint of this can be detected when after being anointed king by Samuel – 10:1 and being given a new heart by the Lord – 10:9, all the tribes come before Samuel and Saul is chosen by lot as king. But he could not be found anywhere because he had hidden among the baggage – 10: 21-22. Is this a sign of timidity or reticence that foreshadows a spirit of fear? There is an ironic incongruity about Saul, designated the king hiding behind the baggage. Yet if we give Saul the benefit of the doubt, is hiding a sign of his lack of confidence, a lack or self-esteem, or feeling unworthy, as he is from the least of the families of the smallest tribe?

We can perceive Saul was fearful when he did not seek the Lord about Goliath's challenge. This fear also surfaces when David has been appointed commander of Saul's army after his victory over Goliath, and David is successful resulting in the song: 'Saul has slain his thousands and David his ten thousands' – 18:7. At this Saul became angry, he was displeased and said, '…what more can he have but the kingdom…Saul was afraid of David because the Lord was with him, but had departed from Saul' – 18:8, 12. We read in 18: 15, 'And when Saul saw that David had great success he stood in awe of him.' An indication of his jealousy. After David kills 200 Philistines in the macabre incident of bringing 200 foreskins to Saul at his request in order to marry his daughter Michal, we read in 18: 28-29, 'But when Saul saw and knew that the Lord was with David and that all Israel loved him, Saul was still more afraid of David. So Saul was David's enemy continually.' Saul's fear is also given as the reason he made the sacrifice to the Lord himself instead of waiting for Samuel to turn up at Gilgal – 15:24-25. Saul's fear of David and his attempts to kill him resulted in David becoming afraid of Saul and fearing for his life. Consequently, David experienced periods of emotional and psychological fear over the years, as Saul pursued him to kill him. Out of just over 70 psalms attributed to David, around half deal with his enemies and his fear of them. Saul's jealousy and fear of David consumed him over the years. His self-indulgent jealousy and fear prevented him from dealing with

Israel's enemies as he sought to kill David and prevented him from sharing in the success of David.

JOAB

Abner was an influential figure in Saul's court. He was his general and kingmaker as he placed Ishbaal Saul's son on the throne. However, when Ishbaal accused him of treason the general ousted him from the throne – 2 Sam. 3: 9. David agreed to an alliance, a covenant with Abner to unite the two kingdoms, as he was going to deliver Saul's kingdom to David. However, Joab returned to the king from a raid and was informed he had let Abner go in peace. Now Joab was David's chief military officer, a powerful, influential and, ambitious man. 'He was cruel, calculating and ready to eliminate any threat to his power.'[30] Joab then goes to David and demands an explanation from him because he believed Abner had come to deceive him – 2 Sam 3:12-13, 22-25. The narrator does not record David's response, but immediately after this encounter, without David's knowledge, Joab orders messengers to bring Abner back, and on his return he defies David and murders him, because he had killed his brother – 2 Sam. 3:27. When Joab follows David's orders and Uriah is killed he captures the city of Rabbah and commands David to come and encamp against the city and take it, otherwise he threatens to name the city after himself – 2 Sam. 12:27-28. Joab also defies David's request that Absalom's life should be spared, and instead ruthlessly killed him – 2 Sam. 18:14. After his death as the king is weeping and mourning the loss of Absalom, instead of celebrating a victory over his enemies that included his son, his mourning resulted in his soldiers being ashamed. Consequently, Joab commands David to go and speak to his army to celebrate their victory, otherwise he threatens that everyone would desert him. So David duly complies – 2 Sam. 18:1-8. In 2 Sam. 19:13 as a political maneuver David appoints Amasa, Absalom's general, a place in his court as commander of his army instead of Joab, which signalled to the rebels that they would be included in his government. Although there is no scriptural record of it, this appointment may have also been motivated by a report that Joab killed Absalom. However, once Joab discovers he has been replaced by Amasa he deceitfully and ruthlessly kills him. He flouts David's political strategy and contributes to the further instability of his rule at a very precarious time. When Joab returns to David's court, the king fails to confront him about this willful act of insubordination.[31]

BLESSING

There are a number of theological themes in the narrative about David and Saul in 1 and 2 Samuel. A major underlying theme is the Deuteronomy blessing and curse decreed by the Lord – Deut. Ch. 28, that those who are obedient and righteous will receive his blessing and those who are not will be cursed-punished. We see evidence of this as Eli's family loses control of the priesthood because his sons are evil – 1 Sam 2: 27-36, 3: 10-14. It is also evidenced in Samuel's family as he appointed his own sons as judges over Israel, but they were also wicked and resulted in the elders rejecting their leadership and asking for a king – 8: 1-6. Saul's punishment was deemed to be because his of disobedience – 15: 10 and the beginning of his downfall. David's successes were due to his obedience to the Lord. However, after his adultery with Bathsheba and murder of Uriah the Lord punished him through his family.

KINGSHIP

In 1 Sam. 8:1-22, we learn that when Samuel was old he appointed his sons judges over Israel. But they did not walk in his ways they took bribes and perverted justice. So because of these things all the elders of Israel came together to Samuel and asked him to appoint a king to govern them like other nations. Samuel is reluctant but prays to the Lord about their request. While the Lord agrees, he tells Samuel to inform the people of the disastrous results this might bring. But they cannot be persuaded to change their mind and insist on a king. Therefore, the issue of kingship becomes a central theme in Samuel, and although it narrates the story of Saul and David as Israel's kings, this is placed within the larger context of God's reign. Consequently, the king's authority is mediated through

God and subservient to him. 'In particular Samuel stresses God's authority as one not dependent on human kingship, but who still chooses to operate within its framework.'[32] David Firth also states that a key issue of the book of Samuel is to record how kingship comes about as it is often regarded as Yahweh's concession rather than his choice. However, there are two places where kingship is announced in advance of its request. At the end of Hannah's Song in 1 Sam. 2:10 that refers to what Yahweh will do with and through his king and also in 2:35 that also refers to God's anointed. Apart from interpreting this as relating to Israel's kings, there may be a prophetic interpretation that ultimately points to Christ. He suggests that the flaw with the elders' request for a king in 1 Sam 8:4-5, is that it denies Yahweh's kingship over the nation as they want the king to lead the nation into battle. Although Israel's request for a monarch is sinful in its initiation, a workable model is available if both king and people submit to Yahweh, hinted at in 10:25 and explicitly in Ch. 12. Firth says:

> Human kingship, however, is always seen in terms of Yahweh's kingship, and cannot be interpreted independently of it. In particular, human kingship is one manifestation (but only one) of Yahweh's reign, since human kingship always stand under Yahweh's authority.[33]

Although it is not stated, at the heart of the issue is, 'In whom does Israel put her trust? And in whom is the king going to put his trust?' Not long into his reign, Saul becomes more like the king Samuel warned about in 8:10-18, while David demonstrates that Yahweh's anointed has to wait for his timing and not take the kingdom forcefully. While David due to his serious sins does not turn out to be perfect, he differs from Saul in one crucial aspect. He accepts Yahweh's right to discipline and judge him, whereas Saul resists. David's election turns out to be pivotal because the high point of the theology of kingship is the Davidic Covenant established by the initiative of Yahweh – 2 Sam. 7: 1-17.[34] Despite David's serious sins, because he repented and accepted the Lord's judgment and punishment, the Lord committed himself in a covenant with David so that Christ would be descended from his family line.

DELIVERANCE

A major theme in David's life is deliverance by the Lord. David leads a charmed life and is a survivor because the Lord was with him and rescued and delivered him from his enemies. The first speech the narrator records him making is when he comes before Saul and offers to fight Goliath. Recounting his exploits as a shepherd David concludes by saying, 'The Lord who delivered me from the power of the lion and the bear will deliver me from the power of this Philistine' – 1 Sam 17: 34-37. David showed an unusually extraordinary faith in the Lord as a young man, who was unskilled as a soldier, as he predicted the Lord would deliver him from Goliath.

After David's opening speech, there are many occasions when David experiences the Lord's deliverance. As early on as 1 Sam. 18:14 the narrator records – 'And David had success in all his undertakings, for the Lord was with him.' Through God's guidance, David defeats the Philistines –1 Sam. 23:1-4 and avoids Saul's pursuit – 23:10-14. In both instances, David sought the Lord's deliverance by seeking his guidance. In 2 Sam. 5:17-22, the Lord delivers David from the Philistines as he seeks God's guidance. Again in 2 Sam. 8:6 we read, 'The Lord gave victory to David wherever he went.'

At a crucial time, David experienced the Lord's deliverance when he may well have lost his life. As he was fleeing from Absalom, with his household and his followers, weeping and covering their heads in shame, he learned that Ahithopel a key member of his court, is among the perpetrators that betrayed him – 2 Sam. 15:30-31: so he prayed, 'O Lord turn the counsel of Ahithopel into foolishness.' In 17:1-14 we learn that the Lord delivered David from Absalom, when he and all the men of Israel chose to ignore Ahithophel's advice to chose twelve thousand men and pursue David that night.

In 2 Sam at the end of Ch. 22 also recorded as Psalm 18, David sings a song that recounts God's deliverance during his life. 'And David spoke to the Lord the words of this song on the day when the Lord delivered him from the hand of all his enemies, and from the hand of Saul.' Craig Morrison says, 'At the beginning of his public life David announced that God would deliver him. Now as his public life draws to a close, David sings that God has done just that…But it is not only the explicit use of the verb 'to deliver' that illustrates the centrality of this theme in the narrative. Between David's opening speech and his song in 2 Sam. 22, the reader observes a series of divine rescues that characterise the David Narrative.'[35]

REVERSAL

The theme about the reversal of fortunes in characters in 1 & 2 Samuel are built into the narrative. The Song of Hannah comes at the beginning of 1 Samuel in Ch. 2 and serves as a thematic and structural introduction.[36] Hannah's suffering because she could have no children was exasperated by her husband's other wife, Peninnah, who had many children and provoked her – 1 Sam 1:6. We are not told what led Hannah to promise to give her son to the Lord if he granted her desire for a child, but she is identified as one of the lowly and needy. Hannah's song rejoices in the Lord who reversed her fortune at the birth of Samuel, and subsequently blessed her with three other sons and two daughters – 1 Sam. 2:21. We then see the reversal of fortune of Samuel as a young lad who went to the temple to minister to the Lord, and as a young man eventually became an esteemed prophet and national leader – 3:19-21. The house of Eli lost its prominent position through the demise of Eli's wicked sons – 3:13 and their fortune was reversed. Saul's fortune was reversed when as an ordinary man he was chosen by the Lord to be Israel's first king – Ch. 9-10, and reversed again when he was rejected – 15:26. David was the youngest in a family of eight brothers but his work as a shepherd had no prospects of improving his lot, but his fortune is dramatically reversed when he is chosen as the future king and mightily anointed with the Holy Spirit – 16:13. In contrast Saul is rejected as king by God and the Spirit of God departs from him and an evil spirit plagues him instead – 16:14.

CRISES

In the books of Samuel Israel constantly faces crises, in fact in the book of Judges the immediate background to 1 Samuel is the recurring crises Israel faced from her enemies that prompted the Lord to raise judges to deliver them. We can discern the crisis of faulty leadership from Eli's sons and Samuel's sons, the crisis of the Philistine threat, the crisis of the lost ark and the crisis of kingship. The failure that emerges from these crises is the failure to trust the Lord. Individuals also face challenging situations and times of crises. As an established prophet, Samuel is confronted by a crisis because of the issue of kingship the elders request. Saul faces a crisis of confidence due to David's success in defeating Goliath and Israel's enemies. Instead of trusting in the Lord he is consumed by envy and becomes self-indulgent in his pursuit to kill David. In turn, David is confronted by the crisis of the maniac jealousy of Saul who is a constant threat to his life. After David's adultery with Bathsheba and the murder of Uriah, his sins result in the biggest crisis in his life, and in his later years, he faces a crisis when he is challenged by his son Absalom for the throne. Crises, whether circumstantial or involving people, challenge whether we turn to the Lord and prayerfully trust him, or seek to resolve matters on our own.

SHEPHERDS

When we picture David as a young shepherd boy looking after sheep, we may have a somewhat romantic image of what this involved. But a shepherd's life was not easy and they spent most of their time outside watching over the herd, no matter what the weather. The shepherd's chief garment is a cloak woven from wool or made from sheepskins, which is sleeveless and hangs like a coat over his shoulders. If the flock of sheep is small, the shepherd can look after them without any help, but if it is too large he would need some help from an hireling. Shepherds often slept near their flock to protect it from robbers or wild animals. The Old Testament shepherd was no wimp. He began as a child, often with a small flock and a lead goat or pet sheep that had been raised from a lamb and he would follow him anywhere. The child was an apprentice and he might begin that job as early as five or six years old, or even accompany an older brother when only four years old. He grew up watching the sheep, being bored, walking around, chasing them away from crops, leading them to water, taking them to green pastures – for years on end. And sometimes he would make a sling and practice with it until he could hit a target at 50 to 100 feet away. It was as a shepherd boy that David acquired the skills, insights and temperament to become David the King.[37] As a shepherd, one of David's responsibilities was to provide food for the sheep. In the springtime, there was an abundance of green pasture, with the sheep grazing near the village where he lived. After the grain had been reaped and the poor gleaned what was left, the sheep fed on what was left.

Shepherds were likely to build permanent sheepfolds in a valley, or on the sunny side of a hill to provide protection from strong winds. The sheepfold is a low building with arches in front of it and a wall forming an outdoor enclosure joining the building. The walls of the enclosure are about three feet wide at the bottom, narrower at the top, and are from four to six feet high. Large stones are used in constructing the outsides of the walls and are also placed at the top, and the centre is filled with smaller stones. Sharp thorn bushes are put on top of this wall to protect the sheep from wild animals or robbers, and there is a gate that is guarded by a watchman. When the weather is mild the sheep are kept in the enclosure at night, but if the weather is stormy, or it is cold, then the sheep are shut up in the interior part of the sheepfold.[38]

It is of interest to note, the Eastern shepherd never drives his sheep as the Western shepherd does. He usually leads them and goes before them, although that does not mean he is always in front of them. Often he will walk by their side or follow from behind, especially if they are headed for the fold in the evening. From the rear, he can gather any stragglers and protect them from the sly attack of a wild animal. If the flock is large, he will be in front and a heifer will follow behind.The shepherd will search for any sheep that is missing from his flock until he finds it. A reminder of Jesus' parable of the lost sheep.

Due to the outdoor nature of the task, shepherds developed a physical strength and toughness, because on occasions they had to protect the sheep from wild animals, as is evident from David's speech to Saul in 1 Samuel 17:34-36: 'Your servant used to keep sheep for his father, and when there came a lion, or a bear, and took a lamb from the flock, I went after him, killed him and rescued it out of his mouth: and if he attacked me I caught him by his beard and killed him. Your servant has killed both lions and bears…' Like other shepherds, David would have carried a rod. This is like a policeman's club made of oak with a knob on the end, into which nails may have been driven to act as a weapon. In Psalm 23 David mentions the rod with the staff. This is a stick five or six feet long and sometimes but not always, has a crook at the end of it which is useful in handling the sheep and for protection. David would also have had a sling, a simple device composed of two strings of rope or leather and a leather pouch for the stone. This was used by swinging it around his head, then letting go of one of the strings to project the stone as a missile. He is likely to have had a dual-piped flute of reed, used as a simple instrument of music in the same way shepherd lads have done for centuries around Bethlehem. David would also have had a pouch in which to carry some bread, cheese, dried fruit and olives. It was into this pouch in 1 Samuel 17:40, that he placed five smooth stones went he went to challenge Goliath.[39]

BACKGROUND

The period in 1–2 Samuel covers just over a century, (probably in the 1070s BC) and ending just before David's death. This was a fortunate time for a small nation like Israel as the powerful nations of Egypt and Mesopotamia were going through periods of unrest and external weakness. Israel lived as interlopers in a land already occupied by a heterogeneous group of people known as the Canaanites, whose strongholds were based at such cities as Hazor and Megiddo. The Jebusites who controlled Jerusalem were a subset of the Canaanites.

The background to 1 and 11 Samuel which originally was one book is the book of Judges, which deals with the history of Israel between the death of Joshua and the transition in the monarchy that began with Samuel. What is significant in the book of Judges is the very diverse religious environment, the nature of the Canaanite gods and the worship associated with them. The Israelites who had been taken out of one polytheistic environment in Egypt and placed in the next generation into another similar culture in Canaan, found it difficult to survive there and remain faithful to their monotheistic faith. Their failure to do so is at the very heart of the account that Judges gives of the fortunes of Israel in the judges period.[40] 'The Canaanites gods became a snare to the Israelites as Joshua warned they would. This led to a weakening of their loyalty to Yahweh and to one another, and spiritual and moral decline.'[41]

Judges portrays Israel as a marginal community because of the power of the Philistines. Judges shows Israel to be a community in moral chaos and involved in brutality – Ch. 19-21, when everyone did what was right in their own eyes. Judges witnesses a shapeless and unstable tribal way of life for Israel, punctuated by times of oppression by her enemies with God raising up judges, such as Samson, Debra and Gideon to save his people, that were followed by times of peace. Israel's lack of a centralised government and standing military left them vulnerable to well their organised enemies such as the Philistines, whose monarchial system supported a powerful standing army. 1 & 2 Samuel portray a radical transformation when ancient Israel became a centralised state ruled by a king, with radical social change and transfer of political power.

PHILISTINES

The Philistines established three coastal city states, Gaza, Ashdod and Ashkelon and later Gath and Ekron were added, creating a confederation of five cities in the Philistine Plain. The reason they extended control in Canaan was not just to dominate and extract taxes, but also to control vital overland routes by establishing military posts and garrisons – 1 Sam. 13, 2, 2 Sam. 23,14. During the period of the judges the Philistines were one of Israel's major enemies – Judges 3: 3, 31, 13:5, 14:4. They appear in the stories of Samson – Judges 14-16 and won a major conflict with Israel during the time of Eli – 1 Sam. 4:1-10. After this victory, they used the road into the Ephraim Mountains and dominated the Via Maris. In 1 Sam. 7:7-11, Samuel gained victory over the Philistines. Before and during the reign of Saul they established their garrisons at strategic points – 1 Sam. 10:5 and on the main roads –1 Sam. 13:17, 14: 15. However, Saul conquered the Philistine fortress at Geba – 1 Sam. 13:3 and ended their domination in Benjamin.[42]

The Philistines had the monopoly on iron metallurgy and they prevented Israelite craftsmen from learning new skills, and subjugated them economically – 1 Sam. 13:19-21. Their military organisation and the quality of their weapons were superior to those of the Israelites. The Philistine material culture was highly developed with well planned urban centres and was also prosperous. They increasingly imported goods from Egypt, Phoenicia and Cyprus. Saul was successful against them in the hill country but not in the open plain. In 1 Samuel 28-31, the Philistines attacked Israel from their bases in the Jezreel Valley on the Via Maris and destroyed the Israelite army and killed Saul and Jonathan on Mount Giboa.[43]

When David was fleeing from Saul, he joined Achish and lived with him at Gath – 1 Sam. 27:2-3. And when he became king he was able to defeat the Philistines and control the territory in the northern plain and the Jezreel Valley and large sections along the Via Maris. Although he broke their military, political and economic power over Israel, David could not destroy the major cities on the southern coast.[44]

NARRATIVE

Paul Borgman says, 'To understand the narratives about David, ancient storytellers relied on techniques of oral repetition requiring skilled listening. From these techniques were discovered the story's embedded meaning, its mysteries of character, action and moral vision. The ancient text involved a circular pattern of repetition that required the listener to remember what has gone before, as the story was being read out aloud time and again, to understand it and reflect on the interlocking patterns of repetition that yield its unique, coherent and compelling unity. Understanding the story will be accomplished by recognising broad patterns of repetition that drive the action and define character.'[45] 'The finest work of Hebrew narrative art' is represented in discrete sequences within the David story – smaller stories complete in themselves, like the ark narrative and the succession narrative.[46]

Craig Morrison highlights that the narrator's style involves not only what he says, but also how he says it – 'the drama of the telling.' This requires an acute eye on the text to observe its structure and to detect the narrator's strategies. David's battles are reported with lighting speed – 2 Sam. 8:1-8, but Tamar is brought into Amnon's web ever so slowly – 13:8-11. The narrator can influence our point of view and guide our judgment of events.[47] Historical narrative because it shapes and organises time, offers only a selection of events that occurred in real time and only captures a small part of David's exploits. Hebrew narrative distinguishes events in the foreground from those in the background. However, the background information is important because it is often critical for interpreting events in the foreground. For example, as the foreground action moves towards Joab's murder of Abner, the Hebrew text informs us, 'but David did not know about it – Joab's plot. Although David might benefit from his murder, the background information tells us he had nothing to do with it.[48]

CHAPTER TWO

KINGSHIP

REQUEST FOR A KING

1 Samuel 8:1-9

1 Samuel Chapters 1-7, record the story of Samuel, beginning with his miraculous birth and ending with the capture of the ark through the victory of the Lord over the Philistines. Ch. 7 as a text stands alone and is significant because through the victory over the Philistines the Lord demonstrates his sovereign rule over Israel, and Samuel is established in the role of judge after Eli's death. In Ch. 8, a significant theological context is established that points to a possible crisis for Samuel. Yahweh is Israel's king and yet he will move the nation towards kingship[1] as he agrees to the peoples' request for a king, with Samuel as both priest and prophet being his intermediary.

Toshio says, 'Ch. 8 is among the most significant in the historical books of the Old Testament, marking the transition from judgeship to kingship in ancient Israel.'[2]As such it can be seen as the start of the foundation of the monarchy in Israel and sets the stage for the demise of the judges, including Samuel. We read in 8: 1, that when Samuel was old he appointed his sons as judges of Israel, the initiation of a dynastic succession. This was a new innovation as previously Yahweh was the one who appointed judges. But his sons did not walk in the ways of the Lord, looked for unjust gain, took bribes and perverted justice – 8:4-5. Two important things stand out. Samuel has grown old, implies that many years passed since the victory over the Philistines in Ch. 7. But just as significant, his sons proved to be poor judges. Consequently, the elders came to Samuel, highlighted his age and his son's failure and made a request for him to appoint 'a king to judge us like all the other nations.' In effect, they request a new institution instead of a new judge.[3] Their request was attractive not only because a king would govern and judge them, but also because the people of Israel were scattered across the land and vulnerable to attack from the surrounding nations. And Israel's loose tribal federation often produced more strife than unity, whereas in contrast, their enemies had standing foreign armies. The idea of setting up a central government to recruit their own army was appealing.[4] They wanted to become like other nations, but the Lord had called them uniquely to be his people and were under his covenant protection. Israel was the chosen people of God and they were seeking to identify themselves with other nations in a wordly sense.[5]

We read in Ch. 8:6, 'The request for a king displeased Samuel.' The literal translation is, 'The matter was evil in Samuel's eyes.' Walter Brueggemann says:

> They have struck at the foundational commitment of Israel, the very reason d'etre of this community, which is the practice of justice for all without privilege or preference. The corruption of the old theocratic authority evokes a crisis that cuts deep into Israel's life and faith. The sons of Samuel are engaged in the undoing of the covenantal Israel…Their affront is a statement of fact on which the entire narrative builds.[6]

However, in Deut. 17:14-15, the Lord anticipates the people asking for a king when he says: 'When you come to the land which the Lord your God gives you, and you possess it and dwell in it and then say, 'I will set a king over me, like all the nations that are round about me' – you may indeed set a king over you, him whom the Lord your God shall choose.' It is reasonable to assume that Samuel and the elders knew about the possibility of a king from Deuteronomy. We can understand why Samuel was displeased as it meant the end of his rule as a judge and his family's rule as judges.

In 8:6, the narrator also records that Samuel seeks the Lord's response to their request in prayer. While the request for a king was interpreted by Samuel as a rejection of him and his role as judge, it was also a rejection of his sons taking over his mantle after his death, and he may have felt aggrieved. However, in the Lord's eyes the deeper underlying issue is their rejection of him as Israel's king, although it can be interpreted as an appeal based on Deut. 17:14-15 – as they did not request a specific person to be their king. Nevertheless, their request is acknowledged by the Lord to Samuel in answer to his prayer. He states that their request for a king is one more rejection of the Lord in a long string of rebellions since their Exodus from Egypt. Despite this, the Lord accepts their request and gives a severe warning and a threat about the consequences of living under a king. Twice the Lord commands Samuel to 'hearken-listen' to the people, in 8:7 and 8:9, and in 8:10-18, Samuel spells out to the people in great detail the consequences of living under a king. What this will entail is highlighted by the focus on what the king will *'take'* from the people, with the word take appearing in verse 11, 13, 14, 15, 16 and 17. This indicates that the request for a king will result in oppression and not necessarily justice, as the king will have power to take men and conscript them to serve him in his army, take women to serve in the royal court, take their best lands and give it to the king's servants, and take one tenth of their produce for his servants and take men and women to serve him. The threat that accompanies this warning in v. 18 is, 'And in that day you will cry out because of your king, whom you have chosen for yourselves, but the Lord will not answer you in that day.' The contemporary challenge to us is, 'In whom do we put our trust – in our institutions or the Lord?'

Brueggemann sees this speech by Yahweh through Samuel as, '...the harshest, most extensive criticism of monarchy in the Old Testament. It is one of the most important pieces in the Old Testament on the abuse of public power...The culmination of political power and social organisation in a state brought with it the redistribution and concentration of wealth, the monopoly of land control, and the nullification of local initiatives for justice and well-being.'[7] Yet it is difficult to understand why Brueggemann does not take into account the passage from Deut. 17: 14-15 and interpret the request for a king of the Lord's choice from this perspective. Despite the severe warning from Samuel, the people refused to listen to him and said, 'No! but we will have a king over us, that we may also be like all the nations and that our king may govern us and go out before us and fight our battles' – 8:19. This implies the people failed to put their trust in the Lord and wanted to rely on a king instead. Perhaps it was their intention behind the request that was interpreted as rejection by the Lord, which ultimately was a failure to put their trust in the Lord. Firth says:

> The fundamental sin was to look for an external source of security...This chapter continues to warn against seeking security where that security is not wholly dependent upon faith in God.[8]

He also says, 'Here we see that the elders' request is fundamentally a new idolatry, an attempt to establish a model of government that supplants Yahweh's authority with that of a king.'[9] Yet in the same context he contradicts himself, when he states that Yahweh has reclaimed the initiative since the choice of king is to be his with the government of the people under his reign.[10] So long of course as the king is obedient to the Lord. In due course, as the Lord initiated the Davidic Covenant with David, we may well perceive that the mention of a king in Deut. 17, anticipates God's plan for Christ as his representative king being descended from a king of his own choice. This may explain why the Lord granted the people their request for a king, although biblical commentators tend to voice their surprise at the Lord's decision to grant their request for a king. Brueggemann perceives Yahweh gives permission, but while giving permission disapproval is signalled. Perhaps the narrative has Yahweh already looking past the dispute and past Saul to the coming of David.[11]

SAUL'S ANOINTING

1 Samuel 9: 1-10:16

Chapter 8 ends ambiguously. Samuel sends the people home to their cities with the Lord instructing him to appoint a king, while chapters 9 and 10 record consecutive stories of how Saul was chosen as king. The first story is the ordinary rural account of Saul's secret anointing and the second his public selection, while the third account of his confirmation as king comes in Ch. 11. The first long and rambling story in Ch. 9 traces the way Saul is chosen king. Here he unobtrusively appears on the scene, ignorant of the drama that will culminate in his anointing. His destiny as God's choice is out of his hands. Barbara Green says, 'Many hands propel Saul towards the kingship: the elders who have insisted on a king…the father who sends a son on a quest…the servant who prevents his going back home, the young women who reassure him he is heading correctly, God who has spoken to the prophet, and Samuel himself. Saul's speech we must now notice is tentative in a variety of ways, making a contrast with the insistence of others.'[12] Goldingay suggests that a key motif in Saul's story is announced – Saul is never quite going to be in control of his destiny. He is always being pushed this way and that by people.[13] We can discern God's providential hand of guidance on Saul through others, and in Ch. 11 he will also find himself in the hands of a band of prophets. In Ch. 10 unknown to Saul, God's invisible hand will take hold of him, and 'this unsuspecting, uncomprehending Saul is transformed for the powerful purpose of Yahweh.'[14]

Ch. 9: 1 begins in the same way as Ch. 1:1 – 'There was a man.' The man introduced is Saul's father Kish, from the small tribe of Benjamin, and a man of substance-wealth. Saul is then described as handsome and tall, taller than any man from the shoulders upward. While the English translation describes an impressive appearance, the Hebrew *hendiadys – good,* refers to Saul's nature.[15] The scene set for Saul is a journey with a servant to find his father's lost asses. The irony will be lost on him, but Saul is the one who will be found by the Lord. Toshio Tsumura also suggests, *ahad mehann arim – one from the servants*, probably refers to the head servant and judging from his knowledge of the man of God, the servant may have been Ziba who is mentioned in 2 Samuel 9. Ziba had 15 sons, 20 servants and he held the important position of custodian of the personal property of Saul and his family – 9: 9-10.[16]

The narrator informs us that they made an extensive search without success – 9:4 for three days – 9:20, and Saul is about to give up and return home because his father will be concerned about them. But his servant is resourceful and persuades Saul to find the man of God who will tell them where to find the asses. Initially, Saul appears anxious, reluctant and somewhat uncertain, as they have no gift to give him, but his servant happens to have a small part of a shekel of silver. The unfolding narrative gradually makes it clear that the Lord is guiding Saul to a date with destiny.[17] It is the servant who initiates meeting Samuel and by contrast Saul appears to be hesitant and reluctant to continue. 'There is a certain misguidedness about Saul's actions when compared with those of the servant. It is the latter's initiative and persistence that keep the action moving in the providentially appointed direction.'[18]

On their way up the hill to the city, they meet some young girls coming to draw water and ask if the seer is here. This is a reminder that in God's providence Abraham's servant met Rebekah at a well and Jesus also met the Samaritan woman at a well. Fortuitously, they discover he has just come to the city to make a sacrifice, and the girls give them directions to find him and say – 'Now go up for you will find him immediately' – 9: 13. Here we can discern the Lord's perfect timing as they are about to meet Samuel, for if they had come a day earlier they would have missed him. Saul's encounter with Samuel that is about to take place is particularly significant as it unmistakably reveals to Samuel that he is the one the Lord has chosen. Paul Borgman suggests that Saul's first appearance on the scene reveals an uncertainty in contrast to his servant's resourcefulness. Also, when they meet the girls and ask where to find the seer, the narrator presents them, 'as unusually talkative, in light of the story's economy of detail and dialogue. Are we to understand they are struck by the imposingly tall and handsome young man? Is the audience to wonder about what appears striking, but otherwise proves deficient?'[19] Similarly, W. L. Humphrey, says: '1 Sam. 9-12 corresponds most closely to words about another doomed king, namely Absalom – 2 Sam. 14:25-26. Attention is called to the striking physical appearance of Saul and Absalom, but, unlike the notes of David and Joseph, their other qualities are not detailed. And of neither Saul nor Absalom was it said, 'That the Lord was with him' – 1 Sam. 16: 18, Gen. 39: 2, 3, etc. Therefore, in the narrative,

'Saul appears as a figure of heroic potential, but a subtone of uncertainty as to the direction this potential will take resonates in the background.'[20] Due to a lack of reference to Saul's internal qualities and the Lord being with him, if he is not suited to the task and destined to fail, why is kingship thrust upon him? There is in fact an ambiguity about how we interpret the character of Saul. Long suggests there may be a punitive element in the appointment of Saul. Perhaps the original concession to the peoples' request for a king was an act of divine judgment. 'I gave you a king in my anger, and took him away in my wrath' – Hosea 13:11.[21]

We read in 1 Samuel 9:14-20:

'So they went up to the city. As they were entering the city, they saw Samuel coming out toward them on his way up to the high altar. Now the day before Saul came, the Lord had revealed to Samuel: 'Tomorrow about this time I will send to you a man from the land of Benjamin and you shall anoint him to be prince over my people Israel. He shall save my people from the hand of the Philistines: for I have seen the affliction of my people, because their cry has come to me.' When Samuel saw Saul, the Lord told him, 'Here is the man of whom I spoke to you. He it is who shall rule over my people.' Then Saul approached Samuel in the gate and said, 'Tell me where is the house of the seer?' Samuel answered Saul, 'I am the seer, go up before me to the high place for today you shall eat with me, and in the morning I will let you go and will tell you all that is on your mind. As for your asses that were lost three days ago, do not set your mind on them for they have been found. And for whom is all the longing of Israel? Is it not for you and for all your father's house?'

Saul's reply to Samuel's rhetorical questions is in the form of three questions. 'Am I not a Benjaminite, from the least of the tribes of Israel? And is not my family the humblest of all the tribes of Benjamin? Why then have you spoken to me in this way?' – 9:20. These verses reveal that the Lord's purposes in choosing Saul is because of His concern for His people which he mentions three times to Samuel. 'He is to anoint Saul prince over my people Israel. He shall save my people from the hand of the Philistines, for I have seen the affliction of my people.' – 9:16. This is reminiscent of the Lord seeing the affliction of his people in Exodus 3:7. Brueggemann says, 'This appointment is not for the sake of the monarchy, not to establish a new institution, not to enhance Saul. It is for 'my people' whose affliction has evoked a firm response.'[22] The emphasis on 'save my people' clarifies Saul's role in terms equivalent to those of a judge. The major judges had all saved Israel from an external power and Saul's role is to follow this pattern.[23] God's providential guidance for Saul is complete as the Lord brings about the perfect timing for Samuel and Saul to meet. While Samuel has doubts about selecting a king their encounter is a divine appointment that will dispel any reservations that Saul is the Lord's chosen man. It was the Lord's inscrutable will to choose Saul from the smallest tribe of Benjamin that had almost been wiped out by its wickedness and stubbornness – Judges 19-20.[24] The Lord and Samuel are the only ones who know what is going on when he meets Saul, and it is understandable if Saul is pleased and perplexed by Samuel's enigmatic words to him. Pleased the asses have been found, perplexed by what his cryptic words mean about him and his father's house being 'the longing of all Israel.' Samuel and the Lord know this longing is for a king like other nations, to lead and judge them, and to save Israel in battle. Some biblical commentators are inclined to think the narrative about Saul portrays him negatively and hints that he will be unsuited as king as he seems to be led by others who take the initiative. But the Lord does not inform Samuel that he has any reservations about Saul.

Goldingay captures the unexpected and extraordinary nature of Samuel words to Saul, that he is 'the longing of all Israel,' when he says he dramatically reels 'in astonishment at each sentence that emerges from Samuel's mouth' especially at the one about Saul being the desire of Israel.[25] Saul had no idea what was going on, Samuel's enigmatic words made no sense to him.[26] While they are certainly extraordinary words when he is just looking for information about donkeys, Saul's response shows deference to Samuel and self-deprecation as he acknowledges the insignificance of his tribe. Toshio Tsumura believes, Saul not only understood the meaning of 'the longing of Israel' but also that he was to be their designated prince.[27] Alternatively, Borgman suggests that Saul's reply sounds less like humility than an expression of deep-seated anxiety. As Saul will choose to hide himself when Samuel begins the process of selecting the Lord's choice of a leader for Israel, he appears to have a serious flaw.[28] Why the Lord chose someone who the narrative appears to imply is unsuited to lead, is a question not answered definitively by the text.[29] But this is speculative as Saul's questioning is thoughtful, pragmatic, and sensible. Despite these negative perceptions about Saul's response to Samuel, we may interpret that his response was equally a sign of great humility. He was aware of the insignificance of his family background and that he was in effect unworthy and, 'a poor member of the least of the families of the smallest tribe.' Therefore, we may perceive a lack of confidence due to his lack of self-esteem when he hides behind the baggage – 10:22

Samuel intends to tell Saul about a more important matter than donkeys, but for the moment, he does not answer him. Instead, he invites Saul and his servant to a meal specially prepared for around thirty men and treats him as a special guest, inviting him to sit at the head of a table with his servant. Not only is Saul the guest of honour, a special portion of food has been prepared for him. T. Cartledge believes the portion of meat Samuel reserved for Saul was usually for the priests and had a hidden significance. The banquet is similar to those that were sponsored by Absalom (2 Sam. 15: 1-12) and Adonijah (1 Kings 1: 1-10) as a means of announcing their designs on the throne and seeking popular acclaim as king.[30] Samuel is the only one who knows the significance of this particular meal. Moreover, he gives no explanation to Saul, or the men, about why he is the guest of honour. Equally, the narrator does not elaborate on Saul's response, he leaves that to our imagination. Although he was probably curious about Samuel's intentions and more than a bit surprised to be the special guest of a strange prophet he has just met. Especially, as the only words recorded by Samuel to Saul are somewhat enigmatic. 'See, what was kept, is set before you. Eat, because it was kept for you until the appointed hour that you might eat with the guests' – 9:24. This is the only hint that Samuel the seer has anticipated meeting Saul, and that he has something important on his mind concerning him.

There are no further details about the meal and Samuel has made sleeping arrangements for Saul for the night upon a roof-top. At the break of dawn Samuel escorts Saul and his servant to the outskirts of the city, where he asks him to send his servant ahead to wait for him – 9:25-27. Sending the servant away may have symbolised that from this moment onwards Saul was his own man, had to make his own decision and take responsibility for them and no longer rely on others.[31] The intrigue has been building up to a dramatic climax and all is about to be revealed to Saul, as Samuel reveals 'the word of God' to him. What follows next is the secret anointing of Saul. Up to now, this is the most memorable event in the life of Saul, but it has been conducted in a clandestine manner.

We read in Ch. 10:1, 'Then Samuel took a vial of oil and poured it on Saul's head and kissed him and said, 'Has not the Lord anointed you to be prince over his people? And you shall reign over the people of the Lord and you will save them from the hand of their enemies round about.' Saul's anointing was a sign of God's authority in choosing him and confirming his call to serve the Lord. Samuel tells Saul about his calling to save God's people and also reign over them. 'He will not only do what a judge does but also what a king does…The new mandate and transformation of Saul is so drastic that it requires verification.'[32] Samuel then informs Saul of the three signs that will occur on his way home – 10:2-7. The mundane event of looking for lost donkeys has been the prelude to the most unexpected day in his life. But the narrator is silent about Saul's response, if indeed there was one. Up to now, there has been nothing in Saul's life to prepare him for being anointed by Samuel, and he will receive confirmation from the three signs he predicts will happen, that his anointing is unmistakably the 'word of the Lord.' Bearing in mind Samuel's reluctance about the elders request for a king, what stands out is his obedience to the Lord as he faithfully anoints Saul. This is especially striking, as he is not keen on the idea of a king.

After Samuel anointed Saul, he shows supernatural insight by the predictions he makes. These involve three encounters with three groups of people. In 10:2, he predicts Saul will meet two men, in 10: 3-4, he predicts he will meet three men and in 10:5-6 he predicts he will meet a group of prophets. The first two signs are relatively ordinary in comparison with the third. In the first, the two men he meets will tell him the donkeys have been found and his father is now concerned about him, and the next three men will give him bread. But when he meets the band of prophets this will result in an unforgettable encounter with the Spirit of the Lord. We read in 10: 5-7, 10:

> '...and as you come to the city, you will meet a band of prophets coming down from the high place with harp, tambourine, flute and lyre before them, prophesying. Then the spirit of the Lord will come mightily upon you, and you shall prophesy with them and be turned into another man.Now when these signs meet you, do whatever your hand finds to do, for God is with you. When Saul turned his back to leave Samuel, God gave him another heart: and all these signs came to pass that day. When they came to Gibeah, behold, a band of prophets met him, and the Spirit of God came mightily upon him, and he prophesied among them.

The first two signs Saul came across were external. However, the third sign was an internal experience of God's Spirit, with an outward manifestation. Gibeah was the location for this encounter and in 11:4 it is described as Gibeah of Saul, and was in fact Saul's home town – 10:26. Tsumura informs us, 'Most scholars identify Gibeah of Saul with the modern Tel el-Ful about 3 miles north of Jerusalem.'[33] The Spirit-*ruah* of the Lord is also mentioned at David's anointing, and both Saul and David received the Spirit of the Lord to empower them to serve him. The Hebrew for 'come' referring to the Spirit is 'rush' and this appears only in the Stories of Samson in Judges 14:4, 19, 15:4, Saul 1 Sam. 10: 6, 11: 18: 10 and David in 1 Sam. 16: 13.

The action of the Spirit as he came upon Saul to turn him into another man was on his heart to equip him to fulfill a new role as God's servant. For example, when the Spirit came mightily on Saul in 11:6, it aroused his anger and inspired him to summon God's people to fight the Ammonites. Firth describes the change in Saul as, 'indicating a complete change covering his rational and emotive self.'[34] This is synonymous with Saul receiving another heart that indicates the transforming work of the Spirit, bringing about a deep work in his heart. The confirmation to Saul that this took place happened when he met the band of prophets, and he prophesied as the Spirit came-rushed upon him. This brought about a new understanding of who he was because of God's call and the anointing on his life. The transformation resulted in his new identity as a person. The experience of Peter in the New Testament is similar. In Matt. 16: 18, Jesus said to Peter, 'And I tell you, you are Peter, and on this rock I will build my church.' At Pentecost when Peter and all the other disciples received the Holy Spirit, when the Spirit came upon them with the sound of a mighty, rushing wind, he was transformed from the man who denied Jesus, into Peter the bold evangelist empowered by the Spirit. He was fulfilling his calling in his new identity that Jesus predicted.

Until Saul's meeting with the band of prophets, he has been, 'The silent recipient of this remarkable encounter.' Now, 'Saul engages in self-transcending acts that sweep away conventional perceptions and usual categories of understanding. Saul becomes filled with energy and freedom beyond himself. The narrative strains to find words adequate for the new reality… Saul, by the work of the Spirit, is a genuine newness in Israel… Here, at the edge of newness, is the gift (charisma) of freedom, ecstasy, and self-transcendence yielding to a purpose beyond Saul's own self.'[35] Mary Evans perceives, that Saul emerges onto the scene looking for his father's donkeys as a very ordinary young man, somewhat indecisive and lacking in confidence. But the encounter with the ecstatic prophets will change his life, as he prophesies with them. 'This personal encounter would transform Saul. His awkwardness and lack of confidence would become a thing of the past and his potential for leadership would become a reality.'[36]

The fulfillment of the three signs Samuel predicted especially the last one with the band of prophets, along with Saul's experience of being transformed into another man, with a new heart, were evidence that Samuel's words about his anointing were trustworthy. 'If Saul was to lead God's people in God's way, it was vital that his own faith in God was firmly based.'[37] This would give him confidence for the future, as he reflected on the overwhelming events after meeting Samuel, and his encounter with God and his Spirit.

After Samuel informs Saul of the three signs that will take place on that day, three unforgettable things happened to him. The three predictions of Samuel took place. The Lord gave Saul another heart as soon as he left Samuel, and the Holy spirit came-rushed mightily on him and he prophesied with the band of prophets. 'For Saul his time with the prophets was a high moment of worship, an encounter with God, an experience of true ecstasy.'[38] These events were a powerful confirmation and evidence of the Lord's calling on his life. This was the most remarkable day in Saul's life. He would need time to reflect and come to terms with his new identity, as the Lord's chosen leader of his people. In hindsight, as we know about Saul's failure, the text invites us to see how we can reconcile the fact he received a new heart and was a changed man, and yet still failed to be obedient. God's divine action in Saul's life still required him to be obedient and put his faith in the Lord. His natural temperament the narrative indicates was somewhat reticent and shy, was not suddenly transformed into hi being a confident extrovert. His challenge was to embrace and respond to the divine work of God's Spirit in his heart and life. Perhaps the reason he failed was that his natural character traits prevented him from making the right decisions. Perhaps that is why he failed to listen attentively and grasp the exact obedience that was expected of him. David himself failed in the area of obedience to the Lord when he committed adultery and had Uriah murdered. Despite having a powerful anointing of God's Spirit, David also made disastrous decisions that were to have severe repercussions on his family and reign as king.

After Samuel tells Saul about the three signs that will take place, he then instructs him to go to Gilgal where Samuel will offer sacrifices, and tells him to wait for seven days for him, when he will show him what to do. Brueggemann sees this as an ominous sign that will bear heavily on Saul's future. It highlights Samuel prominence, but will have aggressive repercussion in the future when Saul fails to wait for him.[39]

While Saul's anointing was personal and private, when the Spirit came mightily on him it was in his home town, Gibeah, notorious in Israel's history as a terrible rape and murder there led to a conflict between the tribe of Benjamin and the rest of Israel – Judges 19:22-20. When he prophesied it was witnessed by his neighbours, and as the band of prophets played their musical instruments, their ecstatic speech along with Saul joining in made a considerable impact, that resulted in the proverb, 'Is Saul also among the prophets?' Firth says, But the association of the Spirit of Yahweh with his elective purpose indicates that it is uttered in awe of what has happened.'[40] This was an unusual event to be remembered for a long time to come and Saul's neighbours would have been puzzled about its significance. Especially as Saul comes across as slightly reticent or not overly confident, perhaps like an introvert when we first encounter him. But here he is completely uninhibited under the influence of the Spirit. Saul will emerge from this experience where he has been taken over by the Spirit in a remarkable way as a new person. After the events of this day and the prophets have gone, Saul goes to the high place. He may have gone to worship as there was a shrine there, or he may have gone to his father's house that was near this location.

After Saul's encounter with the prophets ended, he arrives home, and the first person he meets is his uncle who asks him where he went – 10:14. While he tells him about his search for the asses and that they saw Samuel, he did not tell him what he said, or about his anointing, nor about the day he met the prophets. Perhaps Saul is modest or may be feeling out of his depth and anxious. While it is speculative, it is possible that Samuel instructed him not to tell anyone about his anointing, as it hadn't yet publicly been confirmed by all the tribes of

Israel. Also, it may have sounded somewhat incredulous. In 10:16, the narrator belatedly informs us that Saul did not tell his uncle about the matter of the kingdom which Samuel had spoken to him about. This is the only time Samuel told Saul the reason for his anointing was the elders' request for a king.

SAUL'S ELECTION

1 Samuel 10:17-27

10:17-27 *'Now Samuel called the people together to the Lord at Mizpah, and he said to the people of Israel, 'Thus says the Lord, the God of Israel, I brought up Israel out of Egypt, and I delivered you from the hand of the Egyptians and from the hand of all the kingdoms that were oppressing you.' But you have this day rejected your God, who saves you from all your calamities and your distresses, and you have said, 'No, but set a king over us.' Now therefore present yourselves before the Lord by your tribes and by your thousands. Then Samuel brought all the tribes of Israel near, and the tribe of Benjamin was taken by lot. He brought the tribe of Benjamin near by its families, and the family of the Matrites was taken by lot: finally, he brought the family of the Matrites near man by man, and Saul the son of Kish was taken by lot. But when they sought him, he could not be found. So they enquired again of the Lord. 'Has the man come here yet?' and the Lord said, 'Behold he has hidden himself among the baggage.' Then they ran and fetched him from there, and when he stood among the people, he was taller than any of the people, from his shoulders upward. And Samuel said to all the people, 'Do you see him whom the Lord has chosen? There is none like him among all the people.' And all the people shouted, 'Long live the King!' Then Samuel told the people the rights and duties of kingship, and he wrote them in a book and laid it up before the Lord. Then Samuel sent all the people away, each one to his own home. Saul also went to his home at Gibeah and with him went men of valour whose hearts God had touched. But some worthless fellows said, 'How can this man save us?' And they despised him and brought him no present. But Saul held his peace.'*

After Saul said nothing to his uncle about Samuel, the narrative records Samuel calling all the tribes of Israel together at Mizpah. This was an important city that on occasions had a religious significance because Samuel visited Mizpah annually as he judged Israel. This was especially true when he gathered all the people there after their apostasy to pray for them, and the people fasted and repented of their sin against the Lord. But the Philistines heard they were there and came to fight against Israel, so the people asked Samuel to intercede to the Lord to save them, which he did. This resulted in a tremendous victory, indicating the people did not need a king – 7:5-11

While the request for a king only involved the elders with Samuel, and Saul was a special guest with only around 30 men before his anointing, Mizpah was a historic occasion in the life of Israel when the king was elected, involving all the tribes and thousands of people – 10:19. We note that Samuel called all the people to the Lord and not to himself, because the Lord was going to speak to them. The first thing Samuel says to them is, 'Thus says the Lord…' This was a reminder that he was the Lord's spokesman and this was God's word to them. The Lord's message was a reminder of his deliverance for Israel from the Egyptians and other oppressors. This recounted the Lord's faithfulness and goodness and that he could be trusted to save them from the Philistines. The nature of this formal meeting is solemn and has ominous overtones of the Lord speaking to his people after the Exodus. As the Lord reminded his people of his past deliverance, Samuel reminds them of their rejection of the Lord by their request for a king. The Lord's message and Samuel words heighten the tension amongst the people, as there is a solemn tone of judgment implied in them. Samuel points out that the decision to have a king was flawed, but the Lord allows this, and when he says, 'Now, therefore, present yourselves before the Lord by your tribes and your thousands' – 10:19b, Samuel gave them no hint about what was going to take place next. J. Woodhouse perceives this was a frightening scenario, and at this point it sounded as if something terrible was going to happen, a fitting punishment for the apostasy of asking for a king.[41]

However, what now takes place is a selection process of elimination by lot. In Israel, lots were used in various ways to discover the Lord's will. So the people were familiar with the use of lots as a way of determining God's will. For example, to determine guilt – Joshua 7: 14, 1 Sam. 14: 42, Jonah 1: 7 or to apportion land Num. 26:55, Joshua 14: 2.[42] And in Acts 1: 26 the disciples cast lots to see who would replace Judas. The first lot from the tribes drew the tribe of Benjamin, the second lot from the clans of Benjamin drew the clan of the Matrites, and the third lot of the men from this clan resulted in Saul's name being drawn and selected as God's choice, in a religious process that is liturgical and sacramental.[43] But when they looked for Saul he could not be found. Was this an indication of his reluctance as God's choice? Instead of asking his clan where he was, they asked the Lord to tell them. Saul's reason for hiding as the drawing of lots began is not explained. He may have been hiding because he interpreted Samuel's ominous note in v. 19, as a sign of God's judgment and the drawing of lots was to find the guilty party. Or he may have lacked self-confidence, or was anxious, or afraid. As Saul had had a remarkable experience leading up to his private anointing, it is somewhat surprising that he chose to hide. This appears to contradict that he was a new man with a new heart. But whatever his reason, the Lord tells Samuel where he is, and he is then brought and presented to all the people. When he appears, Samuel declares at this public assembly that Saul was the man the Lord had chosen. Ironically, having been hiding, when he turns up he is not questioned about his action. Instead, the people celebrate and shout, 'Long live the king!' – 10:24. R. Alter perceptively suggests, as Saul has been dragged out of hiding, to distract the attention from his action, Samuel carries out a public relations gesture when he points to this strapping young man, and says, 'Do you see who the Lord has chosen? There is no one like him among all the people' – 10:24.[44] Shaul Bar believed the ceremony at Gilgal strengthened Saul's kingship by bringing the Israelite tribes in the Trans-Jordan under the authority of the new king. Having freed the Israelite tribe from the oppression of the Ammonites it was the right time to make Saul king. This ceremony signified his undisputed authority as king over Israel.[45]

Although Saul was the Lord's chosen leader, neither the Lord or Samuel had called him 'king.' This title was the public recognition of the leader the people had requested. But Saul was not the peoples' choice, he was chosen by the Lord. The term 'chosen' is a significant biblical word when God is the subject. For example, God chose Abraham, He chose Israel, He now chooses Saul. Firth highlights how the Lord reconciled the peoples' request for a king, with the Lord's choice of Saul.

> There is a profound tension lying at the heart of this passage – 10:17-27, a tension only partly resolved, between what Yahweh agrees to do and what Yahweh desires to do. The request for kingship has not taken Yahweh by surprise, even though the motivation behind it rejected his final sovereignty over the nation. Although kingship was within his purposes, the model sought by the people was not. Samuel's task was to mediate Yahweh's decision so that the people understood the fault of their request, and yet show that Yahweh had still chosen a king for them, a choice made clear through the process by which Saul was chosen. By reminding the people of their initial failure and then restating, and perhaps expanding, the 'justice of kingship', Samuel is able to provide a mechanism by which the peoples' request for a king is reshaped, so that it has the potential to conform to Yahweh's will for the nation.[46]

Now that Saul has been publically acclaimed king, Samuel supervises the decisive shift of the legal and political foundations of Israel,[47] as he tells the people the rights and duties of kingship he records in a book before the Lord – 10:25, some of which may have been based on the duties of a king in Deut. 17. These represented a legal agreement between the king and the people, confirmed by the seal of witnesses,[48] which was stored before the Lord in the sanctuary at Mizpah. However, having warned the elders about the potential abuses of kingship that

Samuel pointed out in Ch. 8, to ensure the limitation of the king's rule the document stored in the Lord's presence served as the official guidelines.[49] After the rights and duties were recorded Samuel sent the people to their homes and Saul also returned to his home at Gibeah, along with 'the men of valour whose hearts the Lord had touched' – 10:26. However, not everyone supported the selection of Saul and some men questioned his ability to save them, perhaps because he had been hiding in the baggage, and gave him no gifts. But Saul aware of this kept his peace – 10:27. Keeping quiet at this news may be seen as compatible with Saul's reticent personality, although it can be interpreted positively as well as negatively. It can be seen as wise to ignore them, or a sign of weakness. But this is balanced by the fact a group of men 'felt a divine impulse to join him.'[50] J. Woodhouse discerns profound truths from the public selection of Saul, who was in fact Lord's choice of their leader. Saul like the other people went home at Samuel's instructions, a sign of his submission to the prophet, which implies he was still in charge. God outmanoeuvered the people who wanted a king so they could be like other nations. They now had the Lord's choice and it was on his terms.[51] What is striking about Mizpah is that a Philistine garrison was stationed at this location, but Samuel does not tell Saul to imminently launch an attack on them. Some biblical commentators believe that Saul failed to take the initiative and attack the Philistines after Samuel anointed him and told him of the three signs that would happen to him that day, he said, 'Now when these signs meet you, do whatever your hand finds to do, for God is with you' – 10: 7. This is an ambiguous and cryptic command and if Samuel had intended Saul to attack the Philistines after he anointed him, he could have instructed him to do so.

SAUL'S KINGSHIP

1 Samuel 11: 1-15

Saul's initial anointing was in a clandestine manner, he was then publically elected by lot, now after a famous victory over the Ammonites, he is formally acknowledged as king at Gilgal. This turns out to be a strategic victory following Saul's public selection that confirmed him as king. 'This victory is Saul's great moment in the life of Israel.'[52] The central theme of Ch. 11:3, 9, 11 is 'deliverance' and casts a link back to Judges.

Although it was the Philistines who were a threat to Israel, here the Ammonites besiege Jabesh-Gilead – 11:1. The elders sought to negotiate surrender by a treaty with Nahash, king of the Ammonites, paying tribute and serving him in return for protection. But he had an aggressive and gruesome policy of gouging out the right eye of his defeated enemies, to cripple, humiliate and disgrace God's people and exert total domination over them.[53] This was his condition for agreeing to a treaty. In Judges 16:21 Samson had his eyes gouged out and in 2 Kings 25:7 Zedekiah also had his eyes gouged out. This is a dramatic opening scene, because 'if there is no one to save us' – 11:3, the men of Jabesh-Gilead will be humiliatingly maimed for life. The elders requested seven days respite to send messengers throughout the territory of Israel to see if they could find someone to deliver them, failing this they would accept Nahash's terms – 11:3. Nahash displayed a confident arrogance by agreeing to their terms, as he presumed no assistance was likely from the dispersed tribes of Israel. However, the elders asked for seven days grace, as Jabesh-Gilead is around 40 miles from Gibeah and they intend to find Saul.

When the messengers from Jabesh-Gilbeh come to Gibeah and tell the people what happened they all wept aloud, and when Saul returns from working in the field, he discovers the news. At this God's Spirit comes-rushes mightily on Saul and his 'anger was greatly kindled' – 11:6. The impact of the Spirit inspires him to action and 'He took a yoke of oxen, cut them in pieces and sent them throughout all the territories of Israel by the hand of messengers saying, 'Whoever does not come out after Saul and Samuel, so shall it be done to his oxen' – 11:7. His action resembles that of a charismatic judge following the treatment of the concubine's corpse in Judges, when the men of Gibeah took a Levite's concubine and raped her and she died. The concubine's cut up pieces – 19:29, sent to all the territories of Israel by the Levite, roused the men of Israel to avenge this crime – Judges 20. Saul's symbolic action as elected king and his appeal to Samuel's authority has the desired effect, as the fear of the Lord falls upon them and they come alongside Saul – 11:8. One or two biblical commentators, believe Saul failed to take the initiative and attack the Philistines after he was anointed and publicly selected king by the Lord, but this incident may explain his apparent inactivity. Firstly, as there was no actual siege from the Philistines after his anointing and selection Saul did take the initiative to attack them. Secondly, it was only on the prompting of God's Spirit when Israel was under the threat of her enemies that he was roused to take action. Thirdly, 'The mention of Samuel suggests that Saul did not see himself acting independently as king. Saul's actions are led by the Spirit, so it is no surprise that the dread of Yahweh came upon the nation.'[54]

All the men of Israel were gathered by Saul at Bezek a couple of miles west of the Jordan and close enough to Jabesh-Gilead to allow them to attack the Ammonites. The actual number of men from Israel 300,000 and 30,000 from Judah is accepted as an error in translation and was likely to be around 5000 men. This appears to be the right number as Nahash would not attack Gilead if he knew around 300,000 men of Israel would oppose him. At this point, the narrative suggests that not only has Saul been roused by God's Spirit to gather all the men of Israel and Judah, but inspired his faith in the Lord to deliver them from the Ammonite. This is reflected in his confident declaration to the messengers, 'Thus shall you say to the men of Jabesh-Gilead, 'Tomorrow by the time the sun is hot you shall have deliverance' – 11:9. This news is a source of great encouragement and joy to the men at Jabesh, who then inform Nahash, 'Tomorrow we will give ourselves up to you, and you may do to us whatever seems good to you' – 11:9-10. This is deceptively an intentionally ambiguous statement that Nahash interpreted as a sign of their surrender. But Saul's military tactic of dividing the men into three companies and attacking unexpectedly early in the morning watch (2-6 am) resulted in a rousing victory that scattered the Ammonites. Brueggemann describes their victory as, 'The power behind the deliverance is the inscrutable working of God's Spirit…Saul is the deliverer promised (9:16) and authorised (10:1).'[55]

After this resounding victory, Samuel is at the scene and the people want to kill those who questioned whether 'Saul shall reign over us?' – 11:12. But Saul takes the initiative to diffuse the situation by declaring, 'Not a man shall be put to death this day, for today the Lord has wrought deliverance in Israel' – 11:14. Saul would have been justified in agreeing to the men being put to death because they questioned his authority as the leader of Israel. But he refrains from being defensive about his status. He does not exhibit any presumption on his part to take the credit or the honour for securing the victory over the Ammonites. Although he took the initiative to gather all the men of Israel and Judah together he knew this was due to the prompting of God's Spirit. It may be reading too much into Saul's response, but if we read in between the lines, his response indicates a Godly reverence and submission, as he acknowledges the Lord was responsible for their victory. Brueggemann says, 'This is not the voice of a self-seeking king. This is the voice, rather, of a judge of the old order who moves only by the energy and momentum of God.'[56]

After this, Samuel takes the initiative to summon the people to Gilgal to renew the kingship there – 11: 14. Although Saul has already been publically elected as God's choice, until now there was no evidence as a leader to support this. His initiative to summon all the men of Israel and their victory was proof to the people of the Lord's calling on his life. Tsumura captures the importance of the occasion at Gilgal. 'The purpose of this occasion seems to be to confirm Saul's kingship which has been formally known though lacking demonstration. It was necessary for *all the people* to acknowledge Saul as the king of Israel *before the Lord.* If the election of Saul as king at Mizpah was political, the (re)confirmation of Saul as king at Gilgal would be religious, that is before the Lord...So the 'renewal' confirmed the religious dimension of the kingship of Saul.'[57] As a result, Samuel, Saul, and all the people worshipped the Lord and 'greatly rejoiced' – 11:15. Saul's private anointing at Ramah indicated to Saul God had chosen him. The ceremony at Mizpah confirmed he was the Lord's choice of leader, now at Gilgal the people affirmed that he was their choice too.[58]

MONARCHY

1 Samuel 12:1-25

Chapter 12 is a moment of national significance for Israel as it marks the turning point between the period of the judges and the monarchy. It is pivotal in anchoring the king and monarchy within the covenant framework of Deuteronomy 28, with its conditions of blessing and curse. With both Saul and Samuel present, there is a contrast between Saul's youthfulness and Samuel's old age. It may have seemed like the old order of rule was being replaced by the new. But, Samuel's speech counters this possible expectation or perception.

Chapter 12 also deals with the transition between the old covenant and the new practice of monarchy. If Saul posed a threat to Samuel it may have been because his political leadership threatened, 'the character of Israel as a covenant community.'[59] Like Moses at Sinai – Exodus 19:7 and Joshua at Shechem – Joshua 24:1, Samuel addresses Israel in 12:1-5, in which he testifies to his faithfulness and vindicates his leadership. In Ch. 12:6-11, Samuel's speech also vindicates the Lord and his deliverance from the time of Moses and Jacob and the judges, against Israel's enemies. Although verses 12-13 mention the peoples' request for a king to fight Nahash, king of the Ammonites, Samuel does not mention the failure of his sons, the reasons the elders request a king like other nations.

In Ch. 12:14-15 we read, *'If you will fear the Lord and serve him and listen to his voice and not rebel against the commandment of the Lord, and if both you and the king who reigns over you will follow the Lord your God, it will be well: but if you will not listen to the voice of the Lord, but rebel against the commandment of the Lord, then the hand of the Lord will be against you.'* Samuel with incisive theological astuteness expounds some of the 'most carefully argued covenant theology that includes the king.'[60] This reiterates the Deuteronomy covenant of blessing and curse giving Israel a stark choice that incorporates the king into this 'rigorous system of reward and punishment.'[61] Brueggemann says:

> The rhetoric of these lines is shrewd and devastating. The king is deliberately subsumed under the conventional structure of blessing and curse. Indeed, the king has no individual role to play but is simply one more member of the covenant community, subject to the same summons, available for the same blessings and curses…The rhetoric in fact denies kingship any theological significance. Theologically these verses nullify the institution of kingship! In the insistent categories of covenant, kingship is an institution that makes no difference, simply does not exist, and is not to acknowledged. All that counts is the torah.[62]

In his speech, Samuel reminds the people their request for a king was wicked and he confirms this by calling on the Lord to send thunder and rain upon the people. After the Lord did this, they greatly feared the Lord and Samuel. So they asked him to pray for them that they might not die, as they acknowledge their request for a king was evil – 7:19. Although the Lord acceded to their request for a king Samuel wants to stress their commitment is to firmly remain on, 'following the Lord and serving the Lord with all their heart' and not to trust in vain things that cannot profit – 12:20-21. In this context, the reference to vain things is undoubtedly their desire for a king, and putting their trust in him instead of the Lord. Samuel then reiterates his commitment to pray for the people (although he doesn't specifically mention praying for Saul), and once again he calls them to be faithful in their commitment to the Lord, to fear him and serve him. Lastly, Samuel reminds them of the disaster that shall happen to them and the king if they are wicked – 12:23-25. Samuel's 'crusty voice of tradition is relentless. It cannot stop until it has sounded the warning one more time...'[63]

J. Woodhouse points out that Samuel's exhortation to Israel to be faithful in their commitment to the Lord, 'was a critical moment in the history of Israel.'[64] Because if they rejected the Lord then the hand of the Lord would be against them. This warning as it appears in Hebrew is devastating, and suggests a comprehensive rejection of Israel.[65]

CHAPTER THREE

SAUL'S REJECTION

SAUL'S ADMONITION

1 Samuel 13: 1-23

A considerable amount of time has passed between Ch. 11 and 13. In Ch. 11 when animated by God's Spirit Saul defeats the Ammonites, he attributes their deliverance to the Lord. But now many years later in Ch. 13, his son Jonathan appears on the scene and is involved in fighting against the Philistines. Chapter 13 turns out to be a pivotal time in the life of Saul, because of the unexpected announcement by Samuel that his kingdom would not be established, as the Lord has found a man to replace him because he offered a sacrifice to the Lord instead of waiting for Samuel to do this. Brueggemann in his inimitable style captures the central drama of Chapter 13 when he says, 'This articulates a stunning theological verdict on Saul.'[1] This chapter is an extraordinary one as it appears Samuel had prior information about Saul's future which he has withheld from him. Namely, that the Lord planned to establish his kingdom for ever' – 13:13. But there are problems with this promise. Firstly, it was never shared with Saul, until now, which is too late. Secondly, perhaps Samuel deliberately withheld this promise from Saul to test him. Thirdly, even if Saul had been aware the Lord would have established his kingdom, he did not know of any condition attached to it.[2] Now it is too late. But, Saul is still king, although his monarchy will not become hereditary.[3]

The narrator begins Ch. 13 with a summary of Saul's reign, and despite a reference to his age, none is recorded. Equally, there is a question mark about the length of his reign due to textual problems, because the text is defective and missing the original numerals.[4] The length of Saul's reign is given as two years although the events in 1 Samuel indicate this was clearly longer. Saul begins his official reign at the start of Ch. 13 and by the end of Ch. 15 he has been rejected, yet he is still in power until the end of Ch. 31. 'His monarchy is short and long, its apparent end deferred past the moment of its actual demise.'[5] Although Saul is God's choice the narrative in Ch. 13 has raised a doubt about his suitability.

One of the reasons for Saul's election was to lead the men of Israel in battle against the Philistine. At the end of Ch. 13 we are told there was no blacksmith in Israel, all the Israelites had to go to the Philistines to sharpen their ploughshares, axe or sickle – 13:19-20. And the Philistines had a highly developed iron metal industry with skilled metal-workers and armourers.[6] This information is out of sequence as in verse 3 we read that Jonathan defeated the garrison at Geba. In Ch. 13 Saul is mobilising his men to fight against the Philistines – 13:15b-23, and initially he selects 2000 men to stay with him and 1000 to be with Jonathan, who successfully defeats the garrison at Geba – 13:3. The downside of this is that the Philistines gather in force to fight against Israel. Being aware that they will respond aggressively Saul calls all the men to join him at Gilgal – 13:4-5. Although the narrator does not say it, we can speculate that Saul sent a messenger to fetch Samuel to Gilgal to come and offer sacrifices and pray to the Lord for victory, as they are outnumbered. Meanwhile, as they are waiting, the Philistines assemble 30,000 chariots, 6,000 horsemen and troops like the sand on the seashore. When the men of Israel saw this vast number of soldiers, their hearts trembled with terror and they hid themselves in caves, in holes, and in cisterns, or crossed to the fords of Jordan – 13:5-7. Saul's army which is a band of volunteers begins to disintegrate and disperse as the men were intimidated and feared for their lives.

We read in 1 Samuel 13:7-18, 'As for Saul he was still at Gilgal, while all the troops went trembling after him. And he waited seven days the time appointed by Samuel, but Samuel did not come to Gilgal and the people were scattering from him. So Saul said, 'Bring the burnt offering here to me, and the peace offerings.' As soon as he had finished offering the burnt offering, behold, Samuel came: and Saul went out to meet him and salute him. Samuel said 'What have you done?' And Saul said, 'When I saw that the people were scattering from me, and that you did not come within the days appointed, and that the Philistines had gathered at Michmash, I said, 'Now the Philistines will come down upon me at Gilgal and I have not entreated the favour of the Lord: so I forced myself and offered the burnt offering.' G. Vreeland reasonably says, 'The narrator does not paint a picture of a malevolent, scheming Saul here. He paints a picture of a clueless Saul…I also think that in the rest of the story, Saul will be clueless with respect to the Philistines, his servants, David, God, and Samuel.'[7] While Saul explains and justifies what he did, his action may reflect that his heart he was fearful, and he did not assert his leadership to prevent his men from deserting him. He compromised his leadership because he admitted that he was afraid of the people and obeyed their voice and listened to them – 15:24. Samuel said to Saul, 'You have done foolishly, you have not kept the commandment of the Lord your God which he commanded you: for now the Lord would have established your kingdom over Israel for ever. But now your kingdom shall not continue: the Lord has sought out a man after his own heart: and the Lord has appointed him to be prince over his people, because you have not kept what the Lord commanded you.' And Samuel arose and went up from Gilgal to Gibeah of Benjamin' – 13:13-15.

P. Long points out that the confrontation between Saul and Samuel at Gilgal marks one of the most perplexing episodes in the Old Testament. On the one hand, given the dire military situation, Saul's decision to proceed with pre-battle sacrifices in the absence of the tardy prophet – 13:8 impresses many readers as entirely justified. The severity of Samuel's rebuke, on the other hand, seems inexplicable.[8] Seeing his army is vastly outnumbered, with the Philistines armed in a superior manner, Saul seeks God's blessing through the cultic offering to raise the morale of his men and secure victory by God's favour, as Samuel the priest has not responded to this crisis in the allotted time. Tsumura perceives that Saul judged the situation pragmatically and not by faith in the Lord, and that he relied on his own judgment rather than the word of the Lord from Samuel. Although no specific command from the Lord is stated by Samuel. 'Saul puts his own thought or judgment over the word of the Lord through Samuel. What he was supposed to wait for was not simply Samuel's physical presence, but for Samuel's intercession and instruction – 12: 23…Saul's disobedience to the commandment of the Lord, whatever it might have been has brought a serious result, the cessation of his kingdom.'[9] Similarly, Diane Edelman posits that Saul's 'tendency is to use human perception instead of inward, divinely inspired perception by aligning his heart with Yahweh's, that led him to fail in restraining the people to obey the divine will.'[10] But the command may not have been the same one as in 10:8 to wait 7 days at Gilgal as that was a number of years earlier. W. Blaikie perceives, 'The real offence of Saul was he disregarded the absence of God's prophet and representative. …If Saul had had a real conviction that all depended at this moment on his getting God's help…he would not have acted as if Samuel's presence was of no moment…God was not a reality to Saul.'[11] Perhaps, 'The reality is Saul has misperceived the subordinate nature of his kingship. In appealing to the military crisis as a forbidding delay, he shows himself to be out of accord with the 'Yahweh war' ideology that informs 1 Sam. 13-14. Yahweh's proven ability to bring victory against a vastly superior enemy.'[12] Samuel's response to Saul's welcome, his deferential greeting and his explanation for the offering are tersely rejected. 'Samuel comes so quickly the reader can only marvel at the timing…But we wonder. It almost appears as a set up, in which Samuel is testing to see how far he can keep Saul under his control and subordinate to his priestly authority.[13] This sounds somewhat like an entrapment by Samuel who delayed his arrival even though he wasn't far away. The implication is that he could have readily chosen to come much earlier, in which case Saul would not have failed. In a somewhat cynical tone, Brueggemann says:

> The commandment that seems to have been broken is, 'Thou shall not violate Samuel's authority.' Saul seems to have acted in innocence, not seeking to undermine the authority of Samuel. Samuel's verdict, however,

> is based on another assessment of Saul's action. Or, if we may judge from the pace of the narrative, we may surmise that Samuel arrives at Gilgal with his dread filled message of rejection already prepared. He need only a pretext for its announcement. And this Saul inadvertently provides...Samuel plays a daring brutal game with Saul's faith, Saul's career, and eventually Saul's sanity.[14]

D. Edelman perceives Samuel's command to Saul in 10:7-8 is confusing and ambiguous. The original audience would have been invited to reflect on the fairness of Saul's rejection and by implication, the fairness of the divine will. She wonders whether v.7-8, 'relayed a deliberately ambiguous paraphrase of a clearer divine message, or whether they were Samuel's creation, without divine backing, intended either to confuse and mislead the royal candidate out of spite or envy, or to test Saul's obedience...The opacity of Samuel's motivations throughout the narrative raises the important question of fairness and the severity of the sentence announced in the light of Samuel's possible contribution to Saul's infraction. The exact nature of the announced rejection is as ambiguous as the instructions following the three-part signs that were broken. First, and foremost, do v.13-14 represent a legitimate prophetic pronouncement expressing Yahweh's will, or are they instead a warning to Saul about his possible future divine rejection, in the light of his failure to obey the earlier directions of 10:8?'[15] While the narrator includes the occasion when the Lord speaks to Samuel and tells him how to recognise his choice of leader for Israel – 9:15, he does not include details about when the Lord spoke to Samuel about his plan to establish Saul's kingdom for ever. The narrator also does not include the details about when the Lord changed his mind concerning Saul. Therefore, we are left to wonder, when did the Lord inform Samuel of his intention to establish Saul's kingdom? And exactly when did the Lord change his mind – was it before or after Saul made the brunt offering?

Assuming the Lord had told Samuel of his intention to establish Saul's kingdom some time before the incident at Gilgal, we are left to wonder why Samuel didn't tell Saul about this. M. Evans, says, 'Is there more here than poor timing on Saul's part, or on Samuel's for that matter? We need to note it is only Samuel's word we heard calling for sacrifices at Gilgal, and in fact only the prophet's report of God's feeling about the dynastic firing.'[16] When Samuel arrives at Gilgal he informs Saul that he has lost the opportunity of the Lord establishing his kingdom for ever, because he has not kept the commandment of the Lord. But, as Samuel does not say to Saul on his arrival, 'Thus says the Lord, your kingdom would have been established for ever' etc, this casts doubt about whether the Lord revealed his plan to Samuel only as he arrived at Gilgal. Perhaps circumstances beyond Saul's control and fate are colluding against him. 'Is Saul a man wrestling with fate and the dark powers which limit him at every point in his effort to reach the thing he has set before him?'[17] Gunn says, 'The judgments against Saul, startling in their severity, are made in the face of his avowal that his action had been taken in good faith.'[18] Gunn also raises the issue of Yahweh's striking disparity of treatment between Saul and David. The disparate treatment of Saul and David directs our attention to the fact that according to the story, good and evil are equally at Yahweh's disposal.[19] We are confronted by the inscrutable will of God as we see a contrast in the way Saul and David are dealt with by the Lord. The narrator will make it clear David is a favourite of the Lord, whereas Saul appears as a victim. 'For David Yahweh is 'Providence.' For Saul Yahweh is 'fate.'[20]

Despite Saul's apparent failure, his son Jonathan will soon show that he trusts the Lord – 14:6-12, and his friendship with David in the future will show he has noble qualities as a future king. Therefore, the judgment Samuel announced on Saul could be interpreted as premature. Saul had been elected, a man after God's heart – choice, but he is not offered any chance of redemption. Whereas after David's serious sins of adultery and murder, the Lord took the initiative through Nathan to prompt David's repentance and restoration. Bearing in mind the opportunities the Lord gave Israel to repent, for example, through the prophet Jeremiah, the complete omission of any 'word' by the Lord through Samuel to Saul to repent, is inexplicable and puzzling. Brueggemann says, 'The verdict on Saul is hard and problematic: first, we do not know what Saul did wrongly, and second, we wonder whence came the resolve for a king, when this first king in fact has had no chance….In these two verses, Samuel cunningly gives and takes away...Clearly, whatever failure there was with Saul's sacrifice is quite a small matter in relation to the transfer of power now announced.'[21]

When Saul greets Samuel, he offers excuses that cast the blame on others for the sacrifice he made. He blames the men who were deserting him. The Philistines who had gathered against Israel. Samuel for not arriving at his appointed time, and the need to seek God's blessing. From a different perspective, Barbara Green perceives the issue of answerability is at stake. 'Saul's incapacity for answerability, both structurally and personally, that the monarch(y) fails is the central assertion.'[22] Saul says, 'I forced, restrained myself to do it' (offer the sacrifice). In effect, he justifies his action instead of accepting responsibility for it and acknowledging that he made an error. Consequently, he shows no sign of contrition or the need for repentance.

> His words pointing out the flaws of others bring in their wake testimony of his own inability to restrain them. Additionally, Saul seems to find it a struggle to manage his own role, and when he pulls himself together, he somehow errs. His language about his own process (the word translated 'forced myself') itself implies that he had to place some effort between what he did and some alternative behaviour.[23]

It is somewhat disingenuous of the narrator, that twice he records Samuel saying Saul had not kept what the Lord commanded him – 13: 13-14, but does not specifically say what this commandment was. Unless, of course, it is to wait for Samuel to arrive, offer the sacrifices as priest and also to intercede and inquire of the Lord what Saul should do. The narrator also fails to report Saul's response to indicate what he understood by Samuel's declaration. Yet the outcome is far-reaching and staggering as the implication is that if Saul had been obedient, Christ would have descended from his family line, in which Jonathan was a suitable heir as king. Saul has only offered the burnt offering, therefore one wonders why Samuel did not proceed to make the peace offering, intercede, seek the Lord's guidance, and call Saul to repent. Samuel comes across as a dogmatic, uncompromising and unsympathetic prophet. He destabilises Saul by withholding the knowledge the Lord would have established his kingdom for ever. Instead, he ruthlessly pronounces judgment. The text invites us to wonder if Saul's psychological instability and paranoia about his successor, David, that will manifest itself, had its roots in this particular incident. As the Lord never sought to remove Saul from his office as king, we are left to wonder if Samuel was somewhat precipitous and shortsighted when he informed Saul the Lord planned to replace him. Why not just tell him he has forfeited the opportunity to have his kingdom established permanently. Saul's instability in the coming days may have begun here. We are left to wonder about the untimely change of mind by the Lord. Why choose, anoint and elect Saul as king, and then reject him, without giving him an opportunity to repent? We are left to wonder whether in fact the Lord did instruct Samuel to inform Saul on this occasion about his dynasty. This action only created a sense of uncertainty and apprehension in Saul's mind about his future, that would have serious repercussions on his relationship with David. Any smooth transition for Saul's successor was now completely out of the question. Ironically, thanks to Samuel's timing, Saul would direct his vengeance on David the anointed future king, waiting in the wings.

From a literary critique, the narrator is economical with the facts after Samuel's indignant judgment on Saul, because what is missing is Saul's response that would have indicated how he understood his message. The omission is too convenient. It seems a mystery why the Lord had already judged Saul and Samuel appears to be just waiting for an opportunity to declare his judgment. Here, Saul is given no voice by the narrator. We have no idea to what extent, if any, how Saul understood Samuel's message. It may have seemed a confusing announcement, incongruous to the imminent threat of the Philistines. Saul has been anointed and elected king without any say-voice in the matter. Now judgment has been passed on him, and again he has no say or voice in the matter. Once Samuel has passed judgment on Saul and promptly departs from the scene, the rest of Ch. 13 is somewhat of an anti-climax. Saul is not offered or given any encouragement or help in any way by Samuel. We could be forgiven for thinking he has it in for him. It almost feels like a conspiracy, that for some reason Samuel was out to get Saul. Despite Saul's apparent failure, Samuel fails to give him any help. He arrived at a time of crisis and his action only deepens this crisis. Samuel has left Saul and his men to an inevitable defeat. His late arrival was disastrous for Saul, and his untimely departure is just as calamitous. This king needed all the help he could get. We are left to wonder why Samuel didn't stay and intercede to seek God's help for his people and exhort Saul to repent. We are left to wonder if Samuel has an ulterior motive for abandoning Saul.

The narrator gives no details about how Saul and the 600 men that were now left with him felt about Samuel's action. Despite the impressive number of the Philistine army and their superior weapons, a full scale battle does not ensue, although they took over parts of the previously held Israelite territory. So Saul and his men retreat to from Gilgal to Gibeah, the only safe way to the territory of Benjamin now that the Philistine army occupied the Michmash area. With a massive advantage of men, the Philistines divide their forces in an attempt to encircle Saul and his men. Victory for the Philistines seems to be inevitable as Saul is vastly outnumbered. His escape seems impossible. Chapter 13 ends on an ominous note as the men of Israel were poorly equipped.

DRAMATIC VICTORY

1 Samuel 14: 1-23

In this chapter, there is a contrast between Jonathan and Saul. Jonathan is young, adventurous, courageous, daring, and he shows a bold initiative against the Philistines, and faith in the Lord. Whereas Saul is burdened by his responsibility as king and Samuel's recent judgment as he faces the Philistines. Jonathan acts without Saul's knowledge which may hint at his lack of confidence that his father would have approved. The narrator describes two high rocky crags, the steep sides of a gorge, with a pass between them that stresses the considerable difficulty in attacking the Philistines. Jonathan's camp and the Philistine camp were visible to each other and within shouting distance. Saul's camp was in the outskirts of Gibeah further back up the hills. Saul's and Jonathan's men were outnumbered, outflanked and ill-equipped.

We read in Ch. 14:6-15: *'And Jonathan said to the young man who bore his armour, 'Come, let us go over to the garrison of these uncircumcised Philistines, it may be that the Lord will work for us, for nothing can hinder the Lord from saving by many or by few' And his armour-bearer said to him, 'Do all that your mind inclines to, behold I am with you, as is your mind so is mine.' Then Jonathan said, 'Behold, we will cross over to the men and we will show ourselves to them. If they say to us, 'Wait until we come to you' then we will stand still in our place, and we will not go up to them. But if they say, 'Come up to us' then we will go up, for the Lord has given them into our hand. And this shall be the sign to us.' So both of them showed themselves to the garrison of the Philistines, and they said, 'Look Hebrews are coming out of the holes where they have hid themselves.' And the men of the garrison hailed Jonathan and his armour-bearer and said, 'Come up to us, and we will show you a thing.' And Jonathan said to his armour-bearer, 'Come up after me, for the Lord has given them into the hand of Israel.' Then Jonathan climbed up on his hands and feet and his armour-bearer after him. And they fell before Jonathan and his armour-bearer killed them after him: and that first slaughter which Jonathan and his armour-bearer made was of about twenty men within as it were half a furrow's length in an acre of land. And there was a panic in the camp, in the field, and among all the people. The garrison and even the raiders trembled. The earth quaked, and it became a very great panic.'*

Jonathan is eager and appears almost impulsive as he seeks to get involved in a skirmish with the Philistines. If he has any advantage, it is that of a surprise attack because the terrain is almost impassable with its high rock-formations. H. Hertzberg says, 'Two features of this landscape are the striking rock-formations known as 'the slippery one' and 'the thorny one.' As far as the approach and the attack are concerned, the whole undertaking is either madness or faith.'[24] Despite taking action on his own with his armour-bearer Jonathan acts on his faith in the Lord. He trusts that as they take action the Lord will confirm if it is his will to give them victory through the sign he seeks – 14: 6-10. When Jonathan speaks about the Philistines as uncircumcised – 14: 6, this reflects what David said about Goliath – 1 Sam. 17: 26. The reference to the Philistines as uncircumcised is an indication that this not an ordinary battle, but 'a crusade, a holy war.'[25] It is a statement of contempt. Long has a striking tribute to Jonathan, as the one who assumes the role of 'confessor of Yahweh.' It is Jonathan who proclaims Yahweh's ability to save 'whether by many or by few' and ultimately, it is he, not Saul, who emerges as the 'representative of true Yahwistic piety.'[26] We are left to wonder how Jonathan's faith and trust in the Lord came about, especially as Saul his father does not show signs of such faith. Instead, he comes across as pious in a pragmatic way. Nevertheless, faith in the Lord is what Jonathan displays when he speaks, and in effect, he lays a fleece before the Lord. 'The primary purpose of the sign is oracular, not merely to discover the psychological state of the Philistines.'[27]

As Jonathan and his armour-bearer show themselves to the Philistines, they mock them saying, 'Look Hebrews are coming out of the holes where they hid themselves.' Their invitation to come up is sarcastic as such an attempt seems impossible.[28] However, Jonathan and his armour-bearer show no signs of fear as they approach to mount a surprise attack on the Philistines, because they are confident in the favourable sign the Lord gave them. As they step out in faith the Philistines they encounter fall before them and are killed, but from a perspective of faith we know they have fallen into the hands of the Lord. Believing that no one could possibly climb up the rocky terrain, about twenty Philistines are slaughtered. The unexpected attack causes confusion and panic in the enemy camp and we read in 14: 15 – 'And there was a panic in the camp, in the field, and among all the people: the garrison and even the raiders trembled: the earth quaked and it became a very great panic.' Jonathan and his armour-bearer could not conceivably cause such havoc. It is the hand of the Lord stretched out against the Philistines that caused the panic, the fear and the trembling. When Jonathan says, 'It may be the Lord will work for us' – 14:6, he is not overly presumptuous. He does not take it for granted the Lord will act, and looks for a sign to confirm the Lord's will Once this is given he steps out in faith trusting the Lord. Long describes the success in this small-scale combat that leads to a much greater victory over the Philistines. 'The ultimate attribution of this 'panic' to divine agency (it became a trembling of God) is consistent with Jonathan's own perspective that Yahweh alone gives victory, and in no wise diminishes the illustrious portrait of Jonathan in the episode.[29]

The confusion and uproar resulting from Jonathan's attack was seen by Saul's watchmen, and his instinctive response is to see who is missing and responsible for what is happening. When he is informed that it is his son Jonathan and his armour-bearer Saul commands the ark of God to be fetched, and he asks Ahijah the priest to carry out a ritual and inquire of the Lord whether to attack the Philistines – 14:18. However, just then, the uproar in the Philistine camp increased more and more, and Saul commanded the priest to stop. Then Saul and all his men rallied and went to the scene of the battle, along with the Hebrews who now deserted the Philistines, and all the men who had hid in caves also came out to join them – 14:19-21. *'And behold every man's sword was against his fellow, and there was very great confusion'* – 14:20. At this scene, we can discern the hand of the Lord that resulted in deliverance and victory over the Philistines – 14:23. Tsumura perceives that Saul's two commands, *'bring near the ark'* and *'withdraw your hand'* reveal his attitude towards divine matters.

> He treats both the divine object and the divine method rather carelessly. Instead of inquiring of the priest, Saul commands him…but at a crucial time, he interrupts the consultation. Saul is a person who prays when he should act, and acts when he should pray. Such inconsistency is one of Saul's characteristics. [30]

Tsumura probes deeper into Saul's action, and I think he is onto something very important about Saul's faith and spirituality. When Saul asks the priest to enquire about God's will, he shows evidence of religious piety rather than a real faith in the Lord. When without a second thought he abandons his quest to inquire of the Lord, this may indicate his lack of submission and trust in the Lord. Although he appears to be pious, his faith may be pragmatic and ritualistic. 'In his relationship with the Lord, Saul was 'rash and presumptuous.' He tried to manipulate the divine will through ritual formality.'[31]

RELIGIOUS RITES

1 Samuel 14:24-52

There is a sharp contrast between 14:23 that declares the Lord delivered Israel and 14:24 where Saul wants to avenge himself on his enemies. He leaves the Lord out of the equation, as he makes no direct reference to him. We read in 14:24, 'And the men of Israel were distressed that day, for Saul laid an oath on the people saying, 'Cursed be the man who eats food until it is evening and I am avenged on my enemies.' So no one ate any food.' This is a flashback that had happened earlier, and so Saul's reason for making this oath may have been because the Philistine army still posed a serious threat and he did not want his troops to desert him. And perhaps because he had prevented the priest from seeking God's will – 14:19, his men had no assurance of victory based on a word from the Lord. Therefore, the implication is that Saul used the oath because the people were apprehensive because of the Philistines and he tried to gain the Lord's favour by the fast of self-denial. The LXX *(a translation of the Hebrew Bible into Greek)* preserves a reading that says, 'Saul committed a very rash act on that day.' NRSV or 'Saul made a great blunder that day.'[32]

As a result of Saul's oath, the men went into battle having eaten nothing. Afterwards they came to the forest where honey was dripping, but they did not eat any of it, as they were afraid because of Saul's oath. However, Jonathan was not present when Saul made his oath and he ate some of the honey. After he ate the honey, he was informed about his father's oath – 14:27-28. Despite their hunger, the men were able to rout the Philistines and as they were hungry, they killed sheep, oxen and calves and ate them with the blood. When Saul was informed about this he said, 'You have dealt treacherously' and commanded every man to bring his ox and ass and slay them on a large stone altar, so they did not sin by eating blood. Saul built an altar to the Lord: it was the first altar that he built to the Lord' – 14: 33-35. His oath not to eat any food was the cause for the peoples' action, but ironically, he failed to see this, and turned to a religious ritual to atone for their sin.[33]

In Ch. 14, the narrative continues with another attack at night against the Philistines planned by Saul, yet he makes no mention about inquiring of the Lord if this was right. The priest took the unusual step of suggesting they seek the Lord's guidance when it should have been Saul who initiated this. This may indicate Saul's declining commitment to discovering the Lord's will.[34] But the Lord did not answer him – 14: 36-37. So Saul called the leaders together to discover whose sin was responsible for the Lord's silence. This ritual involved casting lots and the first one was between the royal household, Saul, Jonathan and the people of Israel. After the lot fell on the royal household, Saul had the lot cast between himself and Jonathan and it fell on his son.

We read in Ch. 14: 43-46:

'At this Saul says to Jonathan, 'Tell me what you have done.' And Jonathan told him, 'I tasted a little of the honey with the tip of the staff that was in my hand: here I am. I will die.' And Saul said, 'God do so to me and more also, you shall surely die Jonathan.' Then the people said to Saul, 'Shall Jonathan die who has wrought this great victory in Israel? Far from it! As the Lord lives, there shall not one hair of his head fall to the ground: for he has wrought with God this day.' So

the people ransomed Jonathan and he did not die. Then Saul went up from pursuing the Philistines, and the Philistines went to their own place.'

When Saul is looking to find the guilty person and he says in v. 39, 'For as the Lord lives who saves Israel, though it be in Jonathan my son, he shall surely die' – his judgment is foolish. And when Jonathan admits he is guilty his father's mental state of mind appears to be unbalanced and unraveling, because instead of recoiling in horror at this news he is determined to kill him, without expressing the slightest sign of remorse. Jonathan's reply sounds almost cynical and incredulous and Saul's men are equally determined Jonathan will not die, and to this effect, they make an oath and save his life when they say, 'that not a hair of his head will fall to the ground.' By his action, Saul is beginning to alienate himself from his son, alienate himself from his men, and soon he will be permanently alienated from Samuel. Long says:

> Rebuked by Yahweh, forsaken by Samuel, at odds with Jonathan, Saul ultimately finds himself completely isolated, alienated by his obduracy even from his own troops.[35]

While Samuel informed Saul about his future, the men of Israel did not know, so he continued as king. Ch. 14: 47-48 are a summary of Saul's success as king over Israel's enemies. The position of this list by the narrator signals that the end of Saul's career has effectively drawn to a close.[36] Long points out that in view of the largely negative portrait of Saul this raises the question of why it is placed here rather than later. He thinks the list of Saul's accomplishments confirms his military ability. But what he finds disturbing is that there is no mention of Yahweh or his involvement with Saul.[37] At the end of Ch. 14, the narrator states there was hard fighting against the Philistines all the days of Saul – v. 52. Saul was chosen as king to deal with the Philistines, but ultimately he failed to achieve this, having squandered much of his reign and energy pursuing David to kill him. Tragically, in time, the Philistines would kill Saul and Jonathan in battle.

FLAWED VICTORY

1 Samuel 1: 1-9

In Ch. 13 Saul discovers his dynasty which could have been established for ever by the Lord, is now never going to happen. But the bad news is just about to get worse, as the climax of Ch. 15 ends with the rejection of Saul as king by the Lord. The start of Ch. 15 records the Lord instructing Saul through Samuel to attack the Amalekites and annihilate them completely, which includes men, women, infants and animals – 15:3. It is not surprising if in the 21st century we find it difficult to reconcile this action and recoil at the thought of it. Our instinctive reaction as Christians is that this is a deeply disturbing, horrific and a shocking command, as it resembles ethnic cleansing. But in its context, this was not unusual in the ancient world. T. Cartledge informs us that, 'In a holy war, the entire enemy nation is perceived as the personification of evil, and in 1 Samuel 15 that is named Amalek.'[38]

The first words of Samuel in 15:1-2 are loaded with significance – *'The Lord sent me to anoint you king over his people Israel, now therefore hearken to the words of the Lord. Thus says the Lord of hosts...'* With his prophetic authority Samuel still exerts control and Saul is still under the Lord's will communicated by Samuel, whose one issue is uncompromising loyalty to Yahweh, as Samuel is his only valid voice.[39] Saul is reminded that he is king only because of 'God's divine consent and his sphere of authority is limited by the demand of obedience to prophetically mediated commands'[40] given by Samuel. The Hebrew in v. 1 adds a sense of urgency to this command. 'Saul is required to listen with the utmost attention to what Samuel is about to say.'[41] He is required to listen carefully and be obedient to God's command. Saul is asked to engage in an act of divine punishment for what the Amalekites did to Israel during her journey out of Egypt – Exodus 17: 8-13.

In Deut. 25: 17-19 we read, *'Remember what Amalek did to you on the way as you came out of Egypt, how he attacked you on the way when you were faint and weary, and cut off at your rear all who lagged behind you: and he did not fear God.*

Therefore, when the Lord your God has given you rest from all your enemies round about in the land which the Lord your God gives you for an inheritance to possess, you shall blot out the remembrance of Amalek from under heaven, you shall not forget.' Before the onslaught on the Amalekites Saul advises the Kenites to leave so they are not killed, because of the kindness they showed to Israel when they came out of Egypt – 15:6. Only one solitary verse, 7, records the comprehensive victory over the Amalekites. But Agag the king was captured alive, and some of the best sheep, oxen, the fatlings and the lambs, and all that was good were kept – 15:8-9.

One verse records the defeat of the Amalekites – v.7, while verses 10-31 are a record of the Lord declaring his rejection of Saul. The ominous announcement in v. 10, 'And the word of the Lord came to Samuel' is a formula that occurs eighty-three times in the Old Testament, usually in the prophetic books. The message from the Lord to Samuel is one of regret, he repents that he made Saul king. Twice in Ch. 15 the narrator records the Lord repented he had made Saul king – 15:11, 35.[42] The Lord also says, 'for he has turned back from following me' – 15:11. This traumatic announcement helps to resolve the ambiguity concerning the Lord's declaration in Ch. 13, that Saul's kingdom would not be permanent. That declaration was tantamount to a warning about not obeying, but now in light of his disobedience the Lord declares his rejection of Saul. Verses 10-24, contrast the Lord's judgment on Saul with his perception on his action. Long's statement about Ch. 13, 'The confrontation between Saul and Samuel at Gilgal marks one of the most perplexing episodes in the Old Testament,'[43] may well be pertinent to this incident in Ch. 15. Because in this ancient drama that is completely alien to our experience we do not relate to God's word to annihilate the Amalekites: and we may well find it difficult to reconcile that Saul was given no opportunity to repent by the Lord when his sin was pointed out to him, whereas when we sin and repent God forgives us through Christ, although of course there may be consequences. As New Testament believers, God's will and God's word in this ancient drama may remain inscrutable.

One of the features about the incident of Saul's rejection is that he takes the initiative to show kindness to the Kenites, advising them to leave before attacking the Amalekites. Saul reciprocates in kindness to the Kenites for the ancient act of kindness shown to Israel at the time of the Exodus.[44] This act of mercy is striking because the Lord did not command it and it is overlooked when the Lord rejects Saul. Now when Saul spares Agag and the people keep back some of the best animals he does not appear to have fully grasped the emphasis on the need for absolute obedience to the Lord's word, and the seriousness of doing exactly as the Lord commanded. J. Woodhouse perceives there is a 'depth of tragedy' in this situation.[45] He likens the severity of the Lord's judgment, that he regretted choosing Saul as king, to the time when the Lord used similar language and regretted making man on the earth – Gen. 6:5-6.[46] One is left to wonder what exactly it is in Saul's spirit or personality, that leads him to fail in listening accurately with his heart to the Lord's word and obeying it. In v. 1 Samuel commands Saul to 'listen to the words of the Lord.' This is the same charge Samuel condemns Saul with in Ch. 13.

SAUL'S REJECTION

1 Samuel 15:10-35

A number of facts strike us after the Lord says to Samuel, 'I repent that I have made Saul king' – 15:10. This message is not actually passed on to Saul. God's divine regret and repentance is all that we hear. Samuel then translates God's word into policy – the Lord has rejected Saul and given his kingdom to a man better than him. While Samuel is angry at the news the Lord repents of making Saul king and he cries to the Lord all night, no response from the Lord is recorded.[47] We can speculate that Samuel was grieved and in tune with God's 'divine pathos.'[48]

Before Samuel meets Saul, he is told that after the victory over the Ammonites, Saul came to Carmel and set up a monument for himself before going to Gilgal. This strategically placed monument at the southern boundaries of Judah, suggests it is the self-aggrandisement out of keeping with the Lord's command.[49] After Moses defeated the Amalekites he also built a monument, an altar to the Lord. That monument celebrated the Lord – 'The Lord is my banner' – Exodus 17:15. But Saul's monument was to himself. Woodhouse captures the seriousness of Saul's action: 'Did this man have no idea what he had done?! The inappropriateness of this monument will be apparent even to Saul, before the end of this day.'[50] Borgman with damning discernment says,

> One who takes time, midstream as it were to build a standing tribute to himself may have an interior problem: a severe case of being 'little in (his) own eyes.' Saul emerges as a fearfully insecure person, one who uses monuments and even God to secure a stable sense of himself and of his significance.[51]

The irony of the situation will be lost on Saul as Samuel meets him. Saul sounds innocently pleased with himself when he greets him saying, 'Blessed be you to the Lord. I have performed the commandment of the Lord.' But Samuel is far from pleased and he has not arrived to congratulate Saul and celebrate with him. Despite reporting the word of the Lord in v. 1, the narrator records no instructions from the Lord about dealing with Saul. Samuel takes it upon himself to interpret the Lord's word into action. Samuel the prophet is no stranger to confrontation and delivering life changing utterances, a habit learned when he was a boy. He is austere, with a holy and righteous intensity. God's word is law and Saul failed to listen and obey it. J. Woodhouse calls Samuel's meeting with Saul 'one of the most spectacular confrontations in the Bible.'[52] But what actually turns out to be spectacular, is Samuel's denouncement of Saul's failure and sin – 15:22-23.

> Behold to obey is better than sacrifice, and to listen than the fat of rams. Rebellion is as the sin of divination, and stubbornness is as iniquity and idolatry. Because you have rejected the word of the Lord, he has also rejected you from being king.

Verses 10-31 are a striking contrast between Saul's perception of events concerning his victory and Samuel's. When Samuel asks why he can hear the noise of animals, in self-defense Saul explains the people spared the best. It is ironical that Saul is condemned for having listened to the people when Samuel himself was told by the Lord to listen to the people and elect a king. Saul then proceeds to incriminate himself when he tells Samuel he spared Agag the king of Amalek. Saul is utterly unaware and unprepared for the tirade of judgment that is now going to be unleashed on him by Samuel. Before announcing judgment on Saul, Samuel cannot resist reminding him of his insignificant background – that 'he is in fact a nobody. This reminder is a severe reprimand'[53] and his status is only due to the Lord's calling and anointing. Samuel's religious denouncement unleashed against Saul is astonishing in its vehemence: rebellion, divination, stubbornness, idolatry, doing evil in the sight of the Lord. Samuel functions from a legalistic covenant perspective and theological framework. Brueggeman insightfully describes this dimension.

> Samuel articulates the most rigorous and demanding claims of covenantal theology. In this presentation, covenant theology is so fixed and demanding that it cannot take into account the historical realities with which Saul had to cope. The strident and uncompromising requirements of this theology make it inevitable and inescapable that Saul will be judged a failure…On a surface reading, the text and Samuel are undisturbed by such destructive rigour. The text proceeds on the unflinching conviction that the old demanding theology is indeed the voice of God. Against that voice, Saul has no chance…But as the text has it, it is the rigour of covenant that finally breaks Saul.[54]

Saul lacks the spiritual awareness of Samuel, and theologically he is out of his depth. Samuel announces judgment on Saul and it is devastating. He uses his authority as a priest, prophet, and as the Lord's emissary, ruthlessly. One wonders why Samuel wasn't more explicit about the necessity of waiting for him to arrive at Gilgal in Ch. 13 despite any extenuating circumstances. Why he didn't make it absolutely clear about the utter destruction Saul had to carry against the Amalekites? The act of vengeance against the Amalekites was the Lord's and not Saul's.

When Samuel arrives at Gilgal, Saul greets him with what David Gunn calls, 'a most astonishing sentence' – 'Blessed be you to the Lord, I have performed the commandment of the Lord' – 15:13.[55] This statement implies that Saul is confident (bearing in mind the incident in Ch. 13) that he has been obedient. Despite Samuel's negative reply in verses 17-20, Saul continues to insist that he has been obedient to the mission the Lord sent him on, and informs Samuel that he has killed everyone except Agag. If we read in between the lines, the implication is he will be killed at Gilgal before the Lord when the sacrifices are made. Sparing Agag raises a question mark as to Saul's intention and potentially left him vulnerable, but Samuel does not bother to question Saul about this.[56] It is clear that Saul does not see any conflict between what he and the people have done and Samuel's interpretation. Gunn says, 'The fact is that as the story has it, neither Saul nor the people were aware there was any significant incompatibility…If we suppose them to have been thus aware then that their action in so risking divine wrath becomes particularly difficult to comprehend, since all they were attempting to do was to honour Yahweh by their actions…Why else should Saul and the people have come to Gilgal, the sanctuary of Yahweh, the scene of sacrifice, if not to do precisely what he claims?'[57]

Samuel's reference to Saul, 'Though you are little in your own eyes' is a reminder of his insignificant background, but it has no bearing on the integrity of Saul's account about the facts, and may reflect a personal grudge or slight against him by Samuel. Saul's disobedience is neither willful nor flagrant and his explanation about the animals and Agag implies he was acting in good faith. The unspoken implication of the text asks, what are the motives of Samuel and God in rejecting Saul?[58]

We read in Ch. 15:24-31: *'And Saul said to Samuel, 'I have sinned, for I have transgressed the commandment of the Lord and your words, because I feared the people and obeyed their voice. Now therefore, I pray pardon my sin, and return with me that I may worship the Lord.' And Samuel said to Saul, 'I will not return with you, for you have rejected the word of the Lord, and the Lord has rejected you from being king over Israel.' As Samuel turned to go away, Saul laid hold of the end of his robe and tore it. And Samuel said to him, 'The Lord has torn the kingdom of Israel from you this day, and has given it a neighbour of yours, who is better than you. And also the glory of Israel will not lie or repent, for he is not a man that he should repent.' Then Saul said, 'I have sinned, yet honour me now before the elders of my people and before Israel, and return with me that I may worship the Lord your God.' So Samuel turned back after Saul, and Saul worshipped the Lord.'*

The narrator records that Saul acknowledges his sin against the Lord – v. 24-25, although he justifies the reason for his failure, and asks Samuel to pardon his sin. But Samuel refuses to return with Saul, who then pleads with him to accompany him, so that he may honour him before the elders of his people and Israel, which implies he wants Samuel to affirm him as king before them. Also, when Saul says to Samuel, 'return with me that I may worship the Lord your God' – 15:30, this may indicate that he acknowledges the Lord has distanced himself from him. In view of the fact Saul so confidently states his integrity and innocence when condemned because of his action by Samuel, it is surprising Saul did not maintain his innocence and challenge Samuel about his outburst and condemnation. But perhaps he knows it is pointless challenging Samuel and has to concede and submit, in order to maintain his support.

There is almost an element of unreality about the accusations Samuel levels against Saul as he escalates the enormity of his sin, in contrast to Saul's belief that he obeyed the voice of the Lord. Samuel mentions rebellion, divination, stubbornness, idolatry and rejecting the word of the Lord. This is a comprehensive accusation of Saul. And although he admits his sin, the narrator does not record Samuel pardoning him. It is difficult to know how much Saul grasped Samuel's indictment against him. Ironically, as he acknowledges his error he shows some self-awareness about his weakness in being influenced and led by the people. Yet it is difficult to know the reality of Saul's confession, especially when he asks Samuel to return with him to honour him before the elders of my people and Israel. Tsumura says, 'Instead of being stricken with the awfulness of his sin, which can be taken away by God alone, Saul is concerned about his relationship with the people and their elders…Instead of honouring the Lord Saul is concerned with his own honour.'[59] In this context, G. Vreeland highlights an important distinction between Saul and David. When David is confronted with his sin by Nathan, he does not argue, he confesses and waits for his sentence, although he lived in denial about his sin or around a year. But when Saul is confronted with his sin, there is a stark difference. He argues about it with Samuel and then caves in, for the sake of convenience and empowerment.[60]

When Samuel tells Saul the Lord has rejected him as king over Israel, the narrator does not record the Lord informing Samuel about this. There is no prophetic declaration, 'Thus says the Lord, he has rejected you as king.' This absence raises an ambiguity about Samuel's declaration. Either, the Lord informed Samuel he has rejected Saul, or Samuel concludes the Lord rejected Saul as he repented he was his choice as king. Samuel has no word from the Lord about how Saul's kingship is going to end, nor how, or when, his successor is going to replace him. This indicates no contingency plan was in place to end Saul's kingship. And it is somewhat enigmatic that the rejection of Saul by the Lord is not announced by Samuel to the people and the elders of Israel as it affects them. When we consider the detailed plans the Lord gave to Moses about constructing the tabernacle and to Solomon about building the Temple, no comparable plan has been presented to Saul to enable him to establish his kingship.

Here is a king who no longer has the Lord's blessing or the support of Samuel, and the people of Israel are totally unaware of it, and remain ignorant about it. Having already pointed out that Samuel undermined Saul in Ch. 13, by telling him his kingdom could have been established permanently, but now will not be, he further destabilises Saul by introducing another element of instability into his reign because of the news the Lord has rejected him. Although it is speculative when Samuel says, 'The Lord has torn the kingdom from you this day and given it a neighbour of yours who is better than you' – this does not necessarily mean this was the word of the Lord. It could be interpreted that Samuel was stating the obvious. A successor would be chosen that reflected his perception. Samuel only said this after Saul tore the end of his cloak. Was it an impulsive outburst from Samuel to mention a successor, or was this an inspired symbolic utterance? As Samuel does not inform the people and elders of Israel that the Lord has rejected Saul as king, and does not inform them a successor will replace him, and also does not inform them that no plan exists for officially selecting a new king – this appears an enigmatic and haphazard way of officially concluding Saul's rejection. One is left to wonder about the ambiguities involved.

When Saul grabs the end of Samuel's cloak to prevent him from leaving it appears a desperate act, because if he went to Gilgal without Samuel, everyone would know he no longer had his support and he would be publically humiliated. So Saul again admits he has sinned and asks Samuel to go with him to Gilgal, to honour him, so that he may worship the Lord. Borgman astutely says:

> Cloaked as a request for Samuel to take him back for purposes of worship, Saul is asking for reinstatement of himself before God and good standing before the people…Bound in with what appears at first glance a quite genuine expression of repentance, turns out to be no true willingness to turn around at all: Saul still fears the people, still wants honour before the people. Contrary to those vows suggesting the genuine repentance of Saul and subsequent unfairness of judgment against a king, the narrative dooms Saul with his own words.[61]

Samuel is a fearsome man and after Saul worships the Lord he unflinchingly puts Agag to death which appears a merciless act that we probably cannot relate to, as the theological context of a holy war where God's enemies were put to death is utterly alien to us and our understanding of the God of the New Testament. After declaring that Saul's dynasty would not be established Samuel must have been aware that Saul was out to kill him as he says as much to the Lord in 16:2. When we read in 16:1 that Samuel was grieving over Saul whom he condemns without any hesitation in Ch. 15, we are left to wonder exactly why he was grieving. Samuel's relationship with Saul hardly suggests his grief is for Saul, although it may be for the failed experiment of kingship. Apart from this explanation no biblical commentator gives a convincing reason for Samuel's grief, although Jobling dares to suggest, 'We can now understand Samuel's unexpected grief over Saul's rejection. He could not prevent kingship but he has achieved the next best thing – a king he can control, a king who is less than a king. Samuel has won his battle with Saul, so he wants to keep Saul as figurehead who conforms to his judgeship's idea of what a national leader can be…The Lord is determined that Samuel will not a second time get a king he can control. This goes a long way to explaining the king making in 16:1-13, where Samuel is deprived of any real control or even understanding of what is going on. He is needed as a functionary: continuity still requires that the last judge be the kingmaker. But this will be a new kind of king, one who is beyond Samuel's reach.'[62]

Ironically, and paradoxically, as it is only Saul's dynasty that has been rejected, and despite the anointing of David in secret, Saul is still left to reign for many years to come.

CHAPTER FOUR

DAVID

DAVID'S ANOINTING

1 Samuel 16:1-16

Shaul Bar, the Professor of Judaic Studies at the University of Memphis points out, 'There is a great similarity in the stories depicting Saul's and David's rise to power.'[1] Just as Saul was invited to a meal in Ch. 9:11-14 before a sacrifice after which he was anointed, Samuel invites Jesse and his sons, along with the elders to a sacrificial feast after his arrival. As Saul was privately anointed in secret, David was also anointed in the same way, as his brothers could not have been there because when he arrived at the confrontation between Goliath and Israel, Eliab his brother 'was not evidently not aware of his brother's new status.'[2] Or, perhaps Eliab did not realise the significance of Samuel anointing David with oil, as Ch. 16:13 records Samuel anointed David in the midst of his brothers. Saul nor David was present at the time of their election, Saul was hiding amongst the baggage and had to be fetched, while David was looking after sheep and also had to be fetched. Both are depicted as insignificant and unworthy. 'Saul said, 'But I am only a Benjaminite, from the smallest of the tribes of Israel, and my clan is the least of all the clans of the tribe of Benjamin' – 9:21, while David is described as the youngest – 16:11. In Saul's story his servant, a young man leads him to Samuel and in David's, a young man advises Saul to bring David to his house.[3] The narrator focuses on the physical appearance of both Saul and David. Saul is described as a handsome young man, standing head and shoulders, above everyone – 9:2, while David is described as handsome, with beautiful eyes – 16:2.

In Ch. 8, the elders take the initiative to come to Samuel and request a king to rule over them, but in Ch. 16, the Lord takes the initiative to inform Samuel about his choice of the new king. Saul was the Lord's choice just as David is now his choice, and life will never again be the same for David, just as it was never again the same for Saul. But, the theological leitmotif of the story of David is that the presence of the Lord was with him and explains the secret of his success –18:14-15.[4] However, 'The subsequent courses of these two men's lives show complexities and avoid any simple deterministic understandings.'[5]

Towards the end of Ch. 15 Samuel announced to Saul that the Lord has rejected him as king over Israel and has given his kingdom to 'a neighbour of yours' and in 15: 34 and 16: 1, the narrator records that Samuel grieved over Saul. Woodhouse says, 'The tragedy of Saul's failure was real, but it was not everything. Samuel was not to be so overwhelmed by the calamity that he failed to see the Lord's hands in it and God's purpose beyond the disaster.'[6] If Samuel was so confident Saul has been rejected why is he grieving, instead of asking the Lord who is going to replace him? Or perhaps he is grieving because he was originally opposed to the idea of a king, and the failure of Saul has confirmed his fears about monarch was a mistake. Is he confused about the way ahead, especially as he knows he is under constant surveillance from Saul[7] who is out to kill him, before he can appoint his successor?

We can understand Samuel's reluctance when the Lord tells him to go and anoint the new king, because if Saul finds out he will kill him. Samuel's concern indicates there is a political rift between him and Saul. The Lord takes this seriously and devises a plan to send Samuel. Despite being initially hesitant, Samuel has a resolute determination to be obedient and as he has learned during his life to faithfully trust the Lord when he speaks to him, even though the Lord has not disclosed to him who the next king is. Without Samuel David could not be identified and the Lord's plan would have been thwarted if Samuel failed to be obedient. Despite being elderly he had learned to hear God's voice and this cannot be underestimated.

Bearing in mind the Lord's detailed plans given to Moses about building the Tabernacle, and his detailed plans to Solomon about building the Temple, it is difficult to comprehend and seemingly out of character that when the Lord selects a new king, there is no plan whatsoever given to Samuel or David, informing him about how he will succeed Saul. If it is hazardous for Samuel to go undercover and in a clandestine manner to anoint the new king, how much more dangerous is it for David once Saul finds out. Brueggemann says, 'It is hazardous to anoint a king when there is already a king!... Samuel by now is surely identified as a traitorous enemy of Saul, and he knows any overture towards a new king is high risk.'[8] We are confronted with the Lord's inscrutable purpose and will in the way in which David was chosen and anointed, and was then left on his own without any guidance or plan about how to succeed Saul as king. By way of contrast when Saul was anointed conditions were attached to his kingship. He was expected to be obedient to the word of the Lord Samuel informed him about.

The irony is not lost on the reader, when in the first half of Ch. 16 unknown to Saul, the Lord chooses David and in the second half, Saul chooses David. 1 Sam. 16:1-2 to 2 Sam. 5:2 is often referred to as, 'The History of David's Rise.' The transition from Ch. 15 to 16 gives no indication of the time that lapsed between the rejection of Saul and election of David. Despite Samuel's concern about his safety, he obediently goes to Bethlehem, a town about five miles south of Jerusalem and eleven miles south of Ramah, Samuel's home. To get from Ramah to Bethlehem he had to journey through Gibeah, Saul's home town. A reluctant Samuel arrives at Bethlehem much to the consternation of the elders, who were terrified by his appearance. News of Samuel's arrival in Bethlehem is not immediately seen to be good news, as he has a fierce reputation as a judge. 'The elders of the city came to meet Samuel trembling, and said to him, Do you come peaceably?' – 16:4. Perhaps, they are afraid because of his reputation and are concerned about the reason for his sudden visit. Or, perhaps they have heard Saul is out to kill him and are terrified in case Samuel has come to elect a new king, because there will be serious recriminations if Saul thinks they have colluded with Samuel.

One of Saul's obvious assets when the Lord chose him was his impressive appearance that enabled him to stand out from his contemporaries. Now that Samuel is looking to identify the new king he is immediately struck by Eliab's physical appearance and thinks he must be the Lord's anointed. 'He looked on Eliab and thought, 'surely the Lord's anointed' – 16:6. Samuel is in danger of making a fatal mistake. Just in time, the Lord informed him, 'Do not look on his appearance or on the height of his stature, because I have rejected him, for the Lord sees not as man sees, man looks at the outward appearance, but the Lord looks on the heart' – 16:7. In verses 6-7 there is an emphasis on looking and seeing. Seeing is a key motif. Appearances can be deceptive. Is this a hint that when Saul was chosen, initially the Lord perceived something lacking in Saul, as the Lord gave him another heart? – 10:9. Although the Lord told Samuel not to focus on the appearance of Jesse's sons, the narrator cannot resist commenting on how good looking David's is, 'he was ruddy, (had fair skin) had beautiful eyes and was handsome' – 16:12. 'Samuel and the narrator are dazzled.'[9] We heard Samuel say in Ch. 13:14, that the Lord had sought out a man after his own heart, which means a man of his choice, rather than someone like the Lord. In Jewish thought, the heart is the core of one's inner self – personality. It is the seat of emotion, understanding, volitional will and conscience. Biblical references to heart are typically a figure of speech of some aspect of human personality. Alter adds, 'the heart is the seat of understanding.'[10] The Lord had set his heart on David. He was God's choice, reflecting his sovereign will, and here he is singled out by the Lord as that man. But there is also a double emphasis on 'heart.' The Lord looked at David with his heart – and he also looked deep into David's heart. The Lord saw beyond the surface into David's soul, his character, personality and spirit. When the Lord chose Saul he had to give him another heart – 10:9 and he was changed into another man – 10:6. However, with David the Lord has a man who does not require heart surgery or transformation. When David challenges Goliath, we see evidence of his faith in the Lord and his relationship with him. Whereas the narrator gives no indication that Saul ever knew the Lord personally in this way, or had such faith in him. Although, what both Saul and David have in common is that after their anointing, the spirit of God came mightily upon them – 1 Sam. 10:10, 16: 13.

After Samuel's arrival when he invites Jesse and his sons to the sacrifice and they consecrate themselves, he is caught out completely by surprise when the Lord rejects each one of them. 'The Lord has not chosen these' – 16:10, records the narrator in a dramatic manner, that increases the suspense. Samuel insists that everyone waits while Jesse fetches his youngest son who is looking after sheep. This waiting is not fortuitous. It is providential for David, although he does not yet know it. At this dramatic and historic scene of David's anointing, the narrator fails to inform the reader of David's response or his father's and brothers' reaction. The only words that matter to him are those spoken by the Lord, 'Arise, anoint him, for this is he' – 16:12. There is only an extraordinary silent anti-climax after David is anointed. Samuel doesn't speak to David. David says nothing. His father and brothers are also silent, or so we imagine. What they said or thought is inconsequential to the narrator. What is important is that the Lord has identified David as his man and he has been anointed. The climax to David's anointing is in 16:13, 'And the Spirit of the Lord came mightily upon David from that day forward.'

DAVID SERVES SAUL

1 Samuel 16: 14-23

Monarchy is a new institution and this evolves in response to circumstances. David's anointing is a low key event. It is not marked by any grand ceremony with important officials attending. It is a clandestine affair hidden from Saul. A modest ceremony for a humble shepherd whose prospects for the future were overshadowed by seven brothers. 'The eighth son is the youngest, surely unimpressive, with no claim to make, and no credentials to present.'[11] David was on the margins of family life. No one in his family thought of fetching him on Samuel's arrival. David is the Lord's unanticipated, chosen and anointed. Firth captures the incongruity of his selection, as he is an unlikely candidate being the youngest son of an undistinguished family, in an otherwise unimportant town.[12] Soon he will be catapulted into the public arena where Saul will contend with him. For Saul there is bad news. 'Once David is on the scene it is difficult not to make him the centre of attention, indeed that is part of the problem in the story: everyone's focus is on David!...Everyone loves David when he arrives in court, that will be the ostensible problem.'[13] Firth highlights two themes in the ensuing narrative about David. Firstly, the Lord is present with David. This is recognised by Saul's servant in 16: 18 and by Saul himself in 18:12, 'Saul was afraid of David because the Lord was with him.' Secondly, everyone is drawn to David even Saul himself.[14] 'And Saul loved David greatly' – 16:21. 'Jonathan loved David as his own soul' – 18:1. 'But all Israel and Judah loved David greatly' – 18:16. Now Saul's daughter Michal also loved David' – 18:20.

After Samuel goes to Ramah, there is a change of scene in v.14 as the narrator takes us to Saul in Gibeah, although there is no indication of the time that lapsed between the two events. While the narrator makes no mention of the Lord's involvement in Saul inviting David into his royal court, we are surely meant to see God's hand on the circumstances that brings them together. Yet as they come together, neither protagonist had any clue about the drama that lay ahead. It is an inescapable fact that there are two stories running parallel to each other. The fate of Saul and the destiny of David, that for better and worse are inextricably intertwined. There is much in the life of Saul and Samuel's dealings with him that we may find hard to reconcile, along with the Lord's rejection of Saul, that may leave us with a certain ambiguity. Equally, we may find it hard to understand why the Lord sent an evil spirit to torment Saul, after God's Spirit departed from him and now rested on David. If losing his anointing and being rejected as king was tragic, Saul now faced the emotional and psychological horrors that an evil spirit inflicted on him.

We read in 1 Samuel 16:14-19:

> Now the Spirit of the Lord departed from Saul and an evil spirit from the Lord tormented him. And Saul's

> servants said to him, 'Behold now an evil spirit from God is tormenting you. Let our lord now command your servants who are before you, to seek out a man who is skilful in playing the lyre: and when the evil spirit from God is upon you, he will play it and you shall be well.' So Saul said to his servants, 'Provide for me a man who can play well and bring him to me.' One of the men answered, 'Behold, I have seen a son of Jesse, the Bethlehemite, who is skilful in playing, a man of valour, a man of war, prudent in speech, and a man of good presence – and the Lord is with him.' Therefore, Saul sent messengers to Jesse and said, 'Send me David your son who is with the sheep.'

Saul's affliction and oppression may seem ancient and distant, but it has reminded me of my experience. Shortly after the doctor diagnosed me with post viral fatique at the start of 1998, I had a picture that described how I felt. It was as if someone had drawn a circle around my emotional life and thrown it away, and also drawn another circle around my spiritual life and thrown that away too. Two friends, one a Christian and the other my next door neigbour, both perceived a change had taken place in me. The former said to me, 'The face is the same and the hair is the same, but is it the same person?' Similarly, my next door neighbour said to my wife, 'Sotirios isn't the same person.' Some years later, I wondered if the symbol of a circle represented a curse inflicted by the occult who prayed against Christian leaders in W. Sussex. Now, writing about Saul, I wonder if the Lord was responsible for my malaise.

After returning to Cambridge in June 1998, at times in the first few months as I was worshipping, there was literally a physical pain in my chest. On one occasion, it felt as if a sword pierced had my heart. There were often times when I experienced a lack of energy, although my main symptoms were internal and unseen. Post viral fatigue was punctuated by the disheartening and frustrating tendency of its fluctuating nature. There were often times when I felt that I was getting better, only to find a negative downward turn would invariably follow. Despite the uplifting occasions, it felt as if a negativity had descended like a cloud and enveloped my heart and spirit. One of the most discouraging symptoms was the feeling that this endless roller coaster cycle of going up and then down was never going to end. I named this, *'the internal horrors'* of post viral fatique. Emotionally, psychologically and also spiritually, it felt as if someone was playing games with me: and in these areas I have been to places I never knew existed. On occasions, I also had the feeling of simultaneously being pulled in two directions. There was the desire to serve the Lord and an opposing force pulling me in the opposite direction. At times, I sensed there was a spirit oppressing me. And while this may sound strange, I wondered if the Holy Spirit and the evil one had been playing a tug of war with my soul. Emotionally, psychologically and spiritually, I experienced a fragmentation that altered the landscape of my inner life and relationships. To be ill at ease in these areas is acutely destablising. Another side effect of the symptoms of post viral fatique, is that you feel you have lost touch with parts of your real self. It is as if aspects of your personality are no longer alive. During the years that this illness persisted, I never took any medication and constantly shared my feelings and thoughts with the Lord.

1 Sam. 16 records a remarkable transition as the Spirit is transferred from Saul to David. 'The Spirit came to David and now the spirit departs from Saul.'[15] Ch. 16:14 marks an unwelcome change in Saul due to an unusual event – he now becomes the recipient of an evil spirit from the Lord that tormented – began to terrorise him. Vreeland describes this as, 'One of the most frightening texts in regards to the movement of the Spirit...we will observe an increasingly agitated Saul. He will become more violent, more insane, and more troubled (demonised) until such time as the situation in this life becomes irredeemable.'[16] This may appear to be a harsh act by the Lord and difficult to understand why it was necessary, yet demands to be explored. Diana Edelman interprets this as a malevolent spirit that will prevent Saul from carrying out his role as king. She believes this punishes the king and people, a direct result of 12:13-15. If the people disobey God's commandments, the 'hand of the Lord' will be against both people and king 12:15.

The punishment was because of peoples' disobedience against the Amalekites in keeping some of the best livestock, and Saul not restraining them and also taking Agag their king alive.[17]

Dave Miller points out, 'The peculiar linguistic features of ancient languages must be clarified and understood in accordance with the way those languages functioned. Specifically, ancient Hebrew was literally loaded with *figurative* language – i.e. figures of speech, colloquialisms and idioms.' His next point is relevant to understanding 16:14: 'It frequently was the case that '(a)ctive verbs were used by the Hebrews to express not the doing of the thing, but the *permission* of the thing which the agent is said to do. God did not directly send on Saul an evil spirit, rather he *allowed* it to happen in view of Saul's own propensity for stubborn disobedience. By these successive acts of rebellion against the will and law of God, King Saul left himself wide open to satanic influence.'[18] The Lord also sent an evil spirit between Abimelech and the men of Shechem; and the men of Shechem dealt treacherously with Abimelech – Judges 9:23. In 1 Sam 18:10 we read, 'And on the morrow, an evil spirit from God rushed on Saul, and he raved within his house.' Also in 19:9 we read, 'Then an evil spirit from the Lord came upon Saul.' Tsumura interprets an 'evil spirit from the Lord' as a linguistic problem. This translation is not adequate to convey for the Hebrew original. He suggests the phrase *ruah-ra-ah*, which is usually translated as 'an evil spirit' should be taken as a construct chain, 'a spirit of evilness (or disaster), since *raah* cannot be an adjective in *ruah haraah* – 16:23 and *ruah* YHWH *raah* – 19:9.'[19] 'This situation is not only a state of fright, but also a state of partly being incapacitated.'[20] The word usually translated evil in Hebrew is grievous.[21]

We can detect certain things about the spirit that tormented Saul. In the worldview of his time, the Israelite belief was that everything was attributable to the Lord. The world of biblical perspective is a world without secondary cause. This assumes that the world is ordered by the direct sovereign rule of God.[22] This belief is expressed by Saul's servants who recognise the source of the grievous spirit troubling Saul. And Saul's servants said to him, 'Behold now an evil spirit from God is tormenting you' – 16:15. This may imply that Saul did not realise God's spirit had departed from him, or he failed to recognise what was troubling him. Similarly, we read about Samson, 'For he did not know that the Lord had departed from him' – Judges 16:20. The grievous spirit was the outcome of the Lord's judgment and in effect punishment on Saul. He was not informed by Samuel or the Lord that his rejection as king had a consequence. Also, the phenomenon that manifested itself was outside of his control. He could not overcome it, or master this spirit himself, he was at its mercy. Although it was not permanent and occurred randomly, it oppressed Saul frequently. Woodhouse thinks Saul's later behaviour suggests a severe mental or emotional disturbance.[23] To what extent was the disturbance in Saul's emotional and psychological equilibrium, a result of his disobedience and a response to his rejection as king and a successor appointed? To what extent, was it a spiritual and theological consequence of God's judgment, manifest emotionally and psychologically in his life? Brueggemann aptly describes Saul's affliction that unknown to him has an ironic solution:

> Saul is indeed a disturbed man, and the disturbance has to do with alienation rooted in a theological disorder. The disorder must be seen, however, as both theological and psychological in order to understand the powerful ministration of David, who is Yahweh's antidote for every ailment in Israel.[24]

S. Bar gives some interesting background information about the term 'servant of the king' which referred to a variety of functions inside and outside the royal court. He points out that the servant had high status close to the king. 'The servants in Saul's story refer to high ranking members of Saul's court, which is made clear from other biblical references – 2 Kings 22: 12, 25:8, 2 Chron. 34: 20.'[25] Over a period of time, Saul's high ranking servants observe his distressing moods and appear more knowledgeable about the problem afflicting him than he is. But they are also aware of the solution. So Saul's servants speak to him and identify the cause of his affliction: 'Behold now, an evil spirit from God is tormenting you' – 16:15. They name what Saul may be reluctant to admit. As his advisors, they recommend the solution. They will find a man who is skilful in playing the lyre so that when the evil spirit from God attacks Saul, he will play it and he will feel better. In the ancient Near East, it was believed the lyre had divine healing power.[26] Saul agrees and commands them to find such a man. 'Astonishingly there was a young man who knew just the right person.'[27] One cannot help but think the advisors had already found a solution, but diplomatically suggest it without sounding as if it was already a fait accompli. When the young man (Edelman thinks he is one of the king's military personnel)[28] describes David without actually mentioning his name, what is extraordinary is the remarkable description he gives to Saul. This servant knows all about David, whereas Saul is ignorant about him. David has been transformed from looking after sheep, to an accomplished soldier. He is a man of valour, and a man of war – 16:18, whose reputation is already known to Saul's servant. His military skill far outshines his musical ability. Moreover, the Lord is with him – 16:18. The young man uses twice as many words to describe David's military skill as he does his musical ability.[29] This is a truly incredible description of David who has been transformed. The reader cannot but wonder whether this description is cloaked in hyperbole to impress Saul. Has the narrator described the David we will come to know, or has he grown and matured in stature? And how does someone in Saul's court knows about him? We do not know. What we do know is the Lord is with him.' This is a 'kind of leitmotiv running throughout the stories of David and Saul.'[30] Instinctively, the reader wonders why Saul hasn't recoiled at the news 'the Lord is with him' as he appears oblivious to the implication of God's presence. The narrator is infuriating as he withholds this information. The implication is David's abilities are the manifestation of divine gifts and therefore divine favour.[31] Brueggemann captures the enigma surrounding David's portrayal. 'The speaker who answers Saul is too eager and knows too much. It is as though this character in the narrative has memorised his long line and is waiting for a chance to speak. He 'over nominates' David, who is overqualified for the job as musician.'[32] Ironically, the qualities ascribed to David are those fitting for a king.[33]

We read in Ch. 16:19-23:

> Therefore, Saul sent messengers to Jesse and said, 'Send me David your son who is with the sheep.' And Jesse took an ass laden with bread and a skin of wine and a kid and sent them by David his son. And David came to Saul and entered his service. And Saul loved him greatly and he became his armour-bearer. And Saul sent to Jesse saying, 'Let David remain in my service, for he has found favour in my sight.' And whenever the evil spirit from God was upon Saul, David took the lyre and played it with his hand: so Saul was refreshed and was well, and the evil spirit departed from him.

When Saul was looking for his father's asses, he was guided by a servant, now as king he is guided once again by another servant. Gunn captures this dramatic scene, 'The economy of the plot is superb and the irony of the situation that is created is quite overwhelming…With an introductory nudge of fate, Saul delivers himself into David's hands…by the introduction of David into his court Saul has begun unconsciously to pave the way for his advancement.'[34] Saul is first to name David rather than his servant, although he must have told him his name and that he looked after sheep. The narrative implies that Saul is oblivious David is his successor and unwittingly invites God's newly anointed into his royal court. We can perceive the Lord is working out his purpose to bring David to the throne and that opportunities to prove himself would come in Saul's service. He will also learn about politics and palace intrigue and how the king uses his power and rules Israel. We cannot help but conclude that the Lord's hand of providence is behind David's invitation into Saul's court. It is a stunning development that will have ramifications for both protagonists.

'And David came to Saul and entered his service. And Saul loved him greatly and became his armour-bearer. Presumably, he found favour when he played the lyre and Saul was relieved from the oppressive spirit. David is the Old Testament Adonis, a strikingly beautiful young man. 'David is irresistible.'[35] Although Saul is named as the first person to love him, some biblical commentators think that the attachment to David refers to a political love. Edleman suggests, 'The failure of Saul's name to appear in the MT after the verb 'loved' in order to signal a change of subject should, therefore, be taken as an indication that David is the intended subject of the phrase in question.'[36] Borgman captures the remarkable impact David has on Saul. 'David says nothing, and does nothing except on request…The first David Saul meets then, is quiet, receptive, and musical – a servant responding to solicitation, not a person initiating action or conversation. The quiescence here is almost a passivity.'[37] Soon everyone will love David for his good looks and his charisma. This somewhat unremarkable scenario where David the musician plays the lyre, will give way to David the remarkable warrior who kills Goliath.

DAVID & GOLIATH
1 Samuel 17:1-58

The story of David and Goliath is one of the best known and loved, thrilling tales in the Old Testament. One that captures our imagination as we visualise David killing Goliath. This dramatic scene 'is a powerful, well crafted narrative capable of sustaining our interest and imagination through its long telling. The story deliberately paced, draws us slowly and steadily into the moment of high tension.'[38] Chapter 17 begins with an ominous threat – 'Now the Philistines gathered their armies for battle.' The narrator describes a stand off between Israel and the Philistines, with each army camped on opposite sides of a valley. Woodhouse points out that the goal of this strategically important battle was to secure the Valley of Elah. The natural point of entry from the Philistine homeland into the Saulide kingdom.[39] In 1 Samuel, the Philistines are constantly in the background threatening Israel. Saul was elected king to deliver Israel from the Philistines but had not accomplished this. The Philistines sought to gain a psychological advantage through Goliath as there was a stalemate, because the valley prevented either side from making an ambush or an unexpected attack, so an impasse occurred.[40] At Goliath's challenge, Saul and his troops are incapacitated with fear, with no leadership initiative by Saul to counter this. Equally, there is no high ranking servant who comes to advise him. Moreover, Saul is no longer embued with God's Spirit and Samuel has retreated from Saul.

Goliath was from Gath the closest Philistine city to this battle line which was the city in 1 Samuel 7 that was restored to Israel. Although at some stage, it must have passed back into the hands of the Philistines. Goliath was just over six cubits tall which is a height of over nine feet, his coat of armour weighed 5000 shekels – 56 kilograms and the shaft of his spear was like a weaver's beam. Goliath was a menacing and terrifying sight. He intimidated Israel and seemed indestructible, invulnerable. Clearly, no ordinary man could possibly defeat him, not even Saul. It is somewhat ironic that this giant of a man goes to such great lengths to protect himself. I have seen a wrestler seven feet tall on the sky sports channel, with lumbering movements and not particularly mobile. Perhaps Goliath's lack of mobility was his weakness hence the reason for with his heavy armour to protect himself. Flush with confidence he challenges Saul's men to select a champion to face him, with the losing side being servants of the conqueror's nation. Goliath's brashness and supreme confidence was mingled with defiance, as he provoked Saul's men with open contempt[41] for forty days and taunted them to face him. We Read in 17:8-10:

> Goliath stood and shouted to the ranks of Israel, 'Why have you come out to draw battle? Am I not a Philistine, and are you not servants of Saul? Choose a man for yourselves and let him come down to me. If he is able to fight with me and kill me, then we will be your servants: but if I prevail against him and kill him, then you shall be our servants and serve us. I defy the ranks of Israel this day: give me a man that we may fight together.'

Goliath's speech is bombastic, pompous, denigrating.'[42] And 'Before Goliath's size, strength and speech, Saul and Israel are shattered.'[43] Saul and all Israel are overwhelmed by this giant of a man and were 'dismayed and greatly afraid' – 17:11. They are faced with the impossible challenge of defeating this champion that creates a tangible tension in the narrative.

After the dramatic confrontation between Goliath and Israel, David is inauspiciously introduced to the scene. Although he is Saul's servant, he still goes back and forth to feed his father's sheep. After a journey of around 12 miles from Bethlehem, he arrives unobtrusively with provisions for his brothers as the stalemate between Goliath and Israel has gone on for 40 days, and he can bring a report to his father about their welfare – 17:18. David is too young to be in Saul's army as we learn from Numbers 1:3, 'From twenty years old and upward, all that are able to go forth to war in Israel: you and Aaron shall number.' From this, we can deduce that David was under 20 years old because he wasn't in the army. However, Jesse's three older sons had gone with Saul to the battle. If Shammah the youngest of the three that went was 20, then that leaves 4 brothers between them and David who may be around 17 years old, and already a strong young man.

David's mundane duty brings him to the excitement of the battle line as both armies square up to each other. 'The military procedure so grips David that for the moment he forgets his commission.'[44] He leaves the provisions with the baggage keeper, a tacit reminder Saul hid amongst the baggage, and goes to greet his brothers, just as Goliath issues his challenge once again to Saul's army. On his appearance, some of the men discuss Saul's offer to the man who defeats him. He has promised great riches and the hand of his daughter in marriage. For the first time since David was introduced in the narrative up to now he has been silent, and for the first time his character is revealed when he speaks. Far from being just a young man who does what he is told, he is now a precocious individual who inquiries, 'What shall be done for the man who kills this Philistine and takes away the reproach from Israel? For who is this uncircumcised Philistine, that he should defy the armies of the living God?' – 17:26.

'The narrative has been arranged so the weighty theological affirmation is placed in the mouth of David.'[45] David's first words that he spoke are truly remarkable and wondrous. They are words imbued with the authority we would expect from one of the Lord's prophets. David expresses a godly contempt and reproach for Goliath the uncircumcised Philistine. He is defiant because he mocked Israel and the Lord. His boldness is not mere bravado or chutzpah. David's speech is a sign of the Spirit's anointing. His words are inspired by God's Spirit.

The defeat of Goliath that will follow is almost tantamount to the realm of fantasy, but first David has to overcome the ridicule of his eldest brother Eliab, who overheard what he had just said. He was angry with David, cynically rebuked him and said, 'I know your presumption and the evil of your heart, for you have come down to see the battle.' And David said, 'What have I done now? Was it not but a word?' And he turned away from him toward another and spoke in the same way, and the people answered him as before' – 17:28-30. Here recorded in the Scripture are the first words David ever uttered.[46] The text invites us to see a parallel between the way Joseph was treated with resentment by his brothers and their sibling rivalry. In his ignorance about David, Eliab totally misunderstood his youngest brother. He witnessed his anointing and perhaps that is why he is resentful, but he doesn't know David is the wave of the future.[47] His rebuke to David is fortuitous because when David repeats his words they are reported to Saul who sends for him. 'As with Joseph's dreams, there is a mysterious, divine plan behind the young man's words.'[48] Although the narrator records that David first speaks to Saul, we can assume Saul initiated the conversation. We read in 17: 32-33, 36-38:

> And David said to Saul, 'Let no man's heart fail because of him: your servant will go and fight with this Philistine.' And Saul said to David, 'You are not able to go against this Philistine to fight him, for you are but a youth, and he has been a man of war since his youth.' David replied, 'Your servant has killed both lions and bears, and this uncircumcised Philistine shall be like

> one of them, seeing he has defied the armies of the living God. The Lord, who delivered me from the paw of the lion and the paw of the bear, will deliver from the hand of this Philistine.' And Saul said to David, 'Go, and the Lord be with you.'

Saul's initial response to David shows he does not know of his anointing by the Spirit. He sees no further than the outward appearance as he makes a contrast between David and Goliath, when he states he has been a man of war since his youth, and David is but a young man. But the text also invites us to see a crucial contrast between David and Saul. B. Green stresses, that the contrast is not simply in confidence, but in knowledge of God. 'Saul says little of God that indicates they are on intimate terms. He has so far shown himself not irreligious at all, but rather non-familiar, non-intuitive about God. David somehow draws on a different fund of experience. What David seems to know already Saul will never learn.'[49] Now he overcomes the second obstacle between him and Goliath, Saul – when he states his credentials for challenging him. Although Saul then clothes David with his armour, he takes this off, as he wasn't used to it. It may have been too large and cumbersome for him as Saul was so tall and he wasn't used to wearing armour. Some biblical commentators interpret Saul clothing David with his royal armour as a symbol of divesting his kingship and bestowing it on David, although the narrator does not comment on this.

David's boldness is surreal, because humanly speaking his confident claim to defeat Goliath is outrageous. He is either arrogant, delusional or foolish – or his words speak of a remarkably confident faith in the Lord. Faith inspired by the anointing of the Spirit, Saul and his men are ignorant about. Although he lacks any formal military training, David's first words – 'Let no man's heart fail because of him, your servant will go and fight with this Philistine' may be intended for Saul. Brueggemann says, 'David's very first word, without elaboration, is a salvation oracle designed to overcome Saul's fear, an assurance of David's own presence and solidarity with Saul.'[50] David's extraordinary claim that he made to Saul who was old enough to be his father, was not in himself, but in the Lord. The Lord saved David from wild animals, and he trusted the Lord to deliver him from this Philistine. David's outlook on the challenge of Goliath was theologically rooted, because he defied the armies of the living God. His confidence to challenge Goliath was also theologically grounded in his faith in the Lord to deliver him. And his speech has 'a disciplined and eloquent theological substance.'[51] David's faith flows from his relationship with the Lord and the Lord's deliverance in his life. A faith that has been reinforced by the powerful anointing of God's Spirit. But there is more to it than that. David's speech is stunning in its impact and leaves us speechless in its audaciousness. For the text invites us to see beyond David's words and grasp that his speech is a prophetic oracle inspired by God's Spirit. What David speaks out aloud, is in reality 'the word of the Lord' against Goliath. And in Scripture when God speaks, his voice brings into being what he declares.

However, for God's word to be fulfilled against Goliath, David had to step out in faith and trust the Lord. We read in 1 Sam. 17:39b-54: 'And David took off Saul's armour. Then he took his staff in his hand and chose five smooth stones from the brook, and put them in his shepherd's bag: his sling was in his hand and he drew near to the Philistine. And he came on and drew near to David, with his shield bearer in front of him. And when the Philistine looked and saw David, he disdained him, for he was but a youth, ruddy and comely in appearance. And he said to David, 'Am I a dog that you come to me with sticks?' And he cursed David by his gods and said, 'Come to me and I will give your flesh to the birds of the air and to the beasts of the field.' Then David said to him, 'You come to me with a sword and with a spear and with a javelin: but I come to you in the name of the Lord of hosts, the God of the armies of Israel whom you have defiled. This day the Lord will deliver you into my hand, and I will strike you down and cut off your head: and I will give the dead bodies of the host of the Philistines this day to the birds of the air and to the wild beasts of the earth: that all the earth may know that there is a God in Israel, and that all this assembly may know that the Lord saves not with sword and spear: for the battle is the Lord's and he will give you into our hand.' When the Philistine began to come near David, he ran quickly toward the battle to meet the Philistine. And David put his hand in his bag and took out a stone, and slung it, and struck him on his forehead: the stone sank into his forehead and he fell on his face to the ground. So David prevailed over the Philistine with a sling and with a stone, and struck the Philistine and killed him. Then David ran and stood over him, and took his sword and drew it out of its sheath and killed him, and cut off his head with it. When the Philistines saw that their champion was dead, they fled. And the men of Israel and Judah rose with a shout and pursued the Philistines as far as Gath and the gates of Ekron, so that the wounded Philistines fell on the way from Sha-araim as far as Gath and Ekron. And the Israelites came back from chasing them, and they plundered their camp. And David took the head of the Philistine and brought it to Jerusalem: but he put his armour in his tent.'

We know very little about David before his challenge to Goliath, apart from the fact he was a shepherd and had been anointed by Samuel. We can but marvel at his Spirit inspired faith and trust in the Lord and his theological awareness of the Lord's character as he challenged Goliath – 'in the name of the Lord of hosts, the God of the armies of Israel' – 17:45b. On the day he faced his enemy, David was God's servant and through him the Lord of hosts revealed his sovereign power in both heaven and earth against Goliath. It is striking that David uses the title 'Lord of Hosts' as this refers to the hosts who surround the Lord's heavenly throne and who praise him and carry out his decisions as sovereign of the world. 'Lord of Hosts' also refers to all the created agencies and forces under the dominion of God, who made and maintains them. And in Hebrew the title 'Lord of Hosts' is *Jehovah Sabaoth* which speaks of God's available power in our time of trouble.

After forty days of challenges and taunts by Goliath, with the narrator recording the speeches in great length, there is a spectacularly short confrontation. David's challenge insults Goliath's pride and arouses his anger. He despises and disdains

David. Full of hubris and heavy with irony, Goliath curses him by his own gods.[52] But little does he know of the humiliation that awaits him. Before David takes the initiative to attack Goliath, he took of Saul's armour, and swiftly took his staff, deftly chose five stones, put them in his bag and confidently approached Goliath with his sling in his hand. His agility is his advantage in contrast to Goliath's slow movement. David was probably aware of the ability of the famous 700 skilled men in Judges 20:16, who were left-handed and could sling a stone at a hair, and not miss it! David knew just how lethal a sling and stone could be in frightening away dangerous animals. Robert Pinsky says, 'The slinger was more mobile than the archer and with a greater accurate range, some say with a more damaging projectile. The Romans had medical tongs designed specific-ally for removing the stones or lead bullets shot by sling to penetrate a soldier's body, as David's stone penetrated the skull of Goliath.'[53] David's trust in the Lord still requires that he attacks Goliath, and as he approaches him, he quickly runs, outmaneuvers him and strikes first, with a stone in his sling that is unleashed with unerring accuracy. We can but admire David's calm and fearless courage, having already determined where to aim at Goliath – in the middle of his forehead. Just the right place to stun him so he loses his balance and falls face down to the ground – just like Dagon in 1 Sam. 5. The text invites us to perceive the Lord's hand was providentially on David's hand as his sling shot stunned Goliath. David is trans-formed into a national hero and Israel's champion, as he runs up to Goliath takes his sword, kills him, and cuts off his head.

As we imagine this scene taking place this must have been an incredible and unbelievable sight, as Saul's men watched David walking away with Goliath's head and his sword in his hands. This was a day that no one would ever forget, especially David. In retrospect, bearing in mind the theological content of David's speeches leading up to his challenge with Goliath, it is surprising that David does not magnify and praise the Lord for his deliverance. Either the narrator failed to record this, or David did not proclaim the Lord's name had been vindicated through this victory. In God's providence, David has been victorious, 'in the face of Saul's impotence.'[54] Borgman captures the aura surrounding the enigma of David, who as Saul's musician is now transformed into Israel's champion.

> The two Davids Saul met couldn't have been more different, to be sure: the one is silent, the other talks: one waits dutifully for a call to actions, like carrying lunch to his brothers or playing music for the king: the other talks without waiting and acts impulsively: the one David is musically gifted, the other militaristically brilliant: the one exercises receptivity, the other initiative…There is the distinguishing but also the melding of David the private man and David the public servant – the quiet lyricist, Israel's talkative warrior supreme. The private and responsive David, lyricist and musician, is alone with the king: the public and initiating David is Israel's champion warrior.[55]

On seeing David defeat Goliath the Philistines fled and the men of Israel pursued them, after which they returned and plundered their camp – 17:51-53. After his victory when Abner brings David to Saul and he asks, 'Whose son are you young man?' – this does not necessarily mean that Saul did not know it was David, as he may have been inquiring about his paternal background. Yet Saul appears confused about David who he welcomed into the royal court as his musician. Saul has already 'loved David greatly' – 16:21 and biblical scholars note the varying and inconsistent sources about Saul meeting him. They do not pretend to answer the intriguing question of why the narrator presents David in this potentially confusing manner.[56] Perhaps when he was with Saul he was not clothed like a shepherd, and when David was brought to Saul and he offered to challenge Goliath the text implies Saul did not recognise who he was. As he was presumably absent from Saul's side for 40 days looking after his father's sheep, dressed like a shepherd, this may account for his poor memory. Also, when David is brought to Saul after his victory over Goliath, he appears not to know who he is. One solution offered by biblical commentators is that the narrator has not recorded the sequence of events in the right order, so in fact this is the first time Saul met David. This would explain why he did not apparently recognise him. It is possible that when Saul referred to him as 'young man' without congratulating him on his victory over Goliath, he may have been diminishing David's success. Because when he speaks to David, it is quite extraordinary that he makes no mention of his victory over Goliath whose head is in his hands. Shaul Bar suggests that when Saul asks David who son he is, he is not looking to identify his father, but his lineage. And that Saul knew David was from the tribe of Judah and that Jacob had predicted kings would descend from Judah – Genesis 49: 8-10.[57] Although the text does not imply this, his inquiry may have reflected whether he saw David as a threat and thought his lineage might qualify him as king in the future.

DAVID'S SUCCESS

1 Samuel 18: 1-30

This is truly and unmistakably a chapter that dazzles our senses, as we try to absorb the action it describes. A number of dramatic scenes that took place over a period of time, are presented in swift succession by the narrator. It is likely that several traditions have been combined in this complex chapter and scholars have struggled to untangle the different sources. For example, 18:1-5 is absent from the Greek version (LXX) of the OT and may not have been part of the original story and summarises what is going to take place.[58] As we know the Lord's anointing rests on David and as he kills Goliath, the text invites us to see that behind the relationships he will form with Saul's family, and despite the intrigue that will entangle them, God's hand of providence firmly rests on David. In the political arena of royal relationships, David was now exposed to this complex drama as his future is played out. Although he is the central player, others will make the moves, except that the main protagonist is the Lord, who will work out his will for David through the devoted friendship of Jonathan. David will have to learn to trust the Lord in the years ahead as Saul seeks to kill him. He will have to trust his life is in the Lord's hands, and that he will deliver him time and time again from Saul.

Once David is installed in the royal court he is embraced by the royal family. Saul takes him to serve in his army. Jonathan makes a covenant friendship with David and Michal, Saul's daughter loves David. All Israel and Judah love David and even Saul's servants love David too. The phenomenal rise to fame for David will also be accompanied by tensions. He is in danger of being overwhelmed by his relationships in the royal family tinged by personal agendas. David is an attractive, charismatic and popular hero. 'And all this seems to happen without David knowing what he is doing, and certainly without his attempting to do it. He is not trying to make friends at court.'[59] But his popularity and success place him in danger as Saul becomes jealous and afraid of his champion, whom he now views with awe, and who he sees as a threat to his kingship. Hertzberg captures David's mesmerising effect on everyone as the Old Testament Adonis. 'David is evidently a man with particularly attractive features...he takes hearts by storm, and everyone falls for him.'[60] After David's victory over Goliath he is now in the king's possession, as Saul takes him and keeps him in his entourage. But he is not the only one who wants a piece of David Jonathan does too. And he is the one who wins him over. As Jonathan's friendship with David evolves, this affects his relationship with Saul and a complex emotional and psychological web is spun involving them all.

In 1 Sam. 14, Jonathan carries out an attack on the Philistine stronghold without first asking for permission from Saul or telling his father about this. Although the narrator does not explain the reason for this, as we read in between the lines, the impression we gain is that Jonathan and Saul have different personalities and temperaments. Jonathan is adventurous while his father is cautious. Jonathan puts his faith in the Lord as he approaches the Philistine Garrison, while Saul restrains his men from joining in the attack and places them under oath. Subsequently, Jonathan inadvertently breaks the oath and when Saul discovers this, he is adamant Jonathan shall die, until his men ransom his life. And when we read that Saul wanted to kill David but Jonathan delighted in him – 19:1, these texts – 14, 19:1, invite us to see the conflict and underlying tension between Jonathan and Saul.

Although the narrator does not say it happened, it is not too fanciful to imagine Jonathan witnessing David killing Goliath, albeit at a distance, and winning his admiration. It is also not too fanciful to imagine Jonathan had already heard rumours about David's anointing. If that happened, then what follows, with Jonathan giving David his armour – all his weapons of war, and his robe and making a covenant with him, makes sense, as he was acknowledging him as the future king. If not, then this was the most dramatic and flamboyant gesture of a royal heir. By Jonathan giving David his robe, his armour and weapons, this could be interpreted as divesting himself as heir to the king, and symbolically transferring the kingship in the future onto David. On the other hand, we may interpret the generosity of Jonathan as a practical gesture, because David had challenged Goliath dressed in shepherd's clothing, and he was in need of armour as a soldier in Saul's army. Hertzberg symbolically interprets Jonathan giving his armour to David. 'It is a recognition of the *alter ego* in the covenant friendship, and clothing especially is so much part of the person who wears it, that the giving of it to another person is equivalent to the giving away of one's own self.'[61] We may detect some hyperbole in this statement, nevertheless, Jonathan giving away something so personal to David was also a gift of considerable value that symbolised his acceptance and support for him, and which bound them together in friendship. Tsumura says, 'The attitude of Jonathan, the crown prince, was thus remarkable and exhibits his unselfish character and personality. Jonathan gave while Saul took.'[62] Equally, we may perceive Jonathan discerned that David was the king in waiting after he defeated Goliath. Although the narrator does not state it, it is likely that when Jonathan gave David his armour and made a covenant with him he did this in private. As David's relationship with Saul deteriorated, we can perceive that the Lord's hand was on his friendship with Jonathan, his staunchest ally, who stood up for him before the king. In 1 Samuel 23: 16-18, while Saul is pursuing David to kill him, Jonathan goes to David and he strengthens him, and acknowledges to David that he shall be king after Saul, and that he would be alongside him.

As has been mentioned in the introduction, David's life was touched by the selfless and sacrificial friendship of Jonathan, seen to be compatible with the classical ideals of friendship. Most ancient authorities believed that friends had to be of equal rank with complete trust and be in total agreement in aims, ambitions and attitudes. They denigrated a friendship entered with the hope of selfish gain, and that a friend should be willing to sacrifice himself and all he possessed for his companion. Aristotle believed that for the sake of a friend one should be willing, if necessary, to 'throw away both wealth and honours and in general the goods that are objects of competition.' Because of his love for David Jonathan willingly gives up any hereditary rights to the throne of Israel, while Saul finds such devotion to a friend incomprehensible and even traitorous. In the classical tradition the ultimate goal of friends should be the rise of 'one's souls in bodies twain.' Such a merger of souls is also a step in the kind of love envisioned during the Renaissance. It was believed that a spiritual union was possible in such friendship, where the union of two souls was seen as the penultimate state, followed – if the love was pure and strong – by a merger with the Godhead.[63]

The statement, 'Jonathan loved David as his own soul' – 18:1, 3, is not one that we are likely to use today to express our attachment, commitment, devotion, or love for someone. While some readers may bestow a homoerotic interpretation on this text, this misses and misinterprets the intention of the narrator, who has already pointed out everyone is captivated by David and loves him. Brueggeman perceives the double implication of this text, that Jonathan's love for David may signify a strong emotional attachment as well as a political commitment.[64] But it is more than that. Jonathan's commitment and devotion to David was not just an emotional attachment. He demonstrated his love for him by being his advocate when his father sought to kill him. Consequently, Jonathan was humiliated by his father because of his commitment to David – 20:30. Firth says, 'The verb 'love' is not so much an emotion or expression of friendship, as a commitment to David's political position.'

Also, that the covenant Jonathan made with David, 'was essentially political seems apparent' as Jonathan gives David his armour and his robe that marks out his special status as the heir to Saul.[65] In making a covenant with David Jonathan committed himself to investing in David's future, as he was the one in a position of influence to help him as the newcomer in the royal court. While biblical commentators see a political slant to Jonathan's love for David, his commitment was not to his advantage. If there was any political benefit, it was for David. To Jonathan David became like a brother and he was a kindred spirit. Tsumura insightfully perceives there was a spiritual aspect to Jonathan and David's relationship as, 'both of them loved and trusted in the Lord and shared the same concerns and convictions: that the victory is by the Lord for His name's sake.'[66] He goes on to say, 'the expression attached to *niqs^{e}rah* refers to 'inseparable devotion' as in a similar expression in Judah's words in Gen. 44:30 (as his life is bound up in the boy's life).[67] Coming from a Greek background I am aware of the deep emotional attachment one may have with others. This may be with a member of your family, or friend, or someone of the opposite sex. After my father died, my mother's life was bound up with mine as she had a strong emotional attachment to me. I had similar strong emotional attachments with my Greek friends that I grew up with. In such friendships, there can be a union of our souls and spirits. With someone of the opposite sex, it may be seen as finding your soul mate and a mutual sense of completeness and wholeness, that involves a deep attachment and commitment to them.

David's success in defeating Goliath, not only won him the friendship of Jonathan, his success in defeating Israel's enemies won him the approval of all the people and Saul's servants too – 18:5. The narrator records the adulation given to David when he was victorious over the Philistines, when the women came to greet him along with Saul, to celebrate their triumphs in a victory parade with musical instruments and joyful songs. They sang: 'Saul has slain his thousands and David his ten thousands' – 18:7. Edelman notes that David as the king elect indirectly bestows upon Israel the blessing the rejected king Saul did could not give. She perceives that David has now become king in all but name.[68] While this is somewhat of an exaggeration Saul took note of the peoples' acclaim about David's successes and his increasing popularity that was beginning to overshadow him. Consequently, Saul was angry and displeased at the women's song. He eyed David from the day onwards and became jealous of him, as he thought to himself, 'What more can he have but the kingdom' – Saul's kingdom – 18:8-9. The women's celebrations are reminiscent of Miriam in Exodus 15:20-21. Freedman notes, 'the very fact that David was accorded equal treatment with the king in the song would be sufficient to arouse the suspicions of any monarch, and especially one insecure in his position and jealous.'[69]

One of the main themes that stands out in Ch. 18 is Saul's fear of David which appears three times, in v. 12, 15, and 29. Shaul Bar says, 'The first time we are told Saul was afraid, the second time that he dreaded him, and the third time Saul grew still more afraid, Saul's enmity towards David increases. This fear of David will play a major role in the ensuing events and feeds Saul's desire to kill David.'[70] Early on in the narrative we glimpse that Saul's temperament was naturally prone to be fearful. We recall him hiding when the king was going to be chosen by lot – 10:22. When he explained to Samuel why he did not kill Agag and kept some of the animals, it was because he feared the people and obeyed their voice – 15:24. Saul's irrational fear of David usurping him as king and killing him consumed his spirit. Borgman says, 'Saul is surely doomed because of his handling of fear. Ridding himself of the competition for the throne reveals a deep anxiety about his standing, a dark soil yielding the fruit of murderous jealousy and manipulation of a realm beyond life that belongs exclusively to God.[71] But David also develops a tendency to have a fearful spirit that began when Saul tried to kill him in the palace with a spear. David had a deep suspicion of Saul and was convinced that he wanted to kill him. Consequently, he left the palace precincts and became a fugitive as Saul pursued him. Just over 70 psalms are attributed to David and around half of these are about his fear because of his enemies who seek to kill him.

On occasions in some of these psalms, one cannot help but think that David is somewhat paranoid because of his fear of his enemies. Yet David's fear is not only because of Saul. As he flees from him, he goes to King Achish and he was very much afraid of him and feigned madness – 21:12-13.

We read in 1 Samuel 18:10-16:

> And on the next day an evil spirit from God rushed on Saul, and he raved within his house while David was playing the lyre, as he did day by day. Saul had his spear in his hand and cast the spear, for he thought, 'I will pin David to the wall.' But David evaded him twice. Saul was afraid of David because the Lord was with him but had departed from Saul. So Saul removed him from his presence and made him a commander of a thousand, and he went out and came in before the people. And David had success in all his undertakings, for the Lord was with him. And when Saul saw that he had great success he stood in awe of him. But all Israel and Judah loved David, form he went out and came in before them.

Brueggemann says, 'Encouraged by the extravagant acclaim of David, Saul begins to perceive David as a threat and competitor. Saul interprets everything about David through the prism of this deep, debilitating suspicion…There is keen irony in the fact that the fearful discernment of Saul and the grand intent of Yahweh, converge in seeing David destined for royal power…Saul's response to this rich irony in which he is enmeshed is a response of poison and pain. Failing to understand his true situation, Saul is placed in an impossible circumstance. David drives Saul wild, but only David can soothe Saul. Saul is left with an endless cycle of rage and comfort, wherein the comforter evokes more rage, which requires fresh comfort.'[72]

There is a certain ambiguity in interpreting Saul's two attempts to kill David by throwing a spear at him – 18:11. Is the evil spirit from the Lord that rushes upon Saul, fuelled by his fear and jealousy so overwhelming that he is out of control and he tries to kill David? Or is Saul in control of his faculties as the narrator records his thoughts? 'I will pin David to the wall.' Most English versions say Saul 'raved' when the evil spirit rushed on Saul, but this is somewhat misleading, as the correct translation is 'prophesied.' Both Firth and Tsumura opt for prophesied that implies for a certain time Saul is under the ecstatic influence of this spirit and subject to it. But this was not the same experience as the time when Saul prophesied with the band of prophets when he was filled with God's Spirit. The effect of the evil spirit rushing on Saul is negative and the ecstatic experience indicates that a dark mood enveloped him, perhaps a fit or convulsions, or psychological disturbance. We do not know whether Saul tried to kill David before or after the influence of the evil spirit wore off, but presumably, David was playing the lyre to soothe him during his attack.

'Saul was afraid of David because the Lord was with him, but had departed from Saul' – 18:12. An important factor overlooked by biblical commentators is that David unreservedly submits to Saul's authority as king. Consequently, his loyalty and obedience resulted in his success as the Lord was with him. Without David's submission to Saul and his authority, the Lord would not have blessed him with his continued success. By acknowledging Saul's authority, David also showed himself to be in submission to the Lord. Despite having been anointed as the future king, never once did he try to usurp Saul's authority or seek to kill him. Sadly, for David, Saul was self-indulgent and abused his authority as he constantly tried to kill David. He was threatened by David's success and his periodic attacks by the evil spirit were having a negative psychological impact, heightened by his jealousy and fear of David. Since God's Spirit deserted Saul and was bestowed on David Saul was abandoned by the Lord and Samuel. He was left on his own to cope with the transition of the monarchy to David who he began to realise was his successor. But neither the Lord, nor Samuel, give Saul any guidance or indication about how, or when, this would take place. He is left to fend for himself, for better or worse. But nothing Saul does will ever make it any better, because he rebels against the Lord's will and is resistant to David succeeding him. The narrator gives no hint how the Lord expected Saul to deal with his unstable position after he was rejected, having welcomed David into his royal court.

One question the text invites us to ask, is why did the Lord put Saul in such a compromised position after his rejection? The other question the text invites us to ask, is what options did Saul have in dealing with David as his successor in waiting? There is no definitive answer to the first question, because it is a mystery why the Lord chose to reject Saul but allowed him to remain in power, with his successor staring him in the face. Also, it was the Lord's inscrutable will that resulted in David being invited into Saul's royal court, and presented him with the dilemma of how to deal with David. Seeing an evil spirit oppressed Saul on a regular basis, and he became jealous and fearful of David, his emotional and mental capriciousness and instability, prevented him from realising that David was not a threat and was not out to kill him.

The narrator does not inform us that Saul sought the counsel of his advisers about whether David posed a threat to his life, although Jonathan assures Saul of David's faithfulness. Saul and all Israel could have benefited from David's achievements, and he could have chosen to love David politically and enjoy his loyalty as a close colleague. Sadly, he chose not to. It is difficult not to come to the conclusion, bearing in mind Saul's rejection and his successor living under his roof, Saul found himself compromised, and without God's blessing or guidance. Consequently, he removed David from his royal court, as his presence was a thorn in the flesh, and made him a commander of a thousand men. It would not be surprising if Saul hoped David would be killed by his enemies, but unsurprisingly as the Lord was with him, he was successful. Here, Hertzberg sees the essential contrast between Saul and David, 'God directs the destinies of the two men and with them…the history of the people of Israel.'[73]

That Saul hoped the Philistines would kill David is attested by his proposition to give David his eldest daughter Merab in marriage if he will fight the Lord's battles for him. The narrator records Saul's thoughts on the matter, 'Let not my hand be upon him, but let the hand of the Philistines be upon him' – 18:17. Saul cannot be seen to be responsible for David's death because of his popularity with all the people. However, David can see through Saul's political scheming and rejects the offer by shrewdly declining it because of his humble origins. David cancels Saul's obligation too.[74] So he outwits Saul. Pinksy says, 'With equal cunning and faked candour, décorously, the young man says that the honour of such a marriage is too great for a man like himself, from a humble family. They are paying one another the compliment of an elaborately feigned respect.'[75] David also lacked a dowry, as Saul had not given him the riches he promised to the man who killed Goliath. But Saul is not to be outdone and connives to snare David so he is killed by the Philistines. But this time Saul instructs his servants to approach David about marrying his daughter Michal on the pretext that the king is delighted with him – 18:22. Yet again David declines the king's offer because of his humble and poor origins because he cannot provide a dowry. For the second time we are reminded Saul broke his promise to David since he had promised great riches to the person who defeated Goliath.

Saul, however, does not take 'no' for an answer and sends his servants to David with a grotesque proposition to marry Michal. The dowry is 100 Philistine foreskins. Despite the risk of being killed by the Philistines which is exactly what Saul hoped would happen to David, he is pleased at the prospect of becoming the king's son-in-law. So David along with his men set out to fulfill the king's gruesome request of a dowry and in fact kill two hundred Philistines. After accomplishing this grisly task and presenting Saul with the dowry he asked for, he has no option but to give Michal his daughter to David as his wife. Saul took advantage of Michal in an attempt to entrap David because he knew she loved him, but the narrator never mentions whether or not David loved her in return. At the conclusion of Ch. 18, Saul acknowledged that the Lord was with David and that all Israel loved him. He became increasingly afraid of him and he was now his enemy continually. David has risen through the ranks and is now legitimately part of the royal family. He is also now Jonathan's brother-in-law and as he continued to be successful against the Philistines, he was making a name for himself – 18:30. 'David's star rises without any special initiative on his part, and it becomes evident to the reader that God is at work in David's life. He succeeds because it is God's good pleasure for him, to follow Saul as king.'[76]

DAVID'S DANGER

1 Samuel 19:1-10

Saul refuses to have his plan to kill David thwarted and his paranoid fear of David and obsessive hatred towards him is firmly entrenched in his mind, as he instructs all his servants and Jonathan to kill him – 19:1. Saul's plan to kill David is to Jonathan's advantage, as he will succeed Saul. Just as Saul had to choose whether to love David politically and benefit from his loyalty, something he chose not to do, Jonathan also had to choose whether to be faithful to his covenant with David. This was a supreme test of his friendship and love for David. But Jonathan is not self seeking like his father and he immediately warns David so that he can hide, as it appears that Saul is not aware of his son's covenant and close friendship with David. Jonathan also tells David he will inform him of any news about the matter – 19:3. He then speaks to his father as his advocate, reassuring Saul of his blamelessness towards him and David's faithfulness in serving the king. He reminds Saul that David risked his life to kill Goliath and does not deserve to be sinned against by the king – 19:4-5. 'Jonathan's speech about David is a masterpiece of compressed rhetoric.'[77] Alter says, 'Saul's paranoia and uncontrolled outbursts manifest themselves in an intermittent cycle. He is amenable to the voice of reason and conscience, and vows in presumably good faith not to harm David. But further evidence of David's military brilliance will unleash another round of violent impulses.'[78] In a moment of clarity, Saul sees things clearly, and he swears to Jonathan David will not die. Jonathan informs David of this news and he returns to the royal court again – 19:6-7. 'Jonathan's diplomacy evidently caught Saul in a moment of sanity. As he recounted David's heroic exploits and faithful service Saul relented.'[79] It was Jonathan's courage and selfless noble character that enabled him to speak the truth to Saul and still be loyal to be both his father and David.

While David trusts Jonathan and returns with him to the royal court as royal musician and army commander, we can imagine him being on edge, suspicious, not trusting Saul, and feeling vulnerable as he anticipated his unpredictable moods. Undoubtedly, David was on his guard and kept a very close eye on Saul whenever he was in his presence playing the lyre. After a brief interlude, David is once again successful against the Philistines – 19:8. The text invites us to perceive that Saul is incensed by David's success and his paranoid jealousy and hatred are reignited. Apparently, Saul has an attack from an evil spirit and tries to kill David with a spear, although he evades him. His worst fears have now been confirmed as Saul once again tried to kill David, so he fled and escaped from him. In the 21st century, it is difficult to interpret Saul's action as a direct consequence of an attack by this evil spirit from God, as this implies the Lord was responsible for provoking Saul to kill David. One has to ask how the narrator knew Saul had such an attack, especially as he already had a spear in his hand when it apparently took place. It does appear incompatible with God's character that he would incite an evil spirit to provoke Saul to kill David his anointed king. Blaming an evil spirit from God who may attack Saul at random and incite him to kill David, is incompatible in the context of the theological truth about God in the OT in the time of David. Here, Brueggemann says, 'We must remember that the world of biblical perspectives is a world without secondary cause. All causes are finally traced back to God who causes all…This narrative simply assumes that the world is ordered by the direct sovereign rule of God.'[80]

SAUL & MICHAL

1 Samuel 19:11-17

Saul has now abandoned his subterfuge and opportunistic efforts to kill David. He is now out of control and once again has given in to his impulse to get rid of him. So incensed is he by his failure and so obsessed with hatred for David that Saul plans to kill him in the morning. That very same night he sends messengers to his house to watch David and ensure he does not escape. Fortunately, for David, Michal his wife is the other person who loved David, whom the Lord used to protect him and save his life, as she warned him of the plot to kill him, so that he fled and escaped from Saul's clutches – 19:11. When Saul sends messengers to bring David to him so he might kill him, he discovers that he has been outwitted by his daughter Michal, who deviously pretends that David forced her to let him go because he threatened to kill her. Saul was thwarted first by his son who loved David and then Michal his daughter who also loved him. Saul is becoming a sad figure, alienating himself from those closest to him. We can but wonder why the Lord allowed Saul to remain king and risked the messy saga of him trying to kill David, his future king, instead of removing Saul in some way. Brueggeman says, 'We seem to be reading a dime-store novel or watching a seedy soap opera…We are treated to calculating human actions that do not conform to our expectations. Something is deeply awry when a future king must crawl through a window, when the wife of a coming king must lie to the father who is still king.'[81] Saul is too late to kill David, and as events will prove, he will always be too late. David will always be one step ahead of Saul, because of Jonathan or because the Lord's providential hand of guidance and protection rests upon his anointed one. But that will not prevent David being pursued by Saul whose desire to kill him will now dominate his life, and now David will experience the emotional and psychological trauma of being a fugitive. No longer is he the conquering hero. Instead, he is the enemy of the king. The text invites us to ask why David did not take Michal with him, as he appears to have left her behind without a second thought. We are left to wonder whether he ever loved Michal, as he makes no effort to see her in the future. David will not see Michal again until he demands her return as his wife for political reasons, although by then she is the wife of Paltiel who loved her – 2 Sam. 3:13-14. Until that time, Michal's last glimpse of David was when he escaped through the window of their walled house.

SAUL & SAMUEL

1 Samuel 19: 12-24

At first glance, verses 18-24 appear to be fairly straightforward and record David escaping from Saul to go to Samuel at Ramah, to let him know what has happened and to seek his help, although when he arrives Samuel says and does nothing – 19:18. When Saul learns about this, on three occasions he sends messengers to get David, but when they arrive they see Samuel and the prophets prophesying, and the Spirit of God comes upon the messengers and they too prophesy – 19: 20-21. So Saul himself goes to Ramah. We read in 19: 22-24:

> And Saul went to Naioth in Ramah: and the spirit of God came upon him also, and as he went, he prophesied until he came to Naioth in Ramah. And he too stripped off his clothes, and he too prophesied before Samuel, and lay naked all that day and all that night. Therefore, it is said, 'Is Saul also among the prophets?'

Samuel's home town of Ramah is only 2-3 miles to the north of Gibeah where David escaped from Saul. It would only take around an hour to get there and Ramah is where Saul first met Samuel. David does not have to do anything to defend himself against Saul's messengers and Saul himself, as God's Spirit comes upon them and they have an ecstatic experience that disarms them. When Saul arrives he too is overcome by God's Spirit and prophesies. His behaviour takes the form of an uncontrolled trance, as he loses all control of himself,[82] and lies naked on the floor for a day and night, incapacitated and humiliated. This is the fourth time David escaped from him and he is protected directly by God's intervention. B. Green says: 'God's Spirit must oppose Saul's lethal determination…Saul determined to stay king no matter what, Saul at cross-purposes with God, is losing the 'one thing needful' distracted from performing his other responsibilities, notably fighting the Philistines…He seems conflicted and in denial as he plans, blames, alibis, pretends.'[83] Brueggemann sees the significance of the ecstatic phenomenon that overtook Saul.

> The pitifully embarrassing scene is that of this once great man, still tall but no longer great…clearly not in control, shamed, now rendered powerless in a posture of submissiveness. This episode is an act of dramatic de-legitimation of Saul.[84]

The hidden implication of the text invites us to compare this scene with the time when Saul is anointed king by Samuel and God's Spirit comes mightily upon him and he prophesies after he meets a band of prophets – 10:9-10. This marks the beginning of Saul's career, whereas by contrast the episode in Ch. 19 signals the end of it. Symbolically, Saul is stripped of his dignity and royal symbols of authority. 'This entire incident, with its focus on Saul, highlights the king's fate as one who has been rejected…he has become the victim of the dark side of the divine spirit.[85] It is a tragedy that Samuel appears to hide behind his prophetic role from Saul in support of David and does not confront Saul face to face, with a word from the Lord (which he could have inquired about) or with a word from his own prophetic authority, to prevent the enmity between him and David escalating. Samuel was the victim of his own fear of Saul which prevented him from intervening and seeking to reconcile Saul with David. He failed to give Saul a word of counsel about his remaining time as king, before David would one day succeed him.

CHAPTER FIVE

DAVID, JONATHAN & SAUL

DAVID & JONATHAN
1 Samuel 20:1-23

Some scholars think that this episode is chronologically out of order, as it is unlikely David still has to determine if Saul's intentions towards him are hostile. Nor is it likely David would be expected or welcome as a guest at the king's new moon celebration. Also, Jonathan appears to be unaware of the latest attempt by Saul to kill David in 19:8-24.[1] This is a moving chapter, because Ch. 20 records the last meeting between David and Jonathan in Ramah, that follows on closely from the one in Ch. 19, (except for Jonathan's brief visit to David at Horeb in the wilderness of Ziph – 23:16-18). The first half of Ch. 20 records a long conversation between David and Jonathan in which the stakes are very high, as the danger to David's life from Saul is very real.[2] B. Green says, 'This long chapter is filled with pairs of verbal exchanges: fifteen of them.'[3]

We read in 20:1-4:

> Then David fled from Naioth in Ramah, and came and said to Jonathan, 'What have I done? What is my guilt? And what is my sin before your father that he seeks my life?' And he said to David, 'Far from it! You shall not die. Behold, my father does nothing either great or small without disclosing it to me: and why should my father hide this from me? It is not so.' But David replied, 'Your father knows well that I have found favour in your eyes, and he thinks, 'Let not Jonathan know this, lest he be grieved.' But truly, as the Lord lives and as your soul lives, there is but a step between me and death.' Then Jonathan said to David, 'Whatever you say, I will do for you.'

While Saul has been overcome by the ecstatic experience of God's Spirit, and stripped naked, David escapes from him in

Naioth and goes to see Jonathan at Ramah, in fear of his life and feeling desperate. Although he is innocent, he is playing on Jonathan's sympathy when he says, 'What have I done? What is my guilt? And what is my sin before your father that he seeks my life?' Although Saul had vowed not to kill David – 19:6, he has now broken his vow. Therefore, David's life is in danger, and he is understandably emotional and melodramatic, perhaps feeling sorry for himself. But Jonathan is his closest and most trusted ally that he is able to share his heart with, and he reassures David that he will not die. While David fears Saul, he avails himself of Jonathan's friendship to discover if he still plans to kill him, and if he is to become a fugitive. Jonathan somewhat naively thinks David is not in danger as his father always confides in him. But David shows himself to be the better psychologist.[4] He has read the situation well as Saul knew his son was close to David and esteemed him highly, so he did not reveal his intention to him. Although in Ch. 19, Saul did ask Jonathan to help kill David, he chose to defend him.

Unfortunately, for David, he will now be a fugitive until the day Saul dies at the end of 1 Samuel. But in this ancient saga, Saul's son will enable David to outwit his father and live. The friendship between Jonathan and David will have political implications for the future as well as dimensions of personal intimacy,[5] as Jonathan takes the initiative to make a covenant with David's house – 20:16. But for now, David takes the initiative and outlines his plan to Jonathan to discover if Saul intends to kill him. In their relationship, 'Jonathan excels in affectionate, unselfish friendship, whereas David is more resolute and superior in intellect.'[6] David outlines his plan to Jonathan so they can discover whether Saul intends to kill him – 20:5-7. David's subterfuge involves Jonathan being deceitful with Saul and he betrays his heightened fear and insecurity, as he becomes even more melodramatic when he appeals to the sacred covenant Jonathan made with him. David's dramatic speech is heightened when he says Jonathan should kill him if he thought there was any guilt in him – 20:8. David almost seems to question Jonathan's integrity and loyalty to him, but in reality, he is testing his commitment. What David betrays in his speech is his vulnerability, as he seeks the reassurance of Jonathan's commitment to him.

David outlines his plan to Jonathan which involves finding out if Saul intends to kill him, or if after his ecstatic experience at Naioth David is safe, and he asks Jonathan to inform him of the outcome – 20:5-11. Jonathan now takes the initiative to reassure David with an oath in the Lord's name that he will let him know what his father's intention is. While David's focus is on the immediate present and the danger Saul poses to his life, Jonathan's speech that follows has a far wider perspective that anticipates the future. 'In this speech, which takes the long view, however, it is as though the danger to David has evaporated and Jonathan is now the one in danger.'[7] Jonathan prophetically anticipates a change in the royal house with David succeeding his father and he asks David to show his loyal love to him and to his descendents – 20: 14-16. 'May the Lord be with you, as he has been with my father' – 20:13, is an implicit recognition David will succeed Saul. Tsumura see this as a key element in Jonathan's speech.[8] McCarter says, 'This gives new clarity to the inevitability of David's succession to the throne.'[9] Jonathan uses the term *hesed* twice, first asking for loyal love towards him (v.14) and loyal love towards his heirs (v.15). Three times in his speech, Jonathan uses the term 'cut off.' Firstly, it is a petition not to 'cut off' covenant loyalty. Secondly, that all of David's enemies will be cut off. Thirdly, it is a petition that the name and house of Jonathan will not be 'cut off.'[10] The concern Jonathan expressed for his descendents, sadly is exactly what happened in 2 Samuel 3-4, when David is ruthless.[11] Jonathan's speech to David ends on a very moving note in 20:15-17: 'If I am still alive, show me the loyal love of the Lord that I may not die, and do not cut off your loyalty from my house for ever. When the Lord cuts off every one of David's enemies from the face of the earth, let not the name of Jonathan be cut off from the house of David. And may the Lord take vengeance on David's enemies. And Jonathan made David swear again by his love for him: for he loved him as his own soul.'

Biblical commentators tend to highlight that David is the one who is always on the receiving end of other people's love, but on this occasion, Jonathan asks David to affirm his love for him by swearing an oath to this effect. David's covenant commitment to him was important, because having looked into the future, Jonathan perceives that his life and that of his descendents are likely to be in danger once David is king, because he knew that kings 'were prone to assassinating all rival families.'[12] D. Edelman says, 'Jonathan then makes David reconfirm the pact by swearing an oath stating his covenantal love, thereby binding the lives of the two together as one.'[13] Firth sees another side to their commitment to one another when he says, 'The personal commitment between them is profoundly political, but both the personal and the political are subjugated to God's will.'[14] Although it is not clear if David swears by his own love for Jonathan, or Jonathan's love for him.[15] But what is clear is that in v. 17 the narrator mentions the word 'love' three times and the loyal love of the Lord once in v. 14. Jonathan's personal commitment to David knows no bounds. His soul is knit to David's and we could well say that his love for him was greater than his love for himself. If Jonathan had not loved David so much, it is unlikely he would ever have become king, because if he had opposed him and sided with his father, David would almost certainly have died. Jonathan's loyal, selfless and sacrificial love and commitment to David is extraordinary, and reflects the heart of a remarkable man, who undoubtedly would have been a great king. Ch. 20:18-23 records their plan to find out if Saul intends to kill David.

SAUL & JONATHAN

1 Samuel 20:24-34

As agreed between the two friends, David goes to the field to wait for Jonathan's message about Saul's response to his absence from the feast. After Jonathan informs Saul of David's excuse for not being there, on the second day of his absence the king is angry with Jonathan. He is furious because he knows that his friendship with David will prevent him becoming king while he is alive, and demands that he brings him to Saul that he may die. This outburst reveals that David's worst fears have now been confirmed. It indicates Saul knows David is destined to become king unless he is killed. When Jonathan defends David and says, 'Why should David be put to death? What has he done?' – 20:32, Saul is incensed because he refuses to betray David and in his blind rage, Saul throws his spear at his son. Jonathan is now doubly certain his father intends to kill David. Brueggemann captures this dramatic scene, 'The narrative turns with electrifying violence.'[16] Saul is incensed because he now knows his son is involved in David's deception against him. 'Saul is not surprised by or deceived by the subterfuge of David. But to have his own son and heir join the charade is a profound humiliation.'[17] Saul is wounded and indignant. His own son has given his allegiance to David.

Jonathan has a price to pay for his allegiance to David. He is insulted and humiliated by his father when Saul says, 'You son of a perverse woman, do I not know that you have chosen the son of Jesse to your own shame, and to the same of your mother's nakedness? – 20:30. 'The expression *son of a perverse woman (na'awat), rebellious woman*, is an insult directed toward Jonathan. *Son* in such a phrase denotes a 'member' of the special class of people who forsake those to 'whom they properly owe allegiance.' The term nakedness *('erwat)* which may refer euphemistically to genitals is used in a curse: *'to the disgrace of your mother's nakedness.'* Here the emphasis is on the disgrace or shame which Saul thinks Jonathan has brought upon himself and his family.'[18] We read in 20:34, 'And Jonathan rose from the table in fierce anger and ate no food the second day of the month, for he was grieved for David, because his father had disgraced him.' 'Jonathan makes a costly and daring choice. He has chosen David. He violates the command to honour his father…In retrospect this is an act of stunning loyalty on Jonathan's part.'[19]

DAVID & JONATHAN

1 Samuel 20:35-42

After Jonathan leaves the feast, he is not rash and does not immediately rush to David in case he is followed. Instead, in the morning as previously arranged with David he meets him in the field, after sending the young lad back to the city – 20: 35-40. We read in 20:41-42:

> And as soon as the lad had gone, David rose from beside the stone heap and fell on his face to the ground, and bowed three times: and they kissed one another, and wept with one another, until David recovered. Then Jonathan said to David, 'Go in peace, forasmuch as we have sworn both of us in the name of the Lord saying, 'The Lord shall be between me and you, and between my descendents and your descendents, for ever.' And he rose and departed, and Jonathan went into the city.

'The narrative has passed its moment of tense drama. Jonathan and David know yet again, what they had known already. David is in deep danger and Saul is beyond reason. It is high narrative art to interest us so passionately in something we had already known.'[20] Surprisingly, biblical commentators do not comment in any significant way about this parting scene, that clearly reveals David's love for Jonathan. David's posture on the ground and bowing three times before Jonathan shows his deep respect for the loyalty of his royal friend. Something which is unique in the OT.[21] Firth thinks this highlights the political dimension of their relationship and sees the kiss as a normal male greeting.[22] Although many centuries distance us from Jonathan and David, we cannot help but be moved by this poignant and intensely personal moment, as we glimpse a rare insight into David's heart when he weeps uncontrollably, because he knows this is a parting of the ways for him and Jonathan. Although Jonathan also wept, we are touched by David's weeping, as the narrator has always freely spoken of Jonathan's love for David. There is a sense of finality and tragedy that their friendship has been untimely severed. There is an air of nobility about Jonathan as he chose to remain loyal to his father rather than desert him to join David. It is tragic, as his choice will cost him his life. Jonathan was compromised and conflicted by his divided loyalties to David and Saul, and we are left to wonder whether he should have chosen David rather than give his allegiance to Saul. Jonathan's counsel as David's right hand man may well have prevented him from committing serious sins and making errors of judgment in the future. The text in Ch. 20 invites us to read in between the lines and perceive that Jonathan was able to remain committed in his covenant relationship with David, because at no time did he show any hostility towards Saul or any desire to replace him as king by military force by staging a coup. Jonathan and David go their separate ways at the end of Ch. 20, not knowing if they would ever meet again. They depart in peace leaving behind the conflict Saul espouses.

DAVID & AHIMELECH

1 Samuel 21:1-9

To all intents and purposes, David is now a fugitive, a man on the run from Saul. It appears somewhat desperate for David to leave without any basic supplies, as he flees to Nob, a city of priests and a sanctuary similar to Shiloh, hoping to find supplies there. But the narrator does not record that David inquired of the Lord and sought his will about what to do. Instead, David resorts to political subterfuge and deception as he tells Ahimelech the priest (the chief priest here)[23] he is on a secret mission for Saul. The priest 'trembles' – is frightened because he assumes something is wrong for David to arrive alone. David persuades Ahimelech to give him the holy bread as he has fled from Saul in panic without any supplies. Presumably David could have sought provision from another source in Nob, but perhaps he didn't want anyone to know where he was. He also asks Ahimelech if he had any weapons because his mission was so urgent he departed without taking any with him. Despite, David's story sounding implausible, the priest offers him the only weapon there is at the sanctuary – Goliath's sword, which he readily takes. Unfortunately, for the chief priest, Doeg, Saul's servant was there when David arrived and he would betray Ahimelech. This incident, 'reflects great haste, urgency, and danger.'[24]

DAVID & ACHISH

1 Samuel 21:10-15

After leaving Ahimelech, David is so desperate he makes an attempt to join Achish, king of Gath. But when his servants recognise David and tell Achish who he is, he feigns madness because he is afraid. David's fame has obviously spread not only because of Goliath but because of the song, 'Saul has slain his thousands and David his ten thousands' Achish's servants were familiar with. This must have become a proverb in Israel and other nations. It is strange that David's sudden behaviour didn't appear strange to them, as he 'made marks on the doors of the gate and let his spittle run down his beard' – 21:13. But the king underestimates him and he is taken in by David's deception, which enables him to flee again. Between chapters 16-19 David has been passive and others proactive, but now when he is desperate, 'he is assertive and prepared to take bold initiatives.'[25] This incident with his attempt to join Achish, only reinforces how desperate David felt his situation was as he was isolated and on his own. B. Green says, 'We have arguably another *mise-en-abyme,* the faceoff of two kings: one feigning madness and the other taken in: one of them shrewd, the other clueless: one residually powerful, one wily.'[26]

DAVID IN MOAB

1 Samuel 22:1-5

After David's plan to join Achish backfires, he escapes to the cave at Adullam. Bethlehem was within a day's walk and the news of David's plight reaches his brothers and his father's house, who all came to join him. Suddenly all those on the margins of society who were disadvantaged for economical or political reasons, come and join David who becomes their leader: and they numbered 400 men. In his concern for his parents who cannot be part of a marauding band of renegades, David goes to Mizpah, to the king of Moab, and requests his parents safety by staying with him. This course of action may seem surprising until we recall that David's great grandmother, Ruth, was from Moab. While David was dishonest with Achish and also deceitful with Ahimelech, his approach to the king of

Moab is truthful. These brief verses mark the transition in David's life and the prophet Gad appears from somewhere, presumably at the Lord's command, to tell him to leave the stronghold and go to the land of Judah.

SAUL THE MURDERER

1 Samuel 22:6-23

While Saul was sitting under the tamaraisk tree at Gibeah he was informed that David had been found. While Saul hoped David would be killed when he was his commander fighting the Philistines, he is now so crazed in his desire to kill David that his obsession about him has escalated to fanatical heights. Saul is unhappy David has escaped from him and he harshly accuses his men for not informing him his own son conspired against him. David appears to be popular with Saul's officers, who are unwilling to give Saul any information about him.[27] At this Doeg speaks up and betrays Ahimelech who helped David, perhaps seeking to ingratiate himself as a foreigner with Saul. His report fuels Saul's own suspicion and he sends for Ahimelech, all of his father's house and all the priests who were at Nob, and accuses them of conspiring against him – 22:9-13. Ahimelech repudiates Saul's charge and he defends David's faithfulness in serving Saul and stresses the honour in which David is held: and he declares that along with his household he is innocent of any crime – 22:14-15. This is an eloquent defense and without actually saying it, he clearly infers David is innocent. Firth says, 'Ahimelech's response is a masterpiece of compressed rhetoric…First he points out that David is a highly important person in the court…David is trustworthy, the king's son-in-law, commander of his body-guard and honoured in the king's house.'[28] Saul is now an unreasonable tyrant who does not respond to the logic of truth Ahimelech has just spoken. So Saul condemns Ahimelech, all his household, and all the priests to death – but his servants would not lay a hand on them – 22:16-17. Their fear of the Lord was greater than their fear of Saul. But Saul's insanity cannot be appeased. He is now beyond reason, and out of control.

> Saul is increasingly living in his own world of terrified fantasy. When Saul finished his tirade, there must have been an embarrassed silence among his followers...No, they had not conspired against Saul. No, they had not withheld information. Rather they had not known. They have no way to answer Saul.[29]

Tragically, Doeg carries out Saul's murderous command and kills all the priests, including the men, women and children at Nob. Only one of Ahimelech's sons, Abiathar, escaped and told David what had happened – 22:18-21. It is doubly tragic, as not only the priests but also the entire town of Nob is killed. Although David acknowledges responsibility for the massacre at Nob as he was aware that Doeg would surely betray him to Saul – 22:332 – this hardly exonerates David. Also, the text is silent as to why Lord did not restrain Saul from this murderous act. One wonders why no one in Saul's army prevented Doeg, a foreigner, from carrying out Saul's instructions. Fortuitously, Abiathar the son of Ahimelech who survives and escapes to David brings with him the ephod. 'This indicates the true priesthood and priestly counsel and the divine oracle have officially moved from Saul to David.'[30] Abiathar would be with David during the remainder of his days as a fugitive and for the rest of his life. He eventually shared the position of high priest with Zadok during David's reign. In the more immediate future Abiathar's association with David is linked to the subsequent events in which he has an important role in inquiring about the Lord's will for David. This tragic episode contrasts Saul as the destroyer of the priesthood of Nob, with David who saves 'the cult of Yahweh from extinction.' This paved the way for the elevation of Jerusalem to the status of the chief sanctuary-city in Israel. The following events will continue to contrast Saul who chases David without priestly guidance, with David who is 'guided by the divine oracle at every turn.'[31]

SAUL PURSUES DAVID

1 Samuel 23:1-29

Chapter 23 is primarily about Saul's attempt to find David to kill him. After David successfully defeated the Philistines at

Keilah having first inquired of the Lord whether to go and fight against them, Saul was told that David had come to Keilah. So he ordered his men to go and besiege David in the town that had gates and bars and no means of escape – 23:1-8. But David knew that Saul was plotting against him and asked Abiathar the priest to bring the ephod and inquire of the Lord whether Saul would come after him and if the men of Keilah would betray him to Saul. And the Lord answered, 'He will come down and the men will surrender you.' At this news, David leaves Keilah with his 600 men and remained in the strongholds in the wilderness, in the hill country of Ziph. And when Saul was told David had left Keilah he gave up looking for him – 23:9-14. Saul will now pursue David until the end of his life. Ironically, for Saul, he never realised that in his pursuit of David, he was also contending against the Lord, and that David would always be one step ahead of him because of the Lord's protection. We might reasonably assume David would be confident because the Lord was with him and that whenever he asked the Lord for guidance he would provide it and protect him from Saul. But the narrator informs us that David was afraid because Saul had come out to seek his life – 23:15. Although the text does not say this, it invites us to assume that providentially Jonathan comes out to encourage David. We read in 23:16-18:

> And Jonathan, Saul's son, rose and went to David at Horesh, and strengthened his hand in God. And he said to him, 'Fear not: for the hand of Saul, my father shall not find you: you shall be king over Israel, and I shall be next to you: Saul my father also knows this.' And the two of them made a covenant before the Lord: David remained at Horesh, and Jonathan went home.

In God's perfect timing, Jonathan secretly and stealthily comes to David, to affirm, encourage and strengthen his hand in God. He has come to strengthen David's faith in the Lord, as opposed to just being encouraged by him. His first words to David are also timely: 'Do not be afraid' as he must have sensed he was afraid of his father's murderous intention towards him. But despite David's precarious circumstances,

Jonathan comes to reassure David about his future and God's purpose for him. Saul will never find him, he will be king after Saul, and Jonathan will serve next to him. Moreover, Saul also knows this is true. These are all extraordinary statements. Jonathan has renounced his claim to be king, and his father also secretly knows David will succeed him. Jonathan's support of David as the future king is quite extraordinary and leaves us speechless in its breathtaking generosity and lack of guile. This is the last time the two dear friends will meet. The last time they will see each other. It is a pivotal and defining moment as Jonathan has given up his right to succeed his father. The two friends seal this historical occasion and its future implications with a renewed covenant.

The narrator uses the clandestine meeting between Jonathan and David to punctuate Saul's pursuit of David. The Zephites then went to Saul at Gibeah and told him that David was hiding amongst them in the strongholds at Horesh and they offered to surrender David into Saul's hands. Saul accepted their offer and asked them to report his movements back to him – 23: 19-24. Both David and Saul have their spies, men who look out for their enemies' movements. Meanwhile, David goes to the wilderness of Maon while Saul and his men continue to look for him. When David is informed about this, he went to the rock which is in the wilderness of Maon. When Saul hears about this, he pursues him. So Saul went on one side of the mountain and David and his men on the other side. Just as Saul was closing in on David, a messenger came to Saul reporting that the Philistines had made a raid, so Saul retreated from his pursuit of David. Therefore, that place was called the Rock of Escape and David went from there and dwelt in the strongholds of Engedi – 23:25-29. Tsumura says, 'The rock is named after this incident in which God divided David and Saul provident-ially.'[32] Just as it seemed David was going to be caught by Saul and his men and killed a fortuitous raid by the Philistines stops him in his tracks. Despite two treacherous attempts to hand David over to Saul, he escapes from seemingly impossible situations. Although the narrator does not say so, the text invites us to discern that God's hand of protection was on

David his anointed king. In fact, the narrator says, 'And Saul sought David every day, but God did not give him into his hand' – 23:14. 'Thus ends one of the most dramatic incidents in 1 Samuel. Behind all these 'happenings' one can certainly recognise God's strong hand of guidance in David's life.

DAVID SPARES SAUL

1 Samuel 24:1-22

Ch. 24 is a pivotal chapter that results in a dramatic acceptance of David as the king elect by Saul. It is a truly momentous acknowledgment of the Lord's will Saul had lived in denial of, and tried to thwart with all his heart. In Ch. 24, Saul's insane pursuit of David sees him in the wilderness of Engedi with three thousand of his crack troops. Ch. 24 closely parallels Ch. 26 that results in the dramatic escalation of momentum leading to Saul's ultimate acceptance that David will be king. In Ch. 24, the incident where David and Saul are fortuitously thrown together in the same cave is a moment of high drama, that looks as if it's going to end in a climactic resolution for David. There is tense anticipation as astonishingly Saul enters a cave to relieve himself, where unknown to him David and his men are hiding, that even a scriptwriter could not have imagined. With Saul alone in the cave, David's men eagerly suggest he kills him as the Lord has put his enemy into his hand. Instead, David only cuts off the edge of Saul's robe that was lying on the ground while he relieved himself. But David then regrets his action, 'afterwards David's heart smote him.' This appears a very dramatic way of saying he regretted his action, unless the implication is the Lord powerfully convicted him. David then persuades his men that he should not kill Saul, the Lord's anointed king and prevents them from attacking him. David's magnanimous action towards Saul allows him to demonstrate his innocence to him. This is the last time that David and Saul will ever meet and their speeches are indelibly and memorably recorded for posterity. We read about their encounter in 23: 8-12, 15-22:

'Afterward David also arose and went out of the cave and called after Saul, 'My lord the king.' And when Saul looked behind him, David bowed his face to the earth and did obeisance. And David said to Saul, 'Why do you listen to the words of the men who say, 'Behold David seeks your hurt?' Behold this day your eyes have seen how the Lord gave you into my hand in the cave, and some bade me to kill you, but I spared you. I said, 'I will not put forth my hand against my Lord, for he is the Lord's anointed.' See, my father, see the skirt of your robe in my hand: for by the fact I cut off the skirt of your robe and did not kill you, you may know and see that there is no wrong or treason in my hands. I have not sinned against you, though you hunt my life to take it. May the Lord judge between me and you, may the Lord avenge me upon you: but my hand shall not be against you…May the Lord therefore be judge, and give sentence between me and you, and see to it, and plead my cause, and deliver me out of your hand.

When David had finished speaking these words to Saul, Saul said, 'Is this your voice my son David?' And Saul lifted up his head and wept. He said to David, 'You are more righteous than I, for you have repaid me good, whereas I have repaid you evil. And you have declared this day how you have dealt with me, in that you did not kill me when the Lord put me into your hands. For if a man finds his enemy will he let him go away safe? So may the Lord reward you with good for what you have done to me this day. And now behold, I know that you shall surely be king, and that the kingdom of Israel shall be established in your hand. Swear to me therefore that you will not cut of my descendents after me, and that you will not destroy my name out of my father's house.' And David swore this to Saul. Then Saul went home: but David and his men went up to the stronghold.'

David's obeisance to Saul, his eloquent and moving speech in which he declares he is innocent, touched Saul's heart and this is witnessed by his men. As in a court case, David appeals to the Lord to judge between him and Saul. But he does more than that, he appeals to the Lord as judge to plead his cause and declare sentence between him and Saul, (that Saul is guilty), and to rescue him from his hand. David's speech is a masterful example of discerning speech attributed to him by one of

Saul's messengers when he recommended him to Saul as his musician – 16:18. Hertzberg says, 'It is dramatic and persuasive rhetoric with multiple levels of meaning, designed to make Saul realise the error of his ways and break of his continued pursuit of the Lord's other anointed.'[34]

In a surprisingly paternal tone, we detect a pathos in Saul's response to David as he now speaks with tragic clarity in his right mind – 'Is this your voice my son David?' Does his regretful tone reflect his self-pity because he is feeling sorry for himself and his failure, rather than for his pursuit of David? Saul's better nature speaks the truth his tortured mind has for so long lived in denial of, as he now publicly acknowledges for the first time that David will be king. Brueggemann masterfully captures the pathos of Saul's speech when he says:

> Saul weeps because he must now face what he has long known. He weeps because he must now confront the truth he has avoided...No wonder he must cry, for he must acknowledge not only that David will win and that he will lose, but that his whole effort to be faithful, to be effective, and powerful, even 'righteous' failed. He has failed because of the 'evil spirit' and because of the resolve of God, because of the cunning of David – and because Saul could finally not be who he wanted so deeply to be. There is here both tragedy and failure. Beneath both tragedy and failure there is the inconsolable, inarticulate, unmeasured pathos of a life gone empty. Saul must weep. He must weep before God and before David. When he has wept, then he can speak. It is his honest, unrestrained weeping that permits him to yield to the now irresistible and obvious future, which is David.[35]

Although it's speculative, we can imagine Saul is touched that David his son-in-law did not kill him. Perhaps that is partly why he wept. In Saul's speech, the reality of David succeeding him as king has finally been accepted by him, so he makes a petition asking David to promise he will not destroy his family in the future. David has already promised this to Jonathan and so he readily agrees, although during his reign as king David will kill a number of Saul's family. There is now no turning back for David. He knows that he cannot go and be in Saul's court once again. Saul has proved that he is not trustworthy and may well turn on David in the future. David chose the much more demanding path of trusting the Lord and his timing for succeeding Saul as king, rather than taking matters into his own hands and killing Saul to take the kingdom for himself. He will now enjoy a brief respite from Saul's pursuit knowing he has acknowledged he is to be his successor and that the Lord's hand is on him. The Lord clearly put Saul into David's hands and demonstrated his sovereign will for David as the future king to succeed Saul. At last, Saul now accepts what he had so long sought to deny, that David was indeed the man the Lord had chosen to replace him. Saul would leave the wilderness of Engedi with the indelible memory of David holding the part of his robe he cut off. It would not be surprising if Saul recalled the time when he tore Samuel's robe as he sought to depart from him. On that occasion, Samuel used the incident as a parable to symbolise the kingdom had been torn from Saul. Samuel's words would have rushed back to the forefront of his mind, 'The Lord has torn the kingdom of Israel from you this day, and given it to a neighbour of yours, who is better than you' – 15:28-29. Now that Saul knew this was David, unlike him, Saul refuses to honour the sacrosanct status of the Lord's anointed.[36]

While David's speech is persuasive and makes a considerable impact on Saul, Edelman strongly suggests that the decisive factor in Saul openly and publicly acknowledging to David that he would be king is because Saul along with David and his men, all knew that the Lord had delivered him into David's hand. She believes Saul is convinced that the Lord is actively seeking to betray him to David and He is conspiring to remove him prematurely. She thinks Saul's active persecution by the Lord led to Saul's confession, rather than David's words and plea to the Lord to be his judge because he was innocent.[37] 'The confrontation has not led to a rapprochement between the king and king-elect, only to an acknowledgment by Saul of the destiny of each, a reassurance from David of his non-hostile intentions towards Saul personally, and an oath by David not to eliminate the Saulide royal house entirely.'[38]

DAVID & NABAL

1 Samuel 25:1-13

The death of Samuel is reported at the start of Ch. 25 in one verse, almost as an afterthought, although all Israel assembled and mourned him. Since he anointed David Samuel has been out of the picture, except for the brief occasion when David came to tell him Saul was out to kill him – 19:18-24. Bearing in mind Samuel's significant leadership in Israel it is surprising the narrator does not honour his achievements.

In the incident that follows about David and Nabal there is a striking contrast between his merciful action towards Saul and his aggressive response to Nabal. This man is introduced by initially describing his wealth and then by contrasting him with his wife. 'The woman was of good understanding and beautiful, but the man was churlish and ill-behaved: he was a Calebite' – 25:3. Firth points out that David addresses him as a kinsman and the speech of the young men he sends to Nabal is carefully constructed to emphasise the kinship relationship between them,[39] which includes a blessing of peace to him, his household and all he has: presumably in the hope this would illicit a favourable response. And as David has been protecting Nabal's shepherds he feels this deserves some reward in return, so he sends ten young men to bring back the provisions he is expecting to receive. However, David is insulted by Nabal's harsh response: 'Who is David? Who is the son of Jesse?' – 25:10. Nabal is indignant. He is dismissive of David, his name and his reputation, denies any knowledge of him and he refutes David's claim of protecting his men. Brueggemann interprets David's request for provisions from Nabal as provocative and creating a crisis. He sees the envoy of young men delivering his message as an act of masterful intimidation. He even sees David's greeting of peace as a threat to Nabal if he does not comply and also views his request for provisions as protection money.[40]

In contrast to his merciful response to Saul, David responds with violent intentions towards Nabal after he is disrespectful and dismissive towards him. The issue Nabal does not seem to have grasped is that David is a fugitive and able to plunder his possessions by force. Perhaps he is a supporter of Saul and thinks he is safe. Firth says, 'It seems Nabal's surliness and failure to recognise his mutual obligations have paved the way for battle. David's anger means he stands on the brink of violence.'[41] His credibility and pride has been challenged by Nabal's foolishness so he prepares to attack.

DAVID & ABIGAIL

1 Samuel 25:14-35

Fortunately, the disaster is averted by one of Nabal's young men when he reports the incident to his wife, Abigail, and confirms that David and his men provided protection. Nabal's churlish nature is also confirmed by the young man when he says to her, 'Now therefore know this and consider what you should do: for evil is determined against our master and against all his house, and he is so ill-natured that one cannot speak to him' – 25:17. As Abigail is an intelligent and prudent woman she prepared generous provisions for her servants to take to David to help appease him, but she did not tell Nabal – 23: 18-19. Abigail's initiative is timely as David is on the way to attack Nabal, who is so incensed by the evil he perceives he did to him, that not one man will be left alive in Nabal's household – 25:21-22. David is in danger of overreacting as he justifies his impending action. Fortuitously, or providentially, just in time, Abigail is on her way to intercept David and prevent the massacre. She is an intelligent woman. In a man's world. In a patriarchal society. We can discern this from her winsome speech in which she appeases David. We read in 25:23-31: 'When Abigail saw David she made haste and alighted from the ass, and fell before David on her face, and bowed to the ground. She fell at his feet and said, 'Upon me alone, my lord, be the guilt: pray let your handmaid speak in your ears, and hear the words of your handmaid. Let not my lord regard this ill-natured fellow Nabal: for as his name is, so is he. Nabal is his name and folly is with him: but I your handmaid did not see the young men of my Lord, whom you sent. Now then, my lord, as the Lord lives, and as your soul lives, seeing the Lord has restrained you from bloodguilt, and from taking vengeance with your own hand, now then let your enemies and those who seek to do evil to my lord, be as Nabal. And now let this present which your servant has brought to my lord be given to the young men who follow my lord. Pray forgive the trespass of your handmaid: for the Lord will certainly make my lord a sure house, because my lord is fighting the battles of the Lord: and evil shall not be found in you as long as you shall live. If men rise up to pursue you and to seek your life, the life of my lord shall be bound in the bundle of the living in the care of the Lord your God, and the lives of your enemies he shall sling out as far as from the hollow of a sling. And when the Lord has done to my lord according to all the good that he has spoken concerning you, and has appointed you prince over Israel, my lord shall have no cause of grief, or pangs of conscience, for having shed blood without a cause or for my lord taking vengeance himself. And when the Lord has dealt well with my lord, then remember your handmaid.'

Abigail's passionate speech is unsurpassed in the Bible for its literary eloquence and excellence for a woman of her time. It is extremely shrewd, as it not only appeases David but also invites him to rescue her in the future. It is a remarkably diplomatic and brilliantly beguiling monologue, made even more remarkable as it is extempore. As she speaks to David, it is clear that she is aware of his reputation, and her words are prophetic in their spiritual discernment about David and the Lord's will for him. Her humble obeisance to David is marked by an intelligent submissiveness that is winsome. Moreover, she also pronounces blessings upon David. Her tremendous initiative has saved her husband's family and all his men from annihilation, as she deflected the blame from Nabal to herself, for not receiving David's messengers and giving them the provisions he requested. Her speech is a virtuoso performance delivered impeccably. After Abigail finishes her speech, David affirms her discretion and diplomacy, and he also discerns the

Lord's providence in prompting her to come to him that averts a disaster. David accepts not only her gifts but also all the words she has spoken to him, and he sends her in peace back to her house. He sends her back with a threefold blessing, 'Blessed be the Lord who sent you: blessed be your discretion: blessed be you' – 25:32-33.

Having returned home Abigail says nothing to Nabal about meeting David, as he was drunk until the morning, so he could experience the full impact of what she had done. On learning about this Nabal's heart died within him. This is open to interpretation and while Tsumura says, 'he probably had a stroke'[42] his heart may well have frozen because of the shock and fear resulting from Abigail's story. Regardless of the exact effect, ten days later the narrator informs us that the Lord 'smote Nabal and he died' – 25:38. David then learns that Nabal has died, presumably from Abigail's messenger. He interprets this as a direct sign of the Lord's vengeance as Nabal had insulted David. He then sends messengers to inform Abigail she is to be his wife. She duly complies and we read in 35: 41-42, 'And Abigail rose and bowed with her face to the ground and said, 'Behold, your handmaid is a servant to wash the feet of the servants of my Lord.' And Abigail made haste and rose and mounted on an ass, and her five maidservants attended her: she went after the messengers of David and became his wife.' Abigail's homage and humility do not mask the fact she has five maidens attending and accompany her to be David's wife! David then takes Ahinoam of Jezreel to also be his wife. While Michal his first wife Saul's daughter was given to another man.

DAVID SPARES SAUL

1 Samuel 26:1-25

'Since Ch. 16, the narrative has been shaped so that Saul and David are on a collision course…In the end, the confrontation of Saul and David has an odd settlement. For a long stretch of the narrative, Saul is the stalker seeking out David… As this narrative begins, however, their roles are reversed… Saul is the hunted one and David the hunter…The narrative concerns the working out of Yahweh's will, which happens through military power and political acts, but seems to have its own odd, inexplicable power.'[43] Once again, Saul pursues David after the Ziphites inform him he is hiding in the wilderness of Ziph. When David hears that Saul is after him again, he send spies who confirm this report. He then goes to the outskirts of Saul's camp and sees the tent where he is staying with Abner, the commander of his army. After this David enlists Abishai's help and at night goes down to Saul's camp to where Saul and Abner are sleeping. We read in 26: 7-12: 'Then Abishai said to David, 'God has given your enemy into your hand this day: now therefore let me pin him to the earth with one stroke of my spear, and I will not strike him twice.' But David said to Abishai, 'Do not destroy him: for who can put forth his hand against the Lord's anointed and be guiltless?' And David said, 'As the Lord lives, the Lord will smite him, or his day shall come to die, or he shall go down into battle and perish. The Lord forbid that I should put forth my hand against the Lord's anointed: but take now the spear that is at his head, and the jar of water, and let us go.' So David took the spear and the jar of water from Saul's head, and they went away. No man saw it, or knew it, nor did any awake: for they were all asleep, because a deep sleep from the Lord had fallen upon them.'

After David left Saul's camp he went to the top of the mountain and called out to Abner and the army and told them he has taken Saul's spear and jar of water and they have failed to protect him. On hearing his voice Saul says, 'Is this your voice, my son David?' And David said, 'It is my voice, my lord, O king' – 26:17. David then pleads his innocence and Saul says, 'I have done wrong: return my son David, for I will no more do you harm, because my life was precious in your eyes this day: behold, I have played the fool and have erred exceedingly' – 26:21. After this David replies, and Saul says, 'Blessed, be you, my son David. You will do many things and will succeed in them' – 26:25. These were Saul's last words to David, he returned home and David also went his separate way.

DAVID & ACHISH

1 Samuel 27-28:2

In Ch. 27, the narrator uses the interior monologue of the characters to reveal their thoughts, so we can understand how they feel. Also the narrative between Ch. 27 to 2 Samuel 1, is seen as 'The Accession Narrative' which describes the events that lead to David becoming the king.[44] Despite Saul's invitation to David to return and be with him, and his acknowledgement he has played the fool, David does not trust Saul, and is even more convinced than ever that he is determined to kill him. And David said in his heart, 'I shall now perish one day by the hand of Saul: there is nothing better for me than I should escape to the land of the Philistines: then Saul will despair of seeking me any longer within the boarders of Israel' – 27:1. This is an unexpected and truly extraordinary decision by David, as on two recent occasions the Lord has clearly delivered David from Saul. Instead of trusting the Lord and seeking his guidance and inquiring what he should do, he trusts in his own insight and judgment. Edelman says, 'David has lost sight of his own special relationship with the Lord as the king-elect and has lost faith in the Lord's continued protection and support. He is no longer relying on the Lord to guide him…'[45] Firth thinks this is too harsh a judgment.[46] However, David's decision is tantamount to denying the Lord's sovereign power to protect him from Saul and also a failure to trust the Lord to give him his peace about his situation. Consequently, as a defector, David is now relying on his own duplicity and wits to survive instead of trusting the Lord.

So David decides to go with his 600 men to Achish at Gath. 'And David dwelt with Achish at Gath, he and his men, and every man with his household, and David with his two wives, Ahinoam of Jezreel and Abigail of Carmel, Nabal's widow. And when Saul was told that David had fled to Gath, he sought for him no more' – 27:3-4. When David first came to Achish on his own after he escaped from Saul, he feigned madness as he was afraid – 21:10. But now he is with his men he no longer has to pretend, and persuades Achish to give him a town to live in. So Achish gave David Ziklag and he lived in the country of the Philistines for a year and four months' – 27:5-7. David's time in Ziklag is punctuated by raids of extreme and indiscriminate violence in which he annihilated the inhabitants of the land. 'And David smote the land, and left neither man nor woman alive' – 27:8-9. And David deceived Achish when he gave him accounts of his raids, and led him to believe he was attacking his own people. 'And Achish trusted David thinking, 'He has made himself utterly abhorred by his people Israel, therefore he shall be my servant always' – 27:12.

David's alliance with the Philistines is outrageous and a very high risk political gamble in which he double crosses Achish. Ch. 27-28:1-2 and 29: 1-11, make no mention of the Lord, and give no theological basis or justification for David's action. What is striking is that David does not inquire of the Lord whether his decision to ally himself with Achish is his will. Neither does he inquire of the Lord about carrying out his ruthless plan to annihilate all his enemies. Equally, there is no word from the Lord that addresses David's actions. We can but speculate that David's charisma is attractive enough not only to fool Achish, but also to influence his marauding bandits who unquestioningly follow him. 'One must pause to marvel at this scene. David is no political innocent: he is ruthless and calculating, confident enough to manipulate Philistine cover for Judahite advantage.'[47] Achish is now so taken in by David's deceitful cunning and his disingenuous strategy, and his trust in him is so complete, that he invites David and his men to join his army to fight against Israel. But more than that, he offers to make him his bodyguard for life – 28:1-2. David has created a considerable problem for himself. He does not seem to be aligning himself with the Lord's will to succeed Saul, as he is now firmly entrenched in the camp of the Philistines, Saul's enemies, his enemies and Israel's enemies. 'Achish's complete trust of David now causes him his greatest difficulty. As the Philistine war camps assemble, Achish is clear that David can have no other expectation than that he and his men join the camp with him. David is seemingly caught in his own cleverness.'[48] Bearing this in mind, David's response to Achish's invitation is somewhat ambiguous – 28:2, as he has no idea how to extricate himself from his dilemma. David is caught in a catch 22 situation. He cannot fight against Israel as this would discredit him, and also make his election as king untenable. 'Achish of course knows nothing of the precariousness of David's situation. He only knows what David has wanted him to know.'[49]

SAUL AT ENDOR

1 Samuel 28:3-25

Saul is about to reap the full wrath of the Philistine army and because of his foolish pursuit of David, he is without David's help and without the Lord's help. As the Philistines gathered their forces together, so too Saul gathered all Israel together. But, 'When Saul saw the army of the Philistines, he was afraid, and his heart trembled greatly. And when Saul inquired of the Lord, the Lord did not answer him, either by *(the legitimate means of dreams),* or by Urim, or by prophets' – 28:5-6. So he commanded his servants to find a medium that he might go and inquire of her, and they found a woman at Endor. But having banned all the mediums and wizards from the land, Saul disguises himself when he goes to visit her at night. He then asks her to divine whatever spirit he wants by name, but she points out Saul's ban and her fear for her life if she complies. However, Saul makes an oath in the Lord's name that no harm will come to her, and asks her to, 'Bring Samuel for me' – 28: 8-10. When the woman sees Samuel, she is alarmed and recognises Saul who has deceived her. After bowing with his face to the ground in obeisance to Samuel, he asks him why he has brought him up, at which he explains his predicament. And Samuel said to Saul, 'Why then do you ask me since the Lord has turned from you and become your enemy? The Lord has done to you as he spoke by me, for the Lord has torn the kingdom out of your hand, and given it to your neighbour David. Because you did not obey the voice of the Lord and did not carry out his fierce wrath against Amalek, therefore the Lord has done this thing to you this day. Moreover, the Lord will give Israel also with you into the hand of the Philistines, and tomorrow you and your sons shall be with me. The Lord will give the army of Israel also into the hand of the Philistines. Then Saul fell at once upon the ground, filled with fear because of the words of Samuel, and there was no strength in him, for he had eaten nothing all day and all night' – 28:16-20. This is a tragic situation for Saul, incapacitated by his justifiable fear of the Philistines. He hoped against hope that in death Samuel will be more compassionate, more merciful than he was in life. Saul is desperate and out of his mind with fear, but even in death Samuel is still the intransigent prophet. A prophet of doom for Saul.

> Even in death Samuel dominates the narrative...Samuel appears in all his unmistakable cantankerousness. Death has not mellowed Samuel. He is in death exactly as Saul knew him in life: unaccommodating, unhelpful, incapable of understanding. Samuel's blissful sleep is disturbed, and he does not like it…Saul lays the fullness of his abandonment and despair before Samuel. Samuel's answer is an imperious, majestic statement. 'Why do you ask me? Samuel's speech is an awesome performance. It is Final and absolute. It allows no appeal, no protest, no argument, no alternative. The narrator does not tell of Samuel's departure…It is the voice that counts. That voice speaks only of death, destruction, nullification. Saul's prospects at the hand of Samuel (and Yahweh) have not changed as much as a syllable since Ch. 15. Everything in Saul's career has been enacted under the aegis of this irrevocable decision. Saul is made aware that he lives under the rule of this unaccommodating God. It is a very different face of God from the one that shines on David.[50]

Despite Saul's crazy foolish pursuit of David, and Samuel's defiant speech condemning Saul, we know that this tragic situation is tinged with great sadness. Saul's heart had trembled greatly when he saw the Philistine army, and in death, Samuel ruthlessly compounded that fear and terror. 'This scene is filled with pathos and anguish.'[51] As we know Saul will die, and his sons, including Jonathan will be killed, could this disaster have been averted? Not to exonerate Saul for his foolishness, but to celebrate the life of Jonathan that deserved to be lived to its full potential. 'The narrative is a reflection on how hard and dangerous is the single voice to which Saul failed to give heed.'[52] Saul is now beaten. An empty shell of a man. A dead man walking. But could Saul have chosen to consult his sons and not engage the Philistines in battle to avoid the tragedy that awaited him – and saved his sons from the fate that only he deserved? And although Samuel's message to Saul foretold his death, we are left to wonder if he could have responded differently to this news to avoid this outcome. There is nothing in the text that categorically states the option of retreating from the Philistines was out of the question.

ACHISH & ZIKLAG

1 Samuel 29-30:1-26

Ch. 29 continues on from Ch. 28: 1-3, where the Philistines gathered their forces for war against Israel. The impending battle was a major showdown between the two nations. The site of the encounter was not held in the border area between the two lands as might have been expected, but in the northern section of Israel's territory. Israel was camped at Jezreel and the Philistines were around 50 kilometres south at Aphek. Jezreel was noticeably outside Philistine territory, however if Saul was successful and consolidated his position in the north, this would have been a threat to the Philistines. This may well explain why the Philistines travelled to take on Israel, and why Saul was so troubled by the completely unexpected arrival of the massive Philistine force.[53]

Up to now, David has artfully deceived Achish, so when the Philistines gathered for battle he was amongst them, but their commanders were rattled to find David with their troops. As they spoke to Achish, they questioned his presence and quoted the famous proverb about him, 'Is not this David of whom they sing to one another, 'Saul has slain his thousands, and David his ten thousands?' Achish in quite an extraordinary speech begins to exonerate David when he says, 'As the Lord lives, you have been honest, and to me is seems right that you should march out and in with me in the campaign: for I have found nothing wrong in you from the day of your coming to me to this day. Nevertheless, the lords do not approve of you. So go back now and go peaceably, that you may not displease the lords of the Philistines'– 29:6-7. David's deceit and subterfuge, is in contrast to Achish's honest, though naive assessment of David. He has taken David to his heart and proved to be honourable, defending him before the Philistine lords, whereas David has been devious and cunning. The text invites us to wonder whether David had found favour with Achish, not just because of his reputation, but because he discerned the Lord was with him. It appears a remarkable statement when he says to David, 'As the Lord lives' – v. 6, as this is a statement of affirmation in the Lord. He was swearing by David's God, the Lord, not by a Philistine god, and indicates the high, but misguided regard in which he held David. Despite his murderous pillaging, he found favour in Achish's eyes, as he was ignorant of this. David even outrageously questions Achish's decision for him to withdraw from the Philistine troops, although he ultimately accedes to his request.

Although there is no mention of the Lord in Ch. 29, apart from a passing reference to David, 'as an angel of the Lord' and no explicit theological content, 'we are dealing with a highly self-conscious theological literature that observes the undercurrent of divine governance without being explicit. The Lord is with David everywhere (18:12, 28). The narrator is not so disbelieving as to perceive the outcome of the narrative is luck…The very same Philistines who will finally dispose of Saul, are the ones who unwittingly rescue David.'[54] This is quite an unusual chapter, as we can interpret the outcome of David's rescue from his perilous situation as fortuitous, or we can discern that the hand of the Lord influenced the outcome.

Having departed from the Philistines no doubt with a great sense of relief, David and his men travel around 50 miles from Aphek and return to a disaster in their city of Ziklag, because of the Amalekites who were recently subject to David's raids – 27:8. Not only have they raided and burned the city as an act of vengeance, they have taken the women and children captive.

And although they killed no one they probably intended to sell them as slaves. It is a distressing and a traumatic time as David and his all men are devastated at the sight of the city that has been destroyed, because they do not know who is responsible and if the women and children are alive. We read in 30: 3-10:

'And when David and his men came to the city, they found it burned with fire, and their wives and sons and daughters taken captive. Then David and the people who were with him raised their voices and wept, until they had no more strength to weep. David's two wives also had been taken captive, Ahinoam of Jezreel and Abigail the widow of Nabal of Carmel. And David was greatly distressed, for the people spoke of stoning him, because all the people were bitter in soul, each for his sons and daughters. But David strengthened himself in the Lord his God. And David said to Abiathar the priest, son of Ahimelech, 'Bring me the ephod.' So Abiathar brought the ephod to David. And David inquired of the Lord, 'Shall I pursue after this band? Shall I overtake them?' He answered him, 'Pursue, for you shall surely overtake and shall rescue.' So David set out, and the 600 men who were with him, and they came to the brook Besor where those stayed who were left behind. But David went on with the pursuit, he and 400 men: 200 stayed behind who were too exhausted to cross the brook.'

We can see a contrast between Saul and David when they are in a crisis. David is now in danger from his own men who threatened to stone him because they held him responsible for what had happened, as under his leadership they had allied themselves with the Philistines and left Ziklag undefended. Not only does David turn to the Lord, he also inquires of the Lord, which he does through the priest and ephod. Whereas Saul did not have access to the Lord for divine guidance as he murdered the priests at Nob and had to go to the witch at Endor. While the Lord is not mentioned in Ch. 27-29, in Ch. 30 he is often referred to, as David has access to the Lord and seeks his divine guidance. Tsumura says, 'Only the intimate relationship with his personal God gave David the strength in such a critical time.'[55] Just as David was strengthened by the Lord's guidance, so too his men were encouraged by David's leadership, as he turned to the Lord who answered him and informed them that they would rescue their families.

Confident because of the Lord's word they would overtake their enemy in obedience to the Lord David and his men set out after them. At the brook of Besor 200 men stayed behind, as they were too exhausted to cross the brook. On their way, they meet an Egyptian, a straggler, who has been left behind by his master because he became ill. After giving him food and water David asks him who he belongs to and where he is from. David's kindness in helping this young man is rewarded when he informs him that he was with the band of men that raided and burned Ziklag. David asks the young man if he will take him to these men, and he replies he will, if David spares his life and does not return him to his master – 30:11-15. The text invites us to interpret this encounter providentially rather than fortuitously, as this young man then lead David to the raiders. While the raiders are celebrating, and self-indulgently eating and drinking and dancing, David and his men launch a surprise attack at first light until the evening and ruthlessly kill them, although 400 young men escape. David rescues his two wives and nothing was missing that they had taken from Ziklag, and that the raiders had not harmed any of their families may imply the Lord's restraining hand was upon them. 'David's triumph over the Amalekites is massive, bloody, and total. Everything is recovered, people and property. Moreover, David seizes flocks and herds.'[56]

After this victory, David and his men return to the 200 men they left at the brook of Besor, who go out to greet David on his arrival. The narrator informs us, some of the base fellows did not want to share the spoil with them, as those who were involved in the battle were the ones who had the right to the spoil. But David, as king-elect, introduces a new social equality when he says, 'You shall not do so, my brothers, with what the Lord has given us: he has preserved us and given into our hand the band that came against us. Who would listen to you in this matter? For as his share is who goes down to the battle, so shall his share be who stays with the baggage, they shall share alike.' And from that day forward he made a statue and an ordinance for Israel to this day' – 23:23-25. 'It must have been politically dangerous to make this act, for he risked alienating the military.'[57] However, David's leadership of his men is unchallenged, as he asserts his authority and rightly attributes their victory to the Lord.

SAUL DIES

1 Samuel 31:1-13

As we learn of the death of Saul's sons and Saul himself, we are left to ruefully ponder that these could have been avoided. If Saul had not forced David to become a fugitive, and had accepted the Lord's will he would succeed him, and had kept him as the commander of his army, his position of strength against the Philistines probably would have been unassailable. Equally, although Samuel's word from the grave to Saul spoke of his death, it is reasonable to assume he had the opportunity to retreat to a safe distance from the threat of the Philistine army. Sadly, and tragically, Saul chose not to embrace David, and chose not to retreat to save his sons, his men, and his life.

In Ch. 28:1, 5 when the Philistines assembled their forces to fight against Israel, and Saul saw the size of their army he was afraid and his heart trembled. This indicates that Saul and his army was vastly outnumbered, so it is no surprise to learn that when the battle progressed the men of Israel fled before the Philistines – 29:1. The text also implies that they targeted Saul and his sons who may have been identified by their armour and royal standard. Saul's sons are overtaken, outnumbered and are killed. The battle is fierce and the Philistines press hard on Saul who is badly wounded by the archers – 31:3. Badly wounded and with no hope of escape from his enemy, Saul knows he is going to die. Rather than be captured, humiliated and tortured by the Philistines, he asks his armour-bearer to kill him, but he refuses to kill the Lord's anointed. 'There is no self-pity here, but courage. The courage is matched (and perhaps evoked) by his contempt for the Philistines. Saul is a man with a last heroic gesture.[58]

We read in 31:7, 'And when the men of Israel who were on the other side of the valley, and those beyond the Jordan saw that the men of Israel had fled and that Saul and his sons were dead, they forsook their cities and fled, and the Philistines came and dwelt in them.' Saul's death led to chaos amongst the Israelites as they abandoned their cities and this enabled the Philistines to control large areas of Israel's north territory, especially the valuable trade routes through Jezreel. Consequently, Israel lost one of its principal areas of income.[59]

As was customary, the Philistines come the next day and plunder from the dead any valuable items, such as any armour. When they found Saul's body, they cut off his head and sent messengers throughout the land to carry the good news to their idols and the people. They put his armour in the temple of Ashtroth, and fastened his body to the wall of Bethsan' – 31: 8-10. Green Says, 'The Philistines construe the death of Saul as a matter of great rejoicing for their people and their gods...both gods and Israel's foes rejoice at the royal death.'[60] 'Theologically, it means the enemy god has been defeated, for when the king dies, the king's god has failed. They make a religious claim. The gods of the Philistines have won.'[61]

The Philistines spread the news about their victory over Saul and his sons, but when the inhabitants of Jabesh-gilead hear about this, the valiant men go at night and recover their bodies, burn them at Jabesh and bury their bones – 31:11-13. The men of Jabesh remembered how many years ago Saul had saved them from a humiliating defeat by the Ammonites. They honour his memory and rescue his body from the humiliation and mockery of the Philistines. They give Saul the dignity and respect of a burial.[62]And then the men fasted for seven days. Hertzberg generously says, 'So Saul's life ends not in dishonour but in honour, as befits the Lord's anointed.'[63]

CHAPTER SIX

DAVID'S REIGN

DAVID'S LAMENT

2 Samuel 1:1-27

An Amalekite messenger who comes to tell David about Saul's and Jonathan's death may have hoped for a reward from him, as he anticipated their deaths would have been good news and welcomed by David as Saul's successor. But he has badly misjudged his character. While Saul's death at the hand of his enemies may have been anticipated in the future by David, the sudden and unexpected news of his and Jonathan's death overwhelmed him with grief. 'And he rent his clothes, as did all the men with him: and they mourned and wept and fasted until evening for Saul and for Jonathan his son, and for the people of the Lord and for the house of Israel, because they had fallen by the sword'– 1:11-13. On further questioning by David the Amalekite is put to death for saying he had slain the Lord's anointed. David knows this was a devastating defeat for all Israel as the whole of the north is now under Philistine rule.[1] Brueggemann captures the dramatic moment as the Amalekite shows David Saul's crown and his amulet to confirm his death. 'The transition from v. 10-11 is a breathtaking moment in the narrative…David responds not in glee but in pathos for the dead king...From the awesome news of a slain king comes David's immediate, seemingly uncalculated grief. David does not celebrate. This David of the narrative is so compelling and convincing because there is an astonishing congruity between David's personal inclination and his political perceptiveness… The narrative is perhaps not concerned with who killed Saul. It is rather preoccupied with David's faithful, magisterial response to Saul's death. David grieves and acts for Saul's honour.[2] And David lamented with this lamentation over Saul and Jonathan his son, and he said it should be taught to the people of Judah. We read in 2 Samuel 19-27:

Thy glory, O Israel, is slain
upon thy high places.
How are the mighty fallen.
Tell it not in Gath,
publish it not in the streets of Ashkelon:
lest the daughter of the Philistines rejoice,
lest the daughters of the uncircumcised exult.

You mountains of Giboah,
let there be no dew or rain upon you,
nor the upsurging of the deep.
For there the shield of the mighty was defiled,
the shield of Saul, not anointed with oil.

From the blood of the slain,
from the fat of the mighty,
the bow of Jonathan turned not back,
and the sword of Saul returned not empty.

Saul and Jonathan, beloved and lovely.
In life and in death they were not divided:
they were swifter than eagles,
they were stronger than lions.

You daughters of Israel, weep over Saul,
who clothed you daintily in scarlet,
who put ornaments of gold upon your apparel.

How are the mighty fallen,
in the midst of the battle.

Jonathan lies slain upon your high places.
I am distressed for you, Jonathan my brother:
very pleasant have you been to me:
your love to me was wonderful,
passing the love of women

How are the mighty fallen,
and the weapons of war perished.

The striking and surprising thing about David's eulogy is that the Lord is not mentioned. David's lament is remarkable, as he does not diminish Saul in his death, even though he sought to kill him. Instead, he displays a magisterial generosity imbued with passion and pathos that is deeply moving and eloquent, that enables Israel to mourn collectively. 'This poem marks a deep, precious, and hurtful moment in the life of Israel … Such poetry serves to give the community time, space and means whereby to treasure and relinquish…David sings with abandonment of the splendour of Saul and Jonathan and the enormous loss Israel now faces…No doubt the language is hyperbolic, but it is not dishonest hyperbolic. Rather, it is a liberated grieving in which Israel is permitted to give expression to this moment of extraordinary defeat…We see Saul and Jonathan together, father and son treasured in Israel, attractive in their appearance, united. The poetry of grief looks past the rancours of father and son, the deception of the son and the rage of the father…Grief has a way of focusing the picture, permitting in hyperbolic expression what is true and best remembered.'[3]

David shares how distraught he is at Jonathan's death. And freely, without any inhibition, he recalls how attractive-lovely Jonathan was and how much he was loved by David and everyone else too. We know this is true, as Saul's men ransomed Jonathan's life when he was foolishly going to kill him – 1 Samuel 14:45. David shares the most intimate feelings of his soul for Jonathan's love. He gives voice to his profound loss and sorrow – David is distressed and distraught for Jonathan who has died. His words are tinged with a deep sense of regret for Jonathan and himself. Jonathan's love for David involved a manly bonding of admiration and respect and deep emotional attachment. He was selflessly committed to David and acknowledged to him that he would be king after his father. Jonathan's support in his covenant friendship with David as Saul sought to kill him saved his life. It is a unique tribute from David to Jonathan to say his love surpassed that of women. It was a manly love. A friendship of deep abiding affection, emotional attachment, and intellectual and political commitment.

TRANSITION IN ISRAEL

After Saul's death, David's accession to the throne does not take place straightaway. The reality is that his path to kingship is messy and complex, and does not run smoothly, as Saul's son, Ish-bosheth, is installed as king by Abner the commander of Saul's army. He is king over Gilead, Ephraim and Benjamin and was king over the northern tribes of Israel for two years. Whereas David was king in Hebron over the house of Judah for seven years and six months – 2:8-11. David has rival claimants to the throne from Saul's family and Abner who is the power behind Ish-bosheth. Shortly after this Abner goes with servants of Ish-bosheth and meets Joab David's commander with his servants, who kill one another – 2:12-17. In Ch. 3:1, we learn that there was a long war between the house of Saul and the house of David, with the house of Saul growing weaker, while David's grows stronger.

In 2 Samuel 3:2-5 we read: 'And sons were born to David at Hebron: his firstborn was Amnon, of Ahinoam of Jezreel, and his second Chileab, of Abigail widow of Nabal of Carmel, and the third Absalom, the son of Ma'acah daughter of Talami king of Geshur: and the fourth Adonijah the son of Higgith, and the fifth Shephatiah, the son of Abital, and the sixth Ithream, of Eglah, David's wife. These were born to David in Hebron.

Abner, Ish-bosheth's commander, falls out with him and tells him he is going to transfer the kingdom from the house of Saul to David. So he sends messengers to David offering to make a covenant with him to bring the northern tribes over to him. David agrees to his offer although he wants his first wife Michal returned to him which Abner agrees to. He then confers with the elders of Israel and persuades them to agree to David being king over them. Subsequently, David meets Abner with twenty men at Hebron and he promises David that all Israel will make a covenant with him, so David sends him on his way in peace – 3:6-21. After this Joab, David's commander, returns from a raid and is told about Abner's visit, and at this news, he confronts David and insists he was trying to deceive him. So without David's knowledge, Joab sends his messengers to bring Joab back, and he kills him. On learning about this,

David instructs Joab and all the people to mourn for Abner. So all the people knew that David was innocent of his death – 3:31-38. And David said, 'The Lord requite the evildoer according to his wickedness' – 3:39. After Solomon is crowned king, David advises him to kill Joab for the murder of Abner and Amasa – 1 Kings 2:5-6. Solomon then sends Benaniah to kill Joab which he does – 1 Kings 2: 28-3:4.

When Ish-bosheth heard that Abner had died, his courage failed him and all Israel was dismayed – 4:1. Shortly after this Ish-bosheth himself is killed and beheaded and Rechab and Banah who kill him fetch his head to David thinking he will be pleased. Instead, David says to them, 'When wicked men have slain a righteous man in his own house, shall I not now require his blood at your hand and destroy you from the earth? – 4:12. So David had them put to death.

DAVID ANOINTED KING

2 Samuel 5:1-16

We read in 5:1-5, 'After this all the tribes of Israel came to David at Hebron, and said, 'Behold, we are your bone and flesh. In times past, when Saul was king over us, it was you who led us out and brought in Israel: and the Lord said to you, 'You shall be the shepherd of my people Israel, and you shall be prince over Israel.' So all the elders of Israel came to David at Hebron before the Lord, and they anointed David king over Israel. David was thirty years old when he began his reign and he reigned forty years. At Hebron, he reigned over Judah seven years and six months: and at Jerusalem he reigned over all Israel thirty-three years.' David's kingdom resulted in a reliable economic order and secure military position, and a political legitimacy among the nations. David's narrative is generally seen by scholars in two distinct units. The Rise of David (1 Sam. 16:1-2 Sam. 5:10) and the Succession Narrative (2 Sam. 9:1-20:26, 1 Kings 1:1-2:46). 'Ch. 5:11-8:18 presents David in his ascendency, whereas the second section presents David in his demise and expresses pathos and ambiguity. They show the painful process whereby this beloved king is transformed into a hardened monarch, who now has more power than popular affection. These chapters invite us to ask about the transformation of David.'[4] Ch. 5: 6-10 sum up David's ascendancy with Jerusalem now established as a new place of residence for David. This is a new beginning and unites the house of Saul and the house of David. It is also David's city that marks his autonomy and has military and political importance. It became a royal city as David extended Jerusalem and he built himself a house and the city became the capital of the nation and a national centre. After he came from Hebron David took more concubines and wives from Jerusalem and he had more sons and daughters. Another eleven children were born to David and Solomon was amongst them – 5:13-15.

THE ARK OF GOD

2 Samuel 6:1-23

The last time the ark was mentioned was in 1 Sam. 5-7:2, after the Philistines returned the ark to Israel because the Lord had afflicted them with tumours. 'And the men of Kir'iath-je'rim came and took up the ark of the Lord, and brought it to the house of Abinadab on the hill: and they consecrated his son, Eleazar to have charge of the ark of the Lord. From the day the ark was lodged there, a long time passed, some twenty years…' – 1 Sam. 7:1. In 2 Sam. 5:19 David inquired of the Lord whether to attack the Philistines and if the Lord would give them into his hand. And the Lord said, 'Go up, for I will certainly give the Philistines into your hand' – 5:20. In 1 Chronicles 13:1-4, David says to the leaders of his army, 'If it seems good to you, and if it is the will of the Lord our God, let us send abroad to our brethren who remain in the land of Israel, and with them to the priests and Levites in the cities that have pasture lands, that they may come together to us. Then let us bring the ark of our God to us: for we neglected it in the days of Saul. And all the assembly agreed to do so, for the thing was right in the eyes of all the people.'

David is a shrewd political monarch as he remembers the ark which Israel had forgotten. He wants to house it in Jerusalem as a symbol of royal approval so the city is seen as the legitimate centre of a new dynasty and a royal city. The ark is also a sign of God's presence and his solidarity with Israel and it signifies the unity between the tribes and clans. Under David to have access to the ark and its old significance, the conservative Israelites have to make a pilgrimage to Jerusalem, to the new city with David's new ideology and power and in so doing they give tacit assent. Therefore, the elaborate ritual of Ch. 6 is to bind together in a visible way the old ritual claims and the new ideology. With Jerusalem as the locus of the Lord's presence Solomon was able to establish the Temple that reflected the new ideology.[5]

We read in 2 Samuel 6:1-11:

'David again gathered all the chosen men of Israel, thirty thousand. And David arose and went with all the people who were with him from Baal-judah, to bring up from there the ark of God, which is called by the name of the Lord of hosts who sits enthroned on the cherubim. And they carried the ark of God upon a new cart, and brought it out of the house of Abinadab which was on the hill: and Uziah and Ahio, the sons of Abinadab were driving the cart with the ark of God: and Ahio went before the ark. And David and all the house of Israel were making merry before the Lord with all their might, with songs and lyres and harps and tambourines and castanets and cymbals.

And when they came to the threshing floor of Nacon, Uzzah put out his hand to the ark of God and took hold of it, for the oxen stumbled. And the anger of the Lord was kindled against Uzzah: and God smote him there because he put forth his hand to the ark: and he died there beside the ark of God. And David was angry because the Lord had broken forth upon Uzzah: and that place is called Perezuzah to this day. And David was afraid of the Lord that day, and he said, 'How can the ark of the Lord come to me?' So David was not willing to take the ark of the Lord into the city of David: but David took it aside to house of Obededom the Gitttite. And the ark of the Lord remained in the house of Obededom the Gittite three month: and the Lord blessed the house of Obededom and his household.

And it was told King David, 'The Lord has blessed the

household of Obededom and all that belongs to him, because of the ark of God.' So David went and brought the ark of God from the house of Obededom, to the city of David with rejoicing: and when those who bore the ark of the Lord had gone six paces, he sacrificed an ox and a fatling. And David danced before the Lord with all his might: and David was girded with a linen ephod. So David and all the house of Israel brought up the ark of the Lord with shouting, and with the sound of the horn.'

Transporting the ark of the Lord to Jerusalem is a truly momentous and prestigious occasion and celebration, that involves 30,000 of the chosen men of Israel and all the people who were with David – 6:1. The ark represented two important things for David. Firstly, it re-engages with Israel's traditional faith. 'It is no wonder the ark evoked such a stupendous celebration.' Secondly, the renewed focus on the ark in Jerusalem is a shrewd political move by David to affirm his new regime as the rightful successor to the old tribal system, and signifies royal legitimacy. 'There is a hint of political calculation and manipulation in David's act.' But the ark is not primarily for David's benefit or sacred propaganda. It must not be treated with familiarity or presumed upon, for the ark represents the holiness and presence of God among his people.[6] Those responsible for the ark knew it must not be touched since this breached the Lord's holiness, and the ark should not have been transported on a cart, so Uzzah dies when he touches it. David was transporting the ark with ulterior motives and Uzzah's death was a timely warning to him from the Lord that the ark was not his to control.[7] His death has a salutary effect on David. He fears the Lord who stops him in his tracks and disciplines him.

> When people are no longer awed, respectful, or fearful of God's holiness, the community is put at risk. David may intend to use the ark for his own purposes, for religious equipment has powerful legitimating effect ...The ark is not merely a useful tool. Beyond its utilisation, there is an awesome presence to which heed must be paid.[8]

After the ark had been in Obededom's house for three months David was told the Lord had blessed him and his household. This prompted David to go and bring the ark to Jerusalem. But after the eventful accident of Uzzah, it is surprising the narrator does not record David now inquired of the Lord about whether to bring the ark to Jerusalem. However as we read in 6:13, 'and when those who bore the ark had gone six paces David sacrificed an ox and a fatling' – this indicates David followed the correct procedure in transporting the ark. This is confirmed in 1 Chron. 15:2-3, 11-15, 25-26.

> Then David said, 'No one but the Levites may carry the ark of God, for the Lord chose them to carry the ark of the Lord and to minister to him for ever.' And David assembled all Israel at Jerusalem, to bring up the ark of the Lord to its place which he had prepared for it…Then David summoned the priests of Zadok and Abiathar and the Levites Uriel, Asaiah, Joel, Shem-aiah, Eliel and Amminadab, and said to them, 'You are the heads of the fathers' houses of the Levites: sanctify yourselves, you and your brethren, so that you may bring up the ark of the Lord, the God of Israel to the place I have prepared for it. Because you did not carry it the first time, the Lord our God broke forth upon us, because we did not care for it in the way that is ordained. So the priests and the Levites sanctified themselves to bring up the ark of the Lord, the God of Israel. And the Levites carried the ark upon their shoulders with the poles, as Moses had commanded according to the word of the Lord…So David and the elders of Israel, and the commanders of thousands, went to bring up the ark of the covenant of the Lord from the house of Obededom with rejoicing. And because God helped the Levites who were carrying the ark of the covenant of the Lord, they sacrificed seven bulls and seven rams.

The arrival of the ark in Jerusalem which David placed inside the tent he pitched is a magnificent historic occasion.

The city of David is now the official shrine where the Lord's presence is acknowledged, marked by extravagant liturgical celebrations – sacrifices, and rejoicing and a communal meal David distributed to all the people – 6:17-20. The event evokes extravagance, for the coming of the ark is the Lord's self-giving to David and to Israel's new political beginning.[9] For the first time, David is now referred to as King David, and his legitimate rule is acknowledged before all Israel, along with Jerusalem as the legitimate shrine and dwelling place of the Lord. David has united the clans and tribes of Israel whose identity as nation now has its central focus in Jerusalem. This is also a memorable occasion as, 'The most remarkable thing about the story is the narrative's insistence that King David assumed the high-priestly role of offering the sacrifices and blessing the people. David could do this because Israel's king was ideally the Lord's representative (God's adopted son, according to psalm 2:7)…Also, as the Deuteronomistic story goes, no high priest has yet been appointed…David's supervision of the sacrifices is also a natural extension of his desire to assure that the ceremony is successful. As David took on the role of representative liturgical dancer for the worshippers, he also presided over the sacrifices, leaving as little to chance as possible.'[10]

The ark was the most important historical sacred relic and tangible memorial, that Moses had constructed and placed in the tabernacle, with specific instructions from the Lord. The ark was a symbol of the Lord's presence with Israel in the wilderness and Moses used to go into the tabernacle where the ark was kept in the holy of holies, and the Lord would speak to him face to face. The ark represented the glory of the Lord that spoke to the religious imagination of the people. 'Nothing in Israel was more holy than the ark. Inside were the two stone tablets on which the Ten Commandments had been engraved by God's own finger, and a jar of manna saved from the wilderness days as a sign of God's loving providence.'[11] We can imagine a tumultuous welcome accompanied the arrival of the ark in Jerusalem, with the people celebrating joyfully and noisily with their musical instruments, and leaping and dancing and praising the Lord, just as David did in his priestly garment. David's heart was full and brimming with exuberant joy which he could not contain so he danced before the Lord. He rejoiced because the ark was now in Jerusalem. He rejoiced because the Lord's presence was symbolically now in Jerusalem the city of David. He rejoiced because the ark's presence in Jerusalem was a symbol of unity amongst Israel. He rejoiced because at last the Lord had established him as king over His people. He rejoiced because his heart was overflowing with worship to the Lord. Even Michal could not spoil this momentous and memorable day despite her sarcastic reaction to David's uninhibited worship.

We read in 6:20-23:

> And David returned to bless his household. But Michal the daughter of Saul came out to meet David and said, 'How the king of Israel honoured himself today before the eyes of his servants' minds, as one of the vulgar fellows shamelessly uncovers himself.' And David said to Michal, 'It was before the Lord, who chose me above your father, and above his house, to appoint me as prince over Israel, the people of the Lord – and I will make merry before the Lord. I will make myself yet more contemptible than this, and I will be abased before your eyes: but before the maids of whom you have spoken, by them I shall be held in honour.' And Michal the daughter of Saul had no child to the day of her death.

Michal judged David's unrestrained celebrations in his scantily clad linen ephod as indecent and vulgar and not befitting a royal person, especially the king. Firth says, 'The emphasis upon exposure is so marked that *glh* (uncover) is used three times. Although she refers to David as Israel's king, she clearly does not consider him worthy of that position.'[12] Perhaps her sarcastic put down reflects her bitterness that David in negotiating a covenant with Abner, Saul's commander, insisted that Michal his wife was returned to him from her husband – 3:13. Perhaps her comment to David reflected her bitterness at her father's death and that Saul should have reigned instead of him. Her pride and bitterness could not see beyond David the man, to the man who was God's anointed king, whom she once loved, whose life she had once saved from Saul: but who never returned to rescue and take Michal from Saul to be with him as his wife. It is a tragic day for her, made even more tragic because by contrast, it was a day of celebration for David, and after this, she bore no children. The text can be interpreted as saying David abstained from a sexual relationship with Michal, (and she probably denied him a sexual relationship too as she despised him) and so no one from Saul's lineage was to be heir to David's throne. The narrator makes no judgment on what happened to her, but the reader feels a measure of sympathy towards Michal at the predicament she found herself in, and the way David treated her like a trophy wife, when he took her from her husband.

THE LORD'S VISION

2 Samuel 7:1-17

2 Samuel Ch. 7 can be seen to represent the high point of the Deuteronomistic History, because here the Davidic dynasty is established.[13] Ch. 7:1-3 indicates that David wanted to build the Lord a house for the ark of the Lord to dwell in. Nathan affirms David's desire that is in his heart because 'the Lord is with you' although he hasn't specifically told him what it is. However, that same night the Lord speaks to Nathan and says, 'Go and tell my servant David, 'Thus says the Lord: Would you build me a house to dwell in?' – 7:5. 'Moreover, the Lord declares to you that the Lord will make you a house. When your days are fulfilled and you lie down with your fathers, I will raise up your offspring after you, who shall come forth from your body and I will establish his kingdom. He shall build a house for my name, and I will establish the throne of his kingdom for ever. I will be his father and he shall be my son. When he commits iniquity, I will chasten him with the rod of men, with the stripes of the sons of men, but I will not take my steadfast love from him, as I took it from Saul, whom I put away before you. And your house and your kingdom shall be made sure for ever before me: your throne shall be established for ever' – 7:11-16.

David's desire to build a house for the Lord embraces his genuine piety and desire for further legitimacy for a dynastic order.[14] But the Lord declined David's desire for him to build a house for the ark of the Lord to dwell in. The Lord will determine the house that will be built for him and he will be the architect of it, just as he was the architect of the ark and tabernacle in the wilderness. The Lord surprises David and speaks to him through Nathan the prophet, which is the longest message from the Lord since he spoke to Moses.[15] 'God is about to shape the course of Israel's history and to reveal David's destiny...God, not David guides Israel's history.'[16] David has to submit to the Lord's authority through Nathan which he accepts, when the Lord informs him that one of his sons shall build him a house, and that David's house, a royal line, will be established permanently. The Lord turns the tables on David and his plans supersedes David's and he reminds him that it was the Lord who took David and established him as king. The Lord's promise to David is full of covenantal language and it is the covenant from which the messianic hope sprang.[17] The unconditional Davidic covenant the Lord promised to establish with David and the building of the temple will have a profound effect on Israel's national and religious life for many centuries.[18] While the inauguration of kingship was a somewhat messy affair, the Lord introduces his detailed plan for David's dynasty that will eventually lead to Christ being descended from David, and incorporate his salvation that will be spectacularly different from the God of the OT who annihilated his enemies.

Up to now, God's blessing on Israel had been founded on the Mosaic covenant in Deut. Ch. 5-6 and 28, a conditional covenant that required obedience to receive blessing, whereas disobedience resulted in punishment and curse. The Davidic covenant established by the Lord is a radical departure from the Mosaic tradition.

> The affirmation of the oracle spoken by Nathan is a daring and serious act of theology...It is almost impossible to sort out in this passage what is genuine faith

> and what is self-serving propaganda...This ideological utterance is the taproot of the messianic idea in Israel ...biblical faith characteristically holds together high faith and political interest...This combination of faith and interest always keeps faith close to the realities of public life...We are not permitted to escape into pure religion that has no risk of contamination.[19]

What has seemed incongruous as I studied 1 and 2 Samuel is that in these Scriptures, there is no reference to, or indication of David's faith expressed in the language of the psalms. Therefore, apart from 1 Samuel 17 when David kills Goliath, where we glimpse his profound faith in the Lord as a young man, it is difficult to reconcile David the warrior who kills Israel's enemies with 'David the sweet psalmist of Israel.' But in Ch. 7 we gain another glimpse into the profoundly spiritual side of David as he goes into the tabernacle where the ark of the covenant is kept and into God's presence and prays a prayer 'of deference and bold demand'[20] in response to the Lord's oracle through Nathan – 7:18. However, 1 Chronicles provides a deep insight into David's spirituality and records David's preparation and provision for Solomon to build the temple, including the plans for its construction. Chronicles also records David's organisation of all the administrative and religious personnel to run the temple.

DAVID'S PRAYER

2 Samuel 7:18-29

'Then king David went in and sat before the Lord and said, 'Who am I O Lord, and what is my house, that you have brought me this far? And yet this was a small thing in your eyes, O Lord God: you have spoken also of your servant's house, for a great while to come and have shown me future generations O Lord God. And what more can David say to you? For you know your servant O Lord God. Because of your promise and according to your own heart, you have done all this greatness to make your servant know it. Therefore, you are great, O Lord God: for there is none like you and there is no God besides you, according to all that we have heard with our ears. What other nation on earth is like your people Israel, whom God went to redeem to be his people, making himself a name, and doing for them great and terrible things, by driving out before his people a nation and its gods? And you did establish for yourself your people Israel to be your people for ever, and you, O Lord God, did become their God. And now, O Lord God, confirm for ever the word which you have spoken concerning your servant and his house, and do as you have spoken: and your name will be magnified for ever, saying, 'The Lord of hosts is God over Israel' and the house of your servant David will be established before you. For you, O Lord of hosts, the God of Israel, have made this revelation to your servant saying, 'I will build you a house.' Therefore, your servant has found courage to pray this prayer to you. And now, O Lord God, you are God and your words are true, and you have promised this good thing to your servant. Now, therefore, may it please you to bless the house of your servant, that it may continue for ever before you: for you, O Lord God, have spoken, and with your blessing shall the house of your servant be blessed for ever' – 2 Sam. 7:18-29.

What is surprising about David's prayer in response to the Lord's oracle about his desire to build a house-temple, is that he makes no mention of the 'house of cedar' he had in mind to build for the Lord, and does not mention the Lord said one of his sons would build this. The Lord's promise will be fulfilled from one of David's descendents from the 'seed' of his body in the future. This language is rich in Abrahamic allusions, especially since David had already fathered many children.[21] While the brief report of David's desire to build the Lord a 'house of cedar' implies his concern is for the Lord, omitting any reference to this in his prayer raises a question mark about his motivation. David's prayer is 'a sequence of deference, doxology and demand,[22] and focuses entirely on the promise that the Lord will permanently establish his house as a royal dynasty. This is significant for David, as he knows that Saul's house was cut off in it prime and the same could happen to his descendents in the future. We have perceived from 1 and 2 Samuel that David is politically and personally ambitious and these twin concepts go hand in hand, as building a temple 'is undoubtedly a mixed act of genuine piety and self-serving interest.'[23] But the Lord had far more ambitious plans than David whose focus is on his dynasty. The Lord is one step ahead of him and has much more transformative plans for his people Israel, and their future. While the Lord is going to bless David, his covenantal promise is not just for his family's benefit, 'since it is characteristic of covenantal texts to look to the Lord's greater purposes. Therefore, the promise moves from David to the nation's future status.'[24]

The composition and structure of David's prayer is extraordinary and leads to 'doxology, praising God for his greatness and uniqueness.'[25] Although there is no reference to the Lord's house in David's prayer his prayer reveals a striking spirituality in response to the Lord's oracle, in which a number of notable features stand out. David includes four rhetorical questions in his prayer, the first two being at the beginning, 'Who am I O, Lord God, and what is my house that you have brought me this far?' – 7:18. David recalls his insignificant roots and also his anointing as the Lord chosen king that evokes a sense of astonishment. He also remembers God's incomparable greatness and salvation on behalf of his chosen people Israel. This is followed by other theological statements in the form of rhetorical questions in 7:20 and 7:23. There is the frequent use of 'servant' language by David in 7:19, 20, 21, twice in v. 27 and 29. This is deferential language and acknowledges the special relationship the Lord had with David, who was his chosen and anointed king. As the Lord's servant, David addresses the Lord in an exalted manner saying, 'O Lord God' which comes in 7:18, twice in v 19, 20, 22, 25, 27, 28 and 29. But he also addresses the Lord whose name is to be magnified as, 'Lord of hosts' in 7:26 and 27. In Ch. 7, verses 18-24 are essentially thanksgiving and verses 25-29 are petition. David's prayer leads to a crescendo as he boldly claims the blessing which the Lord has revealed to him in his oracle through Nathan the prophet. While the Lord has promised his blessing on David's house and his descendents for ever, by faith, he boldly claims God's promise in prayer. Four times in his petition David emphasises God's promise is 'for ever' – 7:25, 26 and twice in v. 29. 'David pushes the dynastic claim to its extreme for all foreseeable generations. The bold prayer of David is a perfect match for the remarkable oracle…The Lord has committed deeply to David, and David will insist on that commitment.'[26]

DAVID'S PROVISION

1 Chronicles 22, 28-29

In the ancient Near East, palace temple complexes communicated the power of a king and his gods to his people and to foreign emissaries. The temple testifies to the Lord's reputation and the international function of the Jerusalem sanctuary. Successful ancient Near Eastern kings were supposed to endow the construction of shrines. Temple complexes and palaces could only succeed with great attention being paid to logistics, and the requisition of extensive sums of labour and materials.[27]

Although David did not build the temple, it was his vision that led to its construction and he contributed in significant ways to this project. 1 Chronicles Ch. 28-29 is an extraordinary record of David's contribution to the plans of the temple. 1 Chronicles 22 is also a unique record of David's identification with the temple as there is no direct parallel to his preparations and speeches in Samuel-Kings. The author of 1 Chronicles heavily relied on a variety of older biblical passages to write most of his material. Allusions are made to Joshua 1: 2-9 and Nathan's oracle in 1 Chron. 17:12-13, mentioned by David in 1 Chr. 22:7-16.[28] To all intents and purposes, the temple was David's temple, as he made comprehensive preliminary arrangements for it to be built, including handing Solomon the plans for its construction, giving gifts of gold and silver, and organising the stonecutters to prepare dressed stones. David went to great pains to provide for the house of the Lord, and he gave 100,000 talents of gold one million talents of silver, bronze and iron beyond weighing as there was so much of it, along with timber and stone, and he also provided craftsmen – 1 Chron. 22:14-15. 'Many scholars consider the astronomical amounts of gold and silver that David provides for the temple project as a form of hyperbole common in the biblical world.'[29] Although the site for building the temple was offered to David as a gift by Ornan, he purchased the ground on which to build it for 600 shekels – 1 Chron. 21:23-25. David also organised the personnel of the temple who were responsible for the sanctuary. 1 Chron. 23 opens with a report of David's organisation of the temple personnel, the Levites, and the priests up to Ch. 26. He made it clear to his son Solomon that the Lord had chosen him to build the temple, and because this was a monumental project, David made extensive preparations and provision for the temple as Solomon was young. David wanted Solomon to be confident that the Lord was with him so he quotes Moses' commissioning to Joshua in Deut 31:7-8: 'Be strong and of good courage. Fear not, be not dismayed' – 22:13. Moreover, he commanded all the leaders of Israel to help Solomon – 22:17. Andrew Hill says, 'David's actual charge to Solomon to build the temple is an invocation or prayer that offers encouragement, delineates the task at hand, and gives assurance of divine help.'[30] We read 1 Chron. 28:11-13

> Then David gave Solomon his son the plan of the vestibule of the temple, and of its houses, its treasuries, its upper rooms, and its inner chambers, and of the room for the mercy seat: and the plan of all that he had in mind for the courts of the house of the Lord, all the surrounding chambers, the treasuries of the house of God, and the treasuries for dedicated gifts, for the division of the priests and of the Levites, and all the work of the service in the house of the Lord.

What also stands out in David's preparations for the temple and his instructions to Solomon in building it, is his exhortation to Solomon to keep the law of the Lord and to be careful to observe the statutes and ordinances which the Lord commanded Moses. In David's commitment to enable Solomon to build the temple, we do not discern any disappointment or resentment at the Lord's decision not to let him to build it. This reflects David's submission to the Lord's authority and to his will, which was revealed to him through the word of the Lord, that came to him by the prophet Nathan, and the word of the Lord that one of his descendents would build the temple – 22:8-9. As God's word came to David before Solomon was born, he spent the intervening years accumulating the material required to build the temple as well as drawing up plans for its construction, and conscripting workers and skilled labourers to work on the temple. A. Hill insightfully says:

> Whether or not the Chronicler's figures are a literary device or reflect reality, most biblical commentators miss the main focus, which is not on the opulence of the temple, but on David's understanding of the inestimable worth of God. More practically, the inventory of materials and roster of ready workers mean that any delay in commencing with the building project is unnecessary, because everything is in place to begin construction.[31]

David's personal exhortation to Solomon in Ch. 22 to build the temple, is now complemented in Ch. 28: 1-8 with the public commission in front of all the officials of Israel, all the army, all the stewards of the land, all the palace officials, and all the mighty men of Israel, in which David shares that the Lord instructed him that a son of his, Solomon, is to build the temple – and in this public assembly David is calling them all to support Solomon in this task. This public transfer of power in front of all the people in the sight of all Israel completes the succession ritual David initiated privately with Solomon. In Ch. 28, the first speech by David in 1-8 exhorts everyone to support Solomon. In the second speech in 28: 9-21 there is the exhortation by David to Solomon to seek the Lord with his whole heart and a willing mind, and the affirmation that the Lord has called him to build the temple, with David handing to Solomon all the plans for building it. In v. 20 David once again encourages Solomon with the Joshua exhortation to, 'Be strong and of good courage and do it. Fear not, be not dismayed: for the Lord God, even my God, is with you. He will not fail you or forsake you, until all the work for the service of the Lord of the house of the Lord is finished.' By addressing Solomon with the Lord's command to Joshua who succeeded Moses, this highlights the Lord's call to Solomon who is to succeed David, to follow in Joshua's footsteps in leading God's people. Hill says, 'Two distinct threads tie Ch. 28 together. 1. The stress placed on obedience by the leadership of Israel, both to God and to Solomon as David's successor and 2, the understanding that the temple-building project really is a divine initiative.'[32]

1 Chronicles incorporates Solomon's commission within a larger context based on the leadership succession from Moses to Joshua, which presents David as a new kind of Moses who acknowledges his unfulfilled dream but prepares a successor to carry on. The chronicler has consciously avoided modelling this transition after the David-Solomon succession in Samuel-Kings, as the latter part of David's reign is dominated by palace intrigue and civil war in a self-destructive manner. So he rewrites the transition of the monarchy according to the Moses-Joshua model to redeem the reputations of David and Israel, as there are larger exegetical, political and social issues at stake, along with issues or national identity and solidarity. Also, David's family situation deteriorated badly in his final years.[33] To re-write the transition of the monarchy was attractive because of David's sin with Bathsheba and the murder of uriah, the sins of Amnon who raped Tamar his sister and Absalom who killed Amon, and his insurrection against David. 'The Chronicler's version of David's last years presents a striking contrast to the stories of adultery, rape, deception, chaos, betrayal and murder found in Samuel-Kings. The Chronicler does not simply contest the version of Samuel-Kings – he creates a comprehensive alternative to it.'[34]

The temple construction becomes a rallying point to support dynastic succession and it validates David's latter reign and provides the impetus for Israel to unite. We may perceive the Chronicler intends David's extensive plans for the architecture of the temple to draw a deliberate parallel between practices of the Tent of Meeting in the wilderness and the Jerusalem temple. He seeks to validate these institutions by making a direct link between them and the institutions of early Israel. Also, as the temple will contain the ark of the covenant in the

Holy of Holies it establishes a new orthodoxy superseding the old order.[35]

David's speech at the beginning of Ch. 29 records the financial provision he has made for the temple, the Lord's house, and is similar to his earlier speeches in 22:2-19 and 28:1-21. After David's speech, he invites everyone to also make their freewill offerings, consecrating themselves to the Lord, which they did – 29:1-9. There are important themes in the peoples' response. All the different people listed by the Chronicler are united. They are also of one mind as they give their freewill offerings to the Lord. All the people give generously and willingly. Their contribution is enormous and almost doubles the gifts of gold and silver made by David. We read in 29:9, 'Then the people rejoiced because these had given willingly, for with a whole heart they had offered freely to the Lord, David the king also rejoiced greatly.' Hill says, 'The issue is not the massing of glittering jewels and precious metals, but the pouring of themselves as God's people into building the temple as a symbol of the wholehearted worship that will soon take place in that sanctuary.'[36] We read David's worshipful response to the peoples' gifts in 29:10-22.

'Therefore, David blessed the Lord in the presence of all the assembly and he said, 'Blessed are you, O Lord, the God of Israel our father, for ever and ever. Yours O Lord is the greatness, and the power, and the glory, and the majesty, for all that is in the heavens and in the earth is yours: yours is the kingdom, O Lord, and you are exalted as head above all. Both riches and honour come from you and you rule over all. In your hand are power and might, and in your hand it is to make great and to give strength to all. And now we thank you our God and praise your glorious name.' 'But who am I, and what is my people, that we should able to offer willingly. For all things come from you and of your own have we given you. For we are strangers before you and sojourners as all our fathers were, our days on the earth are like a shadow and there is no abiding. O Lord our God all this abundance that we have provided for building you a house for your holy name comes from your hand and is all your own. I know my God that you test the heart and have pleasure in uprightness, in the uprightness of my heart I have freely offered all these things, and now I have seen your people who are present here, offering freely and joyously to you. O Lord the God of Abraham, Isaac, and Israel our fathers, keep for ever such purposes and thoughts in the hearts of your people, and direct their hearts towards you. Grant to Solomon my son that with a whole heart he may keep your commandments, your testimonies and your statutes performing all, and that he may build the palace for which I have made provision.' Then David said to all the assembly, 'Bless the Lord your God.' And all the assembly blessed the Lord, the God of their fathers and bowed their heads and worshipped the Lord, and did obeisance to the king. And they performed sacrifices to the Lord, and on the next day offered burnt offerings to the Lord a thousand bulls, a thousand rams and a thousand lambs, with their drink offerings and sacrifices in abundance for all Israel: and they ate and drank before the Lord on that day with great gladness. And they made Solomon the son of David king a second time, and they anointed him as prince of the Lord, and Zadok as priest.'

David's prayer in Ch. 29 is one of ten prayers in Chronicles which divides into three sections. The three stanzas include doxology 10-12, thanksgiving 13-16 and petition 17-19. This is a majestic and magnificent prayer that is profoundly concerned with the heart of worship that David eloquently expresses. The doxology-hymn of praise to God in 10-12 focuses not only on God's relationship with Israel, but also on God's cosmic rule and greatness. This embraces God's kingdom in which everything in creation belongs to him. Appropriately, the doxology ends with thanksgiving to God, not only for God himself, but also for God's 'glorious name.' As David announces the blessing on God on behalf of Israel, this reflects a priestly role. David's thanksgiving in 13-16 is tinged with deference and humility as he says, 'Who am I, and what is my people, that we should be able to give willingly?' He acknowledges on behalf of Israel that their freewill offerings to the Lord originate from him, and in giving to the Lord, they are offering what is already his. Once again there is an emphasis by David, that all that Israel has extravagantly given comes from God's hand in the first place and belongs to him – v.16.

David with the wisdom gained from the failure in his own life, knows there is always the possibility of the hearts of God's people and the heart of Solomon being deflected away from the Lord. His concern is that an ambitious and monumental project such as building the temple should not overshadow peoples' love and obedience to the Lord. Therefore, he prays to the Lord addressing him with the longest divine title in Ch. 29, naming the Lord, 'as the God of all three patriarchs. David prays that the present commitment of the people will be maintained for ever…Such commitment can only come through divine assistance.'[37] The key to this commitment is David's emphasis on the 'heart.' This reflects the Lord's primary concern for God's people which is the uprightness of their hearts, and David prays for the people that the Lord may direct their hearts towards the Lord himself. Moreover, David prays that the Lord will enable Solomon to keep the Lord's commandments, testimonies and statutes with a whole heart. Martin Selman captures the essence of David's prayer: 'This magnificent prayer demonstrates beyond contradiction that Chronicles priority is with the heart of worship rather than its form. It's interest is centred not on David or the temple, but on God himself.'[38] In David's prayer his emphasis on 'the heart' is striking, as he refers to 'heart' five times between 17-19.

DAVID & BATHSHEBA
2 Samuel 11:1-5

2 Samuel 5-10 records the pubic triumph of David after the ark has been brought to Jerusalem, and David's desire to build a house for the Lord is superseded by God's unconditional covenant with him to establish his house-dynasty for ever. In Ch. 9 David fulfills his covenant commitment to Jonathan to show kindness to anyone in his family. This turns out to be his crippled son, Mephibosheth. David gave him all of Saul's land and he lived in the royal court, dining every day with David.

In the context of David's success, Ch. 11:1 records the battle with the Ammonites as he sends Joab to fight them, 'But

David remained at Jerusalem.' An inauspicious act that leads to David's infamous sins and subsequent tragedy in Uriah's family, and also in his family. 'We are about to move from David's public triumph to personal disaster and pathos. From a life under blessing to a life under curse.'[39] The narrator does not embellish his adultery with Bathsheba. 'The action is quick. The verbs rush as the passion of David rushed. The royal deed of self-indulgence does not take long…There is no hint of love – only lust'[40] *David saw her: he inquired about her: he sent for her: he took her: he lay with her: she returned home: she conceived: she told David.* The text screams at us in horror and reduces us to silence. 'We are at a moment of no return for David.'[41]

DAVID & URIAH

2 Samuel 11:6-27

David's sin with Bathsheba has returned to haunt him, as she is pregnant with his child. One act of subterfuge is followed by another act of cunning and deception as David sends for Uriah and invites him to go to his own home, rather than lodge with the king's men. But Uriah the Hittite is a man of honour and sleeps at the king's house with all his servants. Equally, the text does not say whether Uriah suspected David of some scheme, we can only speculate whether a servant had informed him of his wife's presence in David's house. When David questions Uriah's action, he refuses to go to his own home and sleep with his wife, when the ark and all Israel dwell in booths, and the army is camping in the open fields. 'Uriah's words indict David…It is a stunning moment of disclosure and contrast.'[42] David then invites Uriah to eat and drink with him and he gets him drunk, but Uriah does not go to his own home to sleep with his wife, so the child born to Bathsheba would be seen to be his. David has learned the art of political maneuver and instructs Joab to place Uriah in the thick of the fighting so that he will be killed. Joab follows David's instructions and Uriah dies, so he sends a messenger to inform David of the outcome of the battle and news of Uriah's death. When Bathsheba learns of her husband's death, she mourns for him, and after her period of mourning was over, David sent for her, brought her to his home and she became his wife, and she bore him a son. 'But the thing that David had done displeased the Lord' – 11:27.

Whenever I read about David's adultery with Bathsheba and his murder of Uriah, it is always with a sense of sadness. We may well ask, how did David succumb to the temptation of a woman sunbathing, and not only sleep with her but plot the murder of Uriah? Although the evil one is not mentioned in the narrative, from our New Testament perspective we know that the evil one, a cunning and unscrupulous enemy, waited until David was nearly fifty years old to tempt him into committing serious sins. He broke three of God's commandments – covetousness, adultery, and murder. He coveted another man's wife. He committed adultery with Bathsheba and arranged for her husband Uriah to be killed. Undoubtedly, these sins are the most tragic events in David's life, apart from the consequences due to God's punishment. If it was possible to have prevented any sin in David's life, it is the sin with Bathsheba I would choose, as it brought tragedy to Uriah and great tragedy in David's family when the Lord punished him.

It seems almost inconceivable how David could commit such sins completely out of character. It is a salutary lesson for leaders to be aware that the devil is strategically planning their downfall. As we read 2 Sam. Ch. 11, it may appear that David's adultery with Bathsheba just happened and it was an unfortunate accident of circumstances. His army was out at war. He saw her sunbathing from the palace roof and he just succumbed to temptation. Was this a split second of covetous desire, that overpowered David, or was the seed of adultery sown earlier? I am inclined to think it was sown earlier as there are factors to indicate this is what happened.

F. B. Meyer says, 'In direct violation to the law of Moses David took more wives and concubines, fostering in him a habit of sensual indulgence.'[43] We read in 2 Sam. 5: 13, 'Meanwhile David took more concubines and wives from Jerusalem, after he came to Hebron and more sons and daughters were born to David.' Although God's blessing was upon David, taking more wives and concubines specifically disobeyed God's command in Deut. 17: 17: 'And the king shall not multiply wives for himself lest his heart turn away.' David's violation of this command had sown the seed for his adultery with Bathsheba, that led to an insidious erosion of his wholehearted commitment to the Lord, and ultimately to a covetous spirit that resulted in his sin.

C. Martini calls this event in David's life, 'Carelessness in small matters. It was careless of him to glance at Bathsheba. This is the sin of disorder. The arrival due to carelessness, superficiality at a situation becoming more insoluble by the minute.'[44] I am not at all convinced David's adultery was a matter of momentary carelessness, as the wives and concubines he took were the underlying factor that laid the foundation for this sin. The other contributory factor is found at the beginning of 2 Sam. 11: 1, where we read, 'It was spring the time of year when kings go out to battle.' But David abdicated his responsibility to lead his army and instead sent Joab his commander. Although he may have had enough of war, back home alone he is lost for things to do. And while he is having a sabbatical from war, he may have become bored and lost his spiritual discipline of worship and prayer. Having abdicated his responsibility to lead his army, he may have become somewhat complacent and careless in his walk with the Lord. This is the immediate context that exposed David to the temptation of sin.

W. Pink in effect says, David failed to follow the path of duty and forsook his post of obligation. He relaxed when he should have girded his sword.[45] 'Solemn indeed is the contrast presented of David in the two books of Samuel. In the former, he is the conqueror of mighty Goliath: in the latter he is mastered by his own lusts.'[46] With time on his hands and lost for things to do, David probably saw Bathsheba sunbathing on more than one occasion while walking on the palace roof. With nothing to do and with no one around he is attracted to her, and in his imagination, he probably flirts with the idea of sleeping with her. So with time on his hands, and nothing to usefully occupy him, he dwells on this covetous possibility. The seed of adultery has been sown, and he not only embraced it with his imagination, but with his heart too. As there is no one around, and as he is the king and is accountable to no one, he acts on his lustful desire. After all, he is the king, and no one will know what has happened between him and Bathsheba. Meyer says about David's failure, 'One brief spell of passionate indulgence and then his character blasted irretrievably: his peace vanquished: the foundations of his kingdom imperiled: the Lord displeased and great occasion given to his enemies.'[47]

Echoing my thoughts about the contributory factors to David's sin Swindoll says, 'And lest you think David's fall was sudden, instant even, consider Emily Dickinson's piece. 'Crumbling is not an instant's act, a fundamental pause: dilapidation's processes are organised decays. Tis first a cobweb on the soul, a cuticle of dust. A borer in the axis, an element of rust. Ruin is formal devil's work – consecutive and slow. Fail in an instant no man did, slipping is crash's law.'[48]

> We are now at the pivotal turning point in the narrative plot of the books of Samuel. We are also invited into the presence of delicate, subtle art. We are at the threshold of deep, aching psychology, and at the same time about to witness a most ruthless political performance. For David and for Israel, we are at the moment of no return. Innocence is never to be retrieved. From now on, the life of David is marked and all Israel must live with that mark...Behind all the critical scholarly questions, we have the harder questions of human desire and power – desire with all its delight: power with all its potential for destruction...The text is placed at the exact point where the narrative shifts from public triumph – 2 Sam. 5-10 to personal pathos, now to be spun out in the narrative that follows in Ch. 12-20. It is about the transition from a life under blessing to a life under curse.[49]

We see the Lord's perspective on this event in David's life in 2 Sam. 11:27b, 'But the thing that David had done had displeased the Lord.' Tragic consequences were to follow, even 'though the Lord put this sin away so that David would not die'

– 2 Sam. 12:10-12. We see God's verdict on David's sins to covet another man's wife, to commit adultery with her, and then arrange to have Uriah killed in battle that resulted in breaking three of God's commandments. Through Nathan, the Lord said to David, 'Now therefore the sword shall never depart from your house, because you have despised me and have taken the wife of Uriah the Hittite to be your wife. Behold I will raise up evil against you out of your own house: and I will take your wives before your eyes and give them to your neighbour, and he shall lie with your wives in the sight of this sun. For you did it in secret, but I will do this thing before Israel and before the sun' says the Lord – 2 Sam. 12:10-12. Tragic events took place in David's family as his son Amnon committed incest with his sister Tamar, then Absalom her brother planned Amnon's murder – 2 Sam. 13. In time, when Absalom rebelled against his father David he was killed by Joab – 2 Sam. 18:14-15, commander of David's army.

As we read these chapters in 2 Samuel, it is with great sadness that we learn about the tragic events that unfolded in David's family, which the Lord had said would happen, culminating in the death of his son Absalom at which David was heartbroken. His original sin with Bathsheba also led to her husband's death, but now as God's judgment unfolds, David's children appear to be innocent victims caught up in this drama of retribution. If it is correct to interpret the rape of Tamar, the death of Amnon and Absalom as signs of God's retribution on David for his sins, it is difficult to comprehend why God involved his family. Why did the Lord not just punish David? Why involve his children who were innocent victims in this drama of retribution that brought catastrophe to their lives? The fact is the narrator does not know why: and neither do we. The silence of the text makes us wonder about the severity of the Lord's punishment that he exacted on David's children.

In hindsight, we see the Lord gave David a warning about Bathsheba when he made enquiries about her, and was told by one of his messengers that she was the wife of Uriah the Hittite – 2 Sam. 11: 3. Equally, Joab the commander of David's army may well have perceived his motive in placing Uriah in the thick of battle where he was certain to be killed. But if he did, he did not question or challenge David about this. In God's eyes, David's adultery with Bathsheba was a sign of despising the Lord, when he had given him so much. Perhaps if he had not attempted to cover up this sin and have Uriah killed, his punishment from God may not have been so severe. There was a gap of around a year before David repented of his sins against the Lord. During this time, he suppressed his guilt and lived in denial of his sins, but they would not go away, and he had no way of putting things right. It took the courage of Nathan the prophet to confront David about his sins, when the Lord instructed him to do this – 2 Sam. 12, as he told him a parable that appealed to his just nature.

After God's judgment on David, God's inscrutable will is seen in the birth of his son Solomon to Bathsheba. Having been on the fringe of his family life as a shepherd boy and the youngest of eight brothers, David's experience of family life was a poor role model. So it is no surprise he did not have a prominent place in his children's lives. Evidence of this can be seen by his failure to be aware of the situation developing between Amnon and Tamar. Also by his failure to take action when he discovered this, by his failure to be aware that Absalom plotted to have Amnon killed in revenge, and by his failure in not confronting Absalom as he plotted against him – 2 Sam. 15. Life even for God's most accomplished servants may at times embrace great joy and success, along with great failure and regret. At times like this, we are aware of our frail humanity and also of God's mercy. In this context reconciling our neatly packaged doctrine and theology, with the failures in our lives is deeply challenging and humbling.

DAVID & NATHAN

2 Samuel 12:1-15

At the beginning of Ch. 12, we read, 'And the Lord sent Nathan to David.' This almost sounds like an inauspicious moment except for the fact we know how abhorrent David's sin was to the Lord, which displeased Him. David has sinned and he does not know how to extricate himself. He is now a conflicted king trapped in the aftermath of a guilty conscience. For around a year after his adultery with Bathsheba, David lived with the Lord's hand of conviction upon him, and Psalm 32 gives an indication of how he felt during this time. 'When I declared not my sin my body wasted away, through my groaning all the day. For day and night, your hand was heavy upon me: my strength was dried up as by the heat of summer' – 32:4. 'The voice of his bad conscience does not allow him peace of mind. He cries out aloud (groans) as he is tormented daily by fear, in which he discerns the hand of God pressing heavily upon him. He also believes himself to be withering away. These are the physical effects of the inner battle which the man who refuses to acknowledge his sin fights against God.'[50] Weiser captures what the convicting hand of the Lord felt like for David and also feels for us. The Lord would give him no peace in his conscience while he refused to face up to his sin. But this conviction also had a physical impact on him, as there was weariness in his soul and his body. He recognised that physically he was feeling unwell in quite an acute manner when he says, 'my body wasted away' – 'I was groaning all day long' – 'my strength was dried up.' These were the physical repercussions of his sin and were sure signs of the convicting hand of the Lord. We should not be at all surprised when the Lord convicts us of sin in our lives, to find that he assails our conscience and our bodies at the same time. It can be the Lord's way of drawing attention to sin in our lives that we are in denial about.

The Lord took the initiative to send Nathan to David to enable him to acknowledge his sin to the Lord and repent of it. The text implies it was the Lord who revealed to Nathan the parable to tell David, yet it required boldness and courage for him to come and confront the king. This is the first time that Nathan who was a royal court prophet is introduced. Although David is the king, 'prophetic speech is still permitted in Israel, for such speech is constitutive of Israel's self-discernment.'[51] Nathan's appearance before David is a moment of high drama. It is an act of divine sending and contrasts with David who sent for Bathsheba, and sent a message to Joab, to send Uriah to the thick of the battle. In Nathan's parable the love of the poor man's family for the ewe lamb, 'allows us to imagine the extraordinary tender love that Uriah had for Bathsheba. Given what we know about Uriah's fidelity to David and to the Lord, we can readily imagine he was equally devoted to his wife.'[52] Nathan's parable brings the legal case before the king whose duty it is to defend the rights of the poor man. David's moral indignation and outrage is aroused by the rich man who stole the poor man's lamb. Just as David took Uriah's wife, the rich man took the poor man's lamb. 'David's anger was greatly kindled against the man and he said to Nathan, 'As the Lord lives the man who has done this deserves to die, and he shall restore the lamb fourfold because he did this thing and because he had no pity' – 12:5-6.

We do not know if Nathan's audience with the king was a private matter, or whether others were present at the royal court, but it would not be surprising if other dignitaries were there to hear the prophet's message. The climax of Nathan's speech to David is an oracle from the Lord, that must have silenced everyone as the prophet announces judgment on David with the immortal words that have reverberated down history – 'You are the man' – 12:7. And the Lord said to David:

> 'I anointed you king over Israel and I delivered you out of the hand of Saul, and I gave you your master's house, and your master's wives into your bosom, and gave you the house of Israel and of Judah: and if this were too little, I would add to you as much more. Why have you despised the Lord to do what is evil in his sight? You have smitten Uriah the Hittite with the sword and have taken his wife to be your wife, and have slain him with the sword of the Ammonites. Now therefore the sword shall never depart from your house, because you have despised me and have taken the wife of Uriah the Hittite to be your wife.' Thus says the Lord, 'Behold, I will raise up evil against you out of your own house, and I will take your wives before your eyes and give them to your neighbour, and

> he shall lie with your wives in the sight of the sun. For you did it secretly, but I will do this thing before all Israel and before the sun' – 12:7-12.

David said to Nathan, 'I have sinned against the Lord.' And Nathan said to David, 'The Lord also has put away your sin, you shall not die. Nevertheless, because by this deed you have utterly scorned the Lord, the child that shall be born to you shall die.' Then Nathan went to his house – 12:13-14. David had accumulated great political power and success because the Lord has chosen him as king, anointed him with his Spirit and was with him. David sinned as he failed to remember all that the Lord had done for him, and he failed to meditate on these things with a thankful heart.

Psalm 51, in chapter Ch. 7, gives us an insight into David's response as he poignantly repents before the Lord. Seeing that the Lord pronounced the child born to David in his adultery with Bathsheba would die, it is remarkable that Solomon the son born to Bathsheba and David who are now man and wife, found favour in God's eyes. 'And the Lord loved him' and sent a message by Nathan the prophet to inform them the child's name should be Jedidah, – 'beloved of the Lord' – 12:25. The child's name Solomon is derived from *salom* – shalom and his birth occurs outside the judgment on David's immediate family. In the midst of God's judgment on David, we see the Lord's acceptance of Solomon. It is an enigma to try to reconcile this with God's punishment on David's family.

AMNON & TAMAR

2 Samuel 13:1-19

It is unlikely that David's adultery with Bathsheba remained a private affair and those family members close to David would have known about this. We can perceive that Amnon David's first born heir was aware of this, and that David's act of indiscretion fuelled his imagination and lust for his sister Tamar, by another mother. While David's adultery with Bathsheba is told in four verses, Amnon's rape of his sister occupies fourteen. He is aided by a cunning friend to fool David so that he asks Tamar to minister to him while he pretends to be ill.

Ironically, David is unwittingly an accomplice to him as he is out of touch with his children's welfare. Yet Jonadab, Amnon's cousin, has noticed that some-thing in his demeanor troubled him – he looked haggard – 13:4. Tamar was in the king's royal household where no man had access to the virgins and so he was denied access to her. And in many middle-eastern cultures even today, it would be unthinkable for Tamar to visit him in his personal quarters without a chaperone. Bearing this in mind, this is a deliberate, well planned assault on a defenseless woman. There was no consideration at the traumatic effect this would have on Tamar.[53] This was a thoughtless act in a patriarchal system that subjugated women. Tragically, 'The sexual wrong of the father is enacted in a horrific manner by a son.'[54] Once Amnon's plan is put into action when they are alone together, he shamelessly asks Tamar to sleep with him. His sister is not only beautiful she is also intelligent and wise. Her reply shames him as he is undisciplined and spoilt and proves to be both a fool and indescribably stupid. Tamar refuses his advances, 'with a quadruple refusal'[55] and says to him, 'No. my brother, do not force me, for such a thing is not done in Israel: do not do this wanton folly. As for me, where would I carry my shame? And as for you, you would be as one of the wanton fools in Israel. Now, therefore, I pray you, speak to the king, for he will not withhold me from you' – 13:12-13. Sadly. and tragically, he did not listen. Instead, he raped her. Hertzberg captures the seriousness of Amnon's crime: 'He does the wanton folly, folly which is not simply stupidity, but a 'culpable misdemeanor.'[56] A serious assault and crime against the law has been committed.

While Amnon may have initially felt love for Tamar, this is in reality only infatuation that turned out to be lust, for as soon as he slept with her, he hated her and sent her away, which in her eyes, was an even greater sin as he was under obligation to marry her under the law in Israel. 'Tamar's rape is unbearable to read'[57] and we recoil in anger at his physical violence towards her. We can barely begin to imagine the revulsion, the shame, the humiliation and horror, Tamar felt at having been violated by her brother. Her life and future prospects have been ruined by him but she is not going to let his sin remain hidden. Tamar is the king's daughter and she publically announces what has happened. She tears her long robe that the king's daughters wore as a sign of their virginity, put ashes on her head as a sign of mourning, laid her hand on her head and went about crying and wailing. Tamar's response is described by five symbolic actions – she took ashes: she tore her robe: she put her hands on her head: she went along: she cried out. Absalom perceived what had happened and asked if Amnon had been with her, which she must have affirmed. But news of Tamar's mourning also reached David, who when he heard about her rape was very angry – 13: 20-21. In fact the Hebrew word *hrh* translated is 'furious' But the narrator does not record that David confronted him about his sin. We can but speculate that David's sin with Bathsheba compromised him into in-action and impotence to discipline his son. Tamar is the king's daughter and has a high profile in the king's court and her mourning is a public gesture of her humiliation and shame. The scandal committed by Amnon has been made public. David, who should have dealt with it, says nothing and does nothing. 'David fails to execute justice for Tamar which incites his brother Absalom to take matters into his own hand…Had David exercised his authority to punish him for his violent crime, he might have averted the rebellion that nearly destroyed his reign'[58] and may have saved Absalom's life.

ABSALOM & AMNON

2 Samuel 13:20-39

After Amnon raped his sister, Absalom did not speak to him for two full years. The text is silent about why he chose not to go to David and ask him to punish him, but perhaps he feared David would be too lenient. Instead, he planned his own final retribution, meanwhile he allowed him to think he had escaped punishment. Absalom's statement to Tamar, 'Now hold your peace my sister, he is your brother, do not take this to heart' – 13:20, appears heartless and unsympathetic, and Tamar lived in Absalom's house a desolate woman under his care and protection. What she did not know, was the act of vengeance

Absalom in effect as judge, was stealthily plotting to extract his revenge. Absalom's retribution is carefully planned with satisfying irony to reflect Amnon's deceitfulness. Just as he had involved David in deceiving Tamar so now Absalom involves David in deceiving Amnon, by persuading him to invite him to a feast, along with all his other sons Absalom was inviting. Just as he lured Tamar into his home, Absalom lures Amnon into his home territory for a feast, unaware that he was a victim, being set-up to exact justice and retribution for Tamar.

Two years of humiliation for Tamar have passed and having waited two years to extract his revenge Absalom invited all the king's sons and the king and his servants to a feast, but the king declined, so he asked David to let Amnon attend, and although he questioned why, David relented and agreed. Once Amnon was merry with drink, on Absalom's orders his servants killed him. Then all the king's sons fled and David heard that all his sons were dead, so he rent his clothes and began mourning. But Jonadab the son of David's brother came and told David that only Amnon was dead on the orders of Absalom, who knew he had raped his sister Tamar. Then all the king's sons came to David and they and the king's servants all wept very bitterly – 13:23-36. But Absalom fled and went into exile to Talmai king of Geshur and David mourned for his son day after day. Biblical commentators do not know if David was mourning for Amnon or Absalom, but the obvious reading of the text is that David was mourning for Absalom, because he was comforted that Amnon was dead – 13:39. The implication is that justice had been carried out for the rape of his daughter Tamar. Absalom has been in exile in Geshur three years and David longed in his heart to go to see him.

DAVID & ABSALOM

2 Samuel 14-15, 17

Joab was a high ranking official of David's carrying out his instructions as the commander of his army, and a powerful, ambitious and ruthless man who on occasions overruled David. We see this on three specific occasions when he killed Abner who came to reconcile with David – 2 Sam. 3:26-30, and killed

Amasa – 2 Sam. 20. He also killed Absalom for whom David had given specific instructions not to harm in any way – 2 Sam. 18. (In 1 Kings 2: 1-5 David will instruct Solomon to have Joab put to death because of these murders.) But before this happened Joab saw David longed to see Absalom and that his 'heart went out to him' – 14:1, so he arranged for David to be tricked by a woman from Tekoa who pretends she has two sons. One has killed the other and she asks his advice about what to do, which in effect is a parable about David's dilemma about Absalom. At the end of her story which is false, David says, 'As the Lord lives not one hair of your sons head shall fall to the ground' – 14:11. The woman then confronts David about Absalom and he then perceives that Joab is behind her scheme that deceived him, which she confirms – 14:12-20. The woman now speaks freely to David and says his judgment about Absalom affects all the people and he is guilty because he does not bring him to Jerusalem. David's guilt is his inconsistency. He granted mercy to Amnon who was guilty but did not to Absalom.[59] After this David commands Joab to bring Absalom back to Jerusalem and Joab fell on his face to the ground and did obeisance to the king and said, 'Today your servant knows that I have found favour in your sight my lord the king, in that the king has granted the request of his servant' – 13:22. David is aware Joab is an ambitious and although Absalom returns to Jerusalem, in effect he is under house arrest in his own home, as David will not see him. Although David longs to Absalom, his refusal to do so is a public display of his displeasure intended to satisfy courtiers and family members because of Amnon's murder.

The narrator informs us that Absalom was another Adonis just like his father David, 'Now in all Israel there was no one so much to be praised for his beauty as Absalom. From the sole of his foot to the crown of his head, there was no blemish in him. And when he cut the hair of his head (for at the end of every year he used to cut it: when it was heavy on him he used to cut it) he weighed the hair of his head, two hundred shekels by the king's weight' – 14:25-26. Absalom lived in Jerusalem two full years without being summoned into David's presence.

David cannot let his heart capitulate to Absalom nor Joab by welcoming him back into the royal court and its influence and power. Absalom's perfect physical beauty matched David's when he was younger. Just as the narrator could not resist describing David's attractiveness when he arrived on the scene, so now he also cannot resist emphasising his son's. Absalom is attractive and looks like a king and he knows it.

Absalom is frustrated by his estrangement with the king so he sends for Joab as he wants him to mediate between him and the king. As he refuses to come, Absalom burns his fields. Joab then comes to him and demands an explanation. He learns that Absalom wants to come into the king's presence, and if he is guilty let the king kill him, which he knows he will not do. So Joab speaks to David about him, who summons Absalom who comes to the king, bows face down on the ground and David kisses him – 14:28-33. Seven years after Tamar' rape, and five years after Amnon's murder, David sees Absalom and welcomes his son. David has been a conflicted king throughout these years having failed to pass judgment on Amnon for raping Tamar and failing to bring Absalom to justice for the murder of Amnon. He has lived with the emotional and psychological aftermath of his son's sins. David defeated his enemies but he was mastered by his feelings for his children. He has been emotionally weak and too lenient and indulgent as a father that compromised him as the king and his leadership. 'David's over weaning emotional attachment to his sons leads to a questionable assessment of David's character, a serious difficulty, since the entire story is informed by a dynamic concerning questions and answers as to who David is.'[60] The tragic irony about David is that the fearless warrior who killed Goliath, as the youngest of eight sons was on the fringe of family life looking after sheep and did not experience close family relationships. Sadly, after his adultery with Bathsheba and his murder of Uriah, he proves to be emotionally indulgent and conflicted as a father, who is out of touch with his children. Perhaps David indulged his children to compensate for what had been lacking in his life as a young man in his own family. But his lack of knowledge about their affairs meant he did not know what was going on in the royal household. He failed to assert his parental authority and his authority as the king over his household, before and after, his two sons brought tragedy into the royal household.

Absalom has become resentful at the way his father has treated him these past few years, especially after he returned to Jerusalem under house arrest for two years, and he is young whereas David has grown older: and he is an ambitious heir and plans to overthrow David. So he presents himself as an alternative ruler to the king by parading in a chariot with 50 men running before him and dispensing justice at the king's gate. 'And whenever a man came near to do obeisance to him, he would put out his hand and take hold of him and kiss him. Thus Absalom did to all of Israel who came to the king for judgment, so Absalom stole the hearts of the men is Israel' – 15:5-6. After four years, Absalom asks David permission to go to Hebron and make a vow to the Lord which he agrees to. But Absalom sent secret messengers throughout all the tribes of Jerusalem saying, 'As soon as you hear the sound of the trumpet, then say, 'Absalom is king at Hebron' – 15:7-10. It is careless that David did not keep a watchful eye on Absalom and his affairs and also failed to instruct his servants to keep an eye on him. Without David knowing, the support for Absalom in Hebron increases and his conspiracy grew stronger.

David is informed by a messenger that 'the hearts of the men of Israel have gone after Absalom' and to prevent a civil war and Jerusalem being attacked by Absalom, David decides to flee for his life from the city. But his departure is not done in a panic. Instead he strategically conducts a number of important meetings with Ittai (19-23), Abiathar and Zadok the priests (24-29) and Hushai (32-37) and all of David's servants made preparations to leave the city. But he asks Hushai to remain in Jerusalem and pretend to support Absalom while offering him advice to defeat the counsel of Ahithophel, and to inform Zadok and Abiathar whose sons will then tell David what is happening – 15:32-37. The meetings indicate David is careful and cunning and that Absalom has underestimated his father. He is politically shrewd. He has Ittai and the two priests who remained with the ark in Jerusalem spying for him. He shows 'trusting faith and cunning strategy...David does entrust himself to God, but such trust does not entail mindlessness or resignation…David develops a network of military and intelligence agents to outflank Absalom at every turn'[61] We read in 15:30-31, 'But David went up to the ascent of the Mount of Olives, weeping as he went, barefoot and with his head covered: and all the people who were with him covered their heads, and they went up, weeping as they went. And David was told, 'Ahithophel is among the conspirators with Absalom.' (His defection is a major blow to David). And David said, 'O Lord I pray, turn the counsel of Ahithophel into foolishness.' After fleeing from Jerusalem David and his faithful followers arrive weary at the Jordan, while Absalom with his followers arrive at Jerusalem – 16:14-15.

After returning to Jerusalem Ahithophel advises Absalom to allow him to choose 12,000 men and pursue David that night, while David and his men are weary having fled, to kill him and return with all the people – 17: 1-2. However, Absalom asks Hushai to also come and offer his counsel. When he arrives, Hushai suggests an alternative plan to involve Absalom going into battle against David himself. In contrast to Ahithophel's plan, Hushai deliberately proposes a grand strategy to give David time to escape, and he masks his deception behind the rhetoric of hyperbole. When they hear this plan, Absalom and all the men of Israel said, 'The counsel of Hushai is better than the counsel of Ahithophel.' For the Lord had ordained the defeat of his advice – 17:1-14. After this Hushai informs Abiathar and Zadok about Absalom's plans and they send messengers to let David know – 17:15. Without wasting any time, David along with all his people, safely cross the Jordan by daybreak. The Lord acted behind the scenes and unknown to Abslaom and his men influences them to choose Hushai's plan.

God is for David. But he is in this predicament because of his sin against Uriah and his family, as Absalom's rebellion is being played out as part of God's punishment on David. Yet it is difficult to comprehend why the Lord's punishment on him after his adultery with Bathsheba and murder of Uriah should have involved his children. As we are intended to interpret the rape of Tamar by Amnon and his murder by Absalom as a consequence of David's punishment, this had a devastating effect on all their lives, and ultimately David loses two sons and also loses the future life of his daughter who cannot marry. And because David did not punish Amnon, and Absalom was resentful about how David treated him after Amnon's death, he has conspired against David to kill him and replace him as the king. If the Lord's judgment on David's family had not been his punishment, the logical conclusion is that Tamar would not have been raped by Amnon, and Absalom would not have killed him, and in turn, he would not have conspired against David. There almost appears to be a hint of injustice and vindictiveness about God's judgment on David's family, because it caused his children and David so much tragedy and grief. Had Absalom not murdered his brother, by all accounts he would have been more than an able heir to succeed David as king.

ABSALOM'S DEATH

2 Samuel 18-19

The inevitable battle between Absalom and David is about to take place as their armies prepare to fight one another. David organises his men under three leaders, Abishai, Joab and Ittai, with David joining them, but his men insist that he stays behind as the enemy will be out to kill him. So David specifically says to his three leaders, 'Deal gently for my sake with the young man Absalom' – 18:1-5. Although Absalom is now David's enemy, 'There are few narrative episodes concerning David that are more carefully wrought than this, or more poignantly expressed.'[62] Despite Absalom's rebellion against him, David still has powerful paternal feelings for his son. His final wish for Absalom reprises the leitmotif of the king's misguided affection for his son.[63] David was not aware of his rebellion against him in Jerusalem and naively gave him permission to go to Hebron. Now we glimpse the depth of David's love for his son because he wants his life spared.

When the battle takes place, David's men defeat the men of Israel. Absalom is in the forest of Ephraim on a mule and his head with his long hair gets caught up in a large oak tree and he is left hanging suspended in mid air. When this is reported to Joab he goes and immediately without any hesitation throws three darts into his heart and his armour bearers surround and kill him. Whether Joab killed Absalom because he was David's enemy, or because he burned his fields we do not know, but he explicitly ignored David's request. Joab is a military man and may only see that David is compromised if Absalom remains alive. 'As Joab murders the king's son, his power in David's court reaches its apex'[64] This will be seen when Joab orders David to go and address his troops after he learns about Absalom's death. But, for now, they bury Absalom and a Cushite and Ahimaaz the son of Zadok run to tell David the news of their victory, and about Absalom's death – 18:9-23.

When David learns about his son's death, 'he was deeply moved. And went up to the chamber over the gate and wept, and as he went he said, 'O my son Absalom, my son, my son Absalom. Would I had died instead of you, O my son, my son' – 18:33. 'David enters into deep, unrestrained, unguarded grief. This is David's most distressed moment…David's cry is an anguished review of all that could have been and was not…The specifics of the past are much too deep and painful to utter. Now David in his abandon gathers all that past together in the simple, anguished acknowledgement, 'My son.'[65] Morrison says this about David's response to Absalom's death:

> The narrator chooses the Hebrew verb *rgz* to capture David's anguish. This verb describes the 'quaking' of the earth and the heavens (1 Sam 14:15, 2 Sam. 22:8). And it refers to peoples trembling with fear (Isaiah 32:11, 64:2) and panic (Exodus 15:14). Thus David, trembling, panicking and quaking, ascends the gate as he weeps and calls out, 'my son' five times. He utters the universal prayer of parents who have lost a child, 'Would that I had died instead of you.' As a king, he planned the defeat of his rebel son. As a father, he

> mourns his death. This fleeting glimpse into David's soul unmasks the inadequacy of language in such intense moments of human suffering.[66]

When Joab arrives to meet David he was informed, 'Behold the king is weeping and mourning for Absalom.' So the victory that day was turned into mourning for all the people, for the people heard that day, 'The king is grieving for his son' – 19:1-2. On learning about David's response, Joab promptly confronts the king, and he threatens and command him to go and speak to the people. He said, 'You have today covered with shame the faces of all your servants who have this day saved your life, and the lives of your sons and daughters, and the lives of your wives and concubines, because you love those that hate you and hate those who love you. For you have made it clear today that commanders and servants are nothing to you. For today, I perceive that if Absalom were alive and all of us were dead today, then you would be pleased. Now therefore arise, go and speak kindly to your servants, for I swear by the Lord, if you do not go, not a man will stay this night with you, and this will be worse for you than all the evil that has come upon you from your youth until now.' Then the king arose, and took his seat in the gate. And the people were all told, 'Behold, the king is sitting in the gate' and all the people came before the king – 19:5-8. Joab is now at the apex of his power, and he is right in what he says to David. His unsentimental thinking has saved the king and the kingdom for David.

But for David 'The grief is unresolved, as we knew it would be. How odd that no one offers to David any gesture of healing. He is alone in this moment. No one intrudes the king in the midst of his grief…The king lives. Life can go on, but life will never be the same again. The narrative leaves us with the residue of grief unresolved.'[67]

ADONIJAH & SOLOMON

1 Kings 1

We read in 1 Kings, 1:1-8, 'Now King David was old in years and although they covered him in clothes he could not get warm. Therefore, his servants said to him, 'Let a young maiden be sought for my Lord the king, and let her wait upon the king, and be his nurse. Let her lie in his bosom that my lord the king may be warm.' So they sought for a beautiful maiden throughout all the territory of Israel and found Abishag the Shunammite, and brought her to the king. The maiden was very beautiful and she became the king's nurse and ministered to him, but the king knew her not. Now Adonijah, the son of Higgith exalted himself saying, 'I will be king' and he prepared for himself chariots and horsemen, and fifty men to run before him. David his father had never at any time displeased him by asking, 'Why have you done thus and so?' He was also a very handsome man and he was born next after Absalom. He conferred with Joab the son of Zeruiah, and with Abiahar the priest and they followed Adonijah and helped him. But Zadok the priest, and Benaiah the son of Jehoiada, and Nathan the prophet, and Shimei, and Rei, and David's mighty men, were not with Adonijah.'

'In contemporary scholarship, 1 Kings 1-2 if often viewed as the conclusion of a 'Succession Narrative' that begins in 2 Samuel 9. The continuity of these chapters with 2 Samuel is evident: I Kings 1-2 concludes the biography of David.'[68] Mordecai Cogan points out that on a literary level the composition of 1 Kings is often singled out as one of the finest examples of early biblical narrative. The action moves forward mainly through the use of speeches and the use of small nuanced differences in the repetitions the narrator succeeds in characterizing the main protagonists. The opening verses of 1 Kings 1:1-8 sets the stage for the action that takes place on a single day, in and around the royal court of David.[69] Brueggemann believes the beginning of Kings touches on one of the most difficult issues faced in Israel's monarchy: 'the interplay of *raw, crude politics* and the insistence that this particular history is *an arena for God's purposes.* It is not easy to hold together in tension, raw crude politics and the sense of God's purposes, but this narrative is agile and subtle in doing that. 1 Kings 1 is governed by the practice of politics that is calculating, manipulative and at the brink of violence. This makes it clear that biblical faith, especially royal faith, takes place in the real world where stakes are high and the risks are great.'[70] The beginning of 1 Kings 1-2 charts the demise of David, and 'Abishag was sought out to resolve a constitutional crisis, not just to comfort the shivering old king…It was believed there was a definite link between his natural powers and the power and effectiveness of his rule.'[71]

'The reader is introduced to the enfeebled king, a mere shadow of the robust leader he once was.'[72] David is now a frail old man who has lost his virility and the succession for his throne involves Adonijah and Solomon. Adonijah actively seeks to grasp this as he has a legitimate claim to the throne, as he is older than Solomon is. 'Adonijah decides to take pre-emptive steps: he is not waiting for David either to designate a successor or to die. He may well have thought that David was now so ineffective that action was needed as he was used to getting his own way.'[73] However, Bathsheba and Nathan act as advocates on behalf of Solomon, who is a passive bystander. Palace intrigue and scheming by David's sons has been characteristic of his reign and now with David's failing health in old age, Adonijah the eldest of the two sons with the help of military, political and religious leaders, stakes his claim and announces himself as king.

When Nathan discovers this, he tells Bathsheba that David does not know what Adonijah has done. And to save her life and Solomon's life he advises her to go to David and say, 'Did you not, my lord the king, swear to your maidservant saying, 'Solomon your son shall reign after me, and he shall sit upon my throne? Why then is Adonijah king?' Then while you are speaking with the king, I also will come in after you and confirm your words'–1:11-14. Adonijah the son who has been indulged by David acts against his knowledge to succeed him as the king, but he is outmaneuvered by Nathan as Bathsheba goes to David. So she comes to David, bows in obeisance and the king inquires, 'What do you desire?' for although he is frail he knows she must have a reason for seeking an audience with him. But instead of saying 'Did you not?' she says, 'My lord, you swore to your maidservant, by the Lord your God saying, 'Solomon your son shall reign after me and he shall sit upon my throne.' And now behold Adonijah is king, although you my lord do not know it. He has sacrificed oxen, fatlings and sheep in abundance, and has invited all the sons of the king, Abiathar the priest, and Joab the commander of the army. But Solomon your servant he has not invited. And now, my lord the king, the eyes of all Israel are upon you, to tell them who shall sit on the throne of my lord the king after him' – 1 Kings 1:15-20. One theme that stands out in Ch 1 is that of 'knowledge' – specifically David's knowledge is consistently deficient. In 1: 11, Nathan points out to Bathsheba that David does not know Adonijah has become king. In 1:18, Bathsheba says to David, 'And now behold, Adonijah is king, although you my lord the king, do not know it.'[74]

Bathsheba appeals to David's authority as the king and is supported by Nathan who comes to see the king after her and confirms what she has said. So David takes control of the situation and instructs Zadok the priest, Nathan the prophet and Benaiah, to install Solomon as king. David said to them, 'Take with you the servants of the lord and cause Solomon my son to ride on my own mule and bring him down to Gihon. And let Zadok the priest and Nathan the prophet there anoint him king over Israel, then blow the trumpet and say, 'Long live King Solomon.' You shall then come up after him and he shall sit on my throne for he shall be king in my stead, and I have appointed him to be ruler over Israel and over Judah' – 1 Kings 1:32-36. Adonijah like his brother Absalom attempts a coup to replace David and like his brother he underestimates David and his loyal followers. Adonijah acts rashly and has not counted on the resistance of David's followers. He is outmaneuvered by Bathsheba, who 'is daring and imaginative, creating a political crisis from which David can extricate himself only in one way, for he dare not renege on his vow.'[75] Although there is no record of David making such a vow, he does not want Adonijah to stage a successful coup and risk the lives of Bathsheba and Solomon. He demonstrates that although he is old and frail, his word still carries authority with his faithful followers and ensures that Solomon is anointed king.

After David's command to anoint Solomon as king, Zadok, Nathan and Benaiah carry out his command and Solomon is crowned king. 'Then they blew the trumpet and said 'Long live King Solomon.' And all the people went up after him, playing on pipes and rejoicing with great joy, so that the earth was split by their noise.' And Adonijah and all the guests who were with him heard it as they finished feasting. And when Joab heard the sound of the trumpet, he said, 'What does the uproar in the city mean?' – 1:38-41. Just then, Jonathan the son of Abiathar the priest came and told them Solomon had been anointed king. 'Then all the guests of Adonijah trembled and rose and each went his own way. And Adonijah feared Solomon, and he arose, and went and caught hold of the horns of the altar. And it was told Solomon, 'Behold Adonijah fears King Solomon, for he has laid hold of the horns of the altar, saying, 'Let King Solomon swear he will not slay his servant with the sword.' And Solomon said, 'If he prove to be a worthy man not one of his hairs shall fall to the earth, but if wickedness is found in him, he shall die.' So King Solomon sent and they brought him down from the altar. And he came and did obeisance to King Solomon, and Solomon said to him, 'Go to your house' – 1:49-53. Adonijah has no choice but to be completely loyal to Solomon as his life depends on it. 'Solomon is the winner in the deathly contest. David has willed it: Yahweh has blessed it: the military guaranteed it…The throne is now assigned by choreographed intrigue, sacramental acts that smack of cynicism, and guaranteeing military power.'[76]

Adonijah's earlier arrogant confidence is in stark contrast to his panic and submission to Solomon as his life is in danger from the new king. But Solomon is merciful and reconciles himself to his brother. Behind all the subterfuge of Adonijah, and the scheming of Nathan and Bathsheba, the Lord carries out his will for Solomon to be king. R. Nelson says, 'This Yahweh will offend pious sensibilities more than once in the pages to follow. Yahweh's plan and will must be effected, and for God, at least, the end justify the means. The God of the Book of Kings seems willing to go to any extreme to bring about the divine will, even to the point of undercutting divine promises, destroying the temple, dismissing the beloved Davidic dynasty, and nearly liquidating his chosen people… Kings ends in tragic contrast to this hopeful beginning as a powerless descendent of David – Jehoiachin King of Judah, sits on a purely symbolic throne, the servant of a foreign monarch – 2 Kings 25:27-30.'[77]

DAVID DIES

1 Kings 2

David unquestionably had the most eventful, successful and historically significant life in ancient Israel. He was the golden boy of Israel, her Adonis and hero who killed Goliath, and his legacy lives on to this day in modern Israel. Yet it was not a life without tragedy, especially in his family. We may well detect David was somewhat of a broken man towards the end of his life because of the death of Absalom, which he probably never recovered from. 1 Kings 2:1-10 records the end of David's life and his parting words and advice to his son Solomon. 'When David's time to die drew near he charged Solomon saying, 'I am about to go the way of all the earth. Be strong and show yourself a man, and keep the charge of the Lord your God, walking in all his ways and keeping his commandments, his ordinances, and his testimonies, as it is written in the law of Moses, that you may prosper in all that you do and wherever you turn: that the Lord may establish his word which he spoke concerning me saying, 'If your sons take heed to their way, to walk before me in faithfulness with all their heart and with all their soul, there shall not fail you a man on the throne of Israel' – 1 Kings 2:1-4. Ch. 2 launches on themes that will be repeated throughout Kings The first theme is the Deuteronomistic voice that comes in verses 2-4 which speaks through David's speech in the style and vocabulary of Deuteronomy and which will continue to surface at intervals throughout the book of Kings. 'This Deuteronomisitc voice represents the editorial comments of the author of Kings, the Detuteronomistic Historian and also introduces the evaluative key for the rest of Book of Kings. David's farewell speech establishes the theological ideal by which each king to follow will be judged. David foreshadows the high potential reached by Hezekiah and Josiah.'[78]

David's farewell speech is part of the legacy he leaves behind to Solomon. But in the second half of his speech in 1 Kings 2: 5-9, he exhorts Solomon to kill Joab for the murder of two commanders in Israel, Abner and Amasa, and also to kill Shimei who cursed him. There is a clear incongruity between the spiritual and the political aspects of his speech that appear contradictory rather than complementary. The spiritual and political dimensions of David's speech reflect the two sides of his character. As a warrior involved in battles against God's people, in their historical context he saw no contradiction or dichotomy between them. David's piety and pragmatic politics went hand in hand. While it may come as a surprise at the end of David's life to see him exhort Solomon to put to death Joab, we can see this may have been for two reasons. Firstly, because Joab killed innocent men and secondly to protect Solomon from this ambitious and cunning political commander.

The striking aspect of his speech concerns the royal promise by the Lord to David which was originally an unconditional covenant in 2 Samuel 7, but is now a conditional promise recorded in Psalm 132:11-12. The introduction of 'If' means the monarchy of David is subject to the conditions of the Torah. 'In these verses monarchy for the future is held to severe demands, insisting that royal power must be devoted to divine purpose'[79] The conditional promise of v. 4 seems to undercut the unconditional Davidic covenant, and the same conditional promise is repeated in 2 Kings 8:25 and 9:4-6. 'The inclusion of both promises to the house of David would create intense theological dissonance. A closer look, however, indicates the unconditional promises are only offered within the material on Solomon and refer only to the throne of Israel.'[80] 'Then David slept with his fathers and was buried in the city of David. And the time that David reigned over Israel was forty years. He reigned seven years in Hebron and thirty-three years in Jerusalem' – 2 Kings 2:10-11.

CHAPTER SEVEN

DAVID'S PSALMS

INTRODUCTION

The psalms which follow that are attributed to David are from my book, 'The Psalms–Intimacy, Doxology & Theology' – 2012. I have included them as they give an insight into David's faith and spirituality. As I wrote 'David, Jonathan & Saul,' I was acutely aware that David in 1 and 2 Samuel can be seen to be at variance with David in the psalms. In David's psalms (assuming they are written by him) we have an insight into his inner life that the narrator in 1 and 2 Samuel does not have access to. They can be seen to complement the material about David in 1 and 2 Samuel, although we may find it hard to reconcile David the warrior with David in his psalms.

As you study The Psalms, while there are some categories one can readily divide them into they are a complex genre which demand careful study, to discern their significance for faith in the 21st century and the worshipping life of the Church. The Psalms in their diversity can be included in our corporate worship. They can be part of our Scripture readings. Or they can be recited. Or they can be sung. Or our songwriters can compose songs from them and our ministers can preach from them. Through The Psalms, we can learn more about faith, more about prayer and more about song writing, more about worship, more about rejoicing, and more about the Lord too.

The Psalms present us with the challenge of integrating our faith in our relationship with God that involves theology – truth about God and doxology the praise of God – into our corporate worship. The Psalms deal with real experiences in the life of faith of God's people. While some aspects in them may seem strange to us, as Brueggemann points out – 'biblical faith, as it faces life fully, is uncompromisingly and embarrassedly dialogic.'[1] We learn from The Psalms that this dialogue of faith is a normal part of life in the Spirit in our relationship with God and Christ. Through The Psalms, the Lord has also provided us with a biblical framework and model, for sharing our feelings and thoughts with him in his relationship with us.

The Psalms can teach us to delight in the Lord and in his ways and Word, to delight in his presence and in worshipping him. The Psalms point us to an intimacy and close walk with the Lord we can have. The Psalms also enable us to integrate our doctrine and theology with our emotions. 'The Psalms inform our intellect, arouse our emotions, direct our wills and stimulate our imaginations...The Psalms give us theology written in intimate relationship with God and in close touch with life.'[2] 'Responding to God in The Psalms is not mere emotionalism. It is emotion that ultimately responds to the truth about God in his relationship to his people. We see real-life emotion at the footstool of deep theological truth. True worship is not fuelled by emotion: it is emotion fuelled by exciting truth. It is as we fully understand the truth about the nature of God and his relationship to us, that our emotions will be channelled into the praise and worship of God.'[3]

The Psalms not only had an existential relevance for God's people in the Old Testament, but a social, political and spiritual relevance too – and I would suggest they still do today. The Psalms can challenge a nation to turn to the Lord as the living God to follow him and walk in his ways of obedience, holiness, justice, and righteousness. Through The Psalms, the Church can pray in a meaningful way for the nation during their corporate worship: as well as seeing how their faith can impact the social, political and spiritual issues of our day. Many of The Psalms give us an ambitious and prophetic model of praise where the nation/s or the whole earth worship the Lord. This invites God's people to intercede on a national and an international level for this to happen.

PSALM 18
I LOVE YOU LORD

One of the things that clearly stands out in many of the psalms is their spontaneous testimony and witness to God's glory – the focus of which is his goodness and salvation in the life of his people. In these psalms, there is no apparent reticence nor inhibition about declaring what the Lord has done. They are bursting with irrepressible acclaim about the Lord's glory – his character and saving activity. To keep quiet about God's goodness and his salvation may well be tantamount to sin. To remain silent and not thank the Lord for his glory and to not praise him is unthinkable. The psalmists clearly declare their thanksgiving and praise to the Lord and on occasions specifically declare this in the assembly of his people. There are even occasions when the psalmist wants to declare God's glory and praise to nations or to generations yet unborn! These psalms reinforce in a compelling way the place of testimony to the Lord in corporate worship. Bearing witness to God's glory in corporate worship – his character, goodness, and salvation, is a powerful evangelistic witness. It encourages us to have thankful hearts full of praise to the Lord.

Yet it is rare to hear in corporate worship testimonies about the Lord's glory – what the Lord has done in peoples' lives. But on the rare occasion when this has taken place, it has been a powerful witness to God's glory and also a tremendous encouragement to those listening. There are occasions when the Lord touches people's lives through other Christians and these can be a testimony in corporate worship to witness to God's glory and goodness. I have known the Lord touch people's lives in very meaningful and timely ways, yet there has been a lack of testimony to what God has done – although I suspect this is more out of ignorance than design. Individuals do not have to be named who have been a channel of God's blessing, to ensure the glory is given to the Lord. But they or the church should not be embarrassed to share how the Lord has ministered to them through others. What the Lord has done can glorify him in our corporate worship.

1-3 I love you O Lord my strength. The Lord is my rock and my fortress and my deliverer, my God, my rock in whom I take refuge, my shield and the horn of my salvation, my stronghold. I call upon the Lord who is worthy to be praised, and I am saved from my enemies.

P. C. Craigie informs us 'There is some degree of unanimity among scholars that Psalm 18 is ancient and a Royal Psalm, to be dated in the 11th or 10th century BC. It is reasonable to assume that the original form comes from the time of David or shortly after. It may have been used in cultic worship or one of Israel's great annual festivals.'[4] Psalm 18 with 50 verses is one of the longest in The Psalter and a unique feature is the fact it can be found in 2 Samuel 22 where it is virtually identical. Although the superscription here and in 2 Samuel traditionally has David as the author, Goldingay suggests there is no direct evidence for this. He thinks David's serious sins disqualify him from speaking personally in terms of his integrity in v. 20-21, in such unequivocal terms. It is more plausible, that it was written for him, and could account for the objective view of his integrity.[5]J. M. Boice on the other hand, takes it at face value that David is the author and M. Wilcock says, 'Even scholars who hold *of David* does not normally mean *by David,* are likely to make an exception in the case of psalm 18.'[6]

> The psalmist begins his magnificent hymn of praise with a profoundly personal statement: 'I love you.' The verb is unusual but indicates an intimacy in the relationship with God which is reflected throughout the psalm…in a series of dangerous and mortal crises. The psalmist continues by piling up a series of words and epithets in a kind of staccato style, expresses pungently the nature of God, as he has been experienced. The names reflect two themes, though each is closely related to the other: one theme is military (God is deliverer, shield and safe retreat) and the other evokes the rocky wilderness (God is cliff, stronghold and rock).[7]

4-19 'The cords of death encompassed me, the torrents of perdition assailed me, the cords of Sheol entangled me, the snares of death confronted me. In my distress, I called upon the Lord: to my God I cried for help. From his Temple, he heard my voice and my cry to him reached his ears. Then the earth reeled and rocked: the foundations also of the mountains trembled and quaked because he was angry. Smoke went up from his nostrils and devouring fire from his mouth: glowing coals flamed forth from him. He bowed the heavens and came down: thick darkness was under his feet. He rode on a cherub and flew: he came swiftly upon the wings of the wind. He made darkness his covering around him, his canopy thick clouds dark with water. Out of the brightness before him there broke through his clouds hailstones and coals of fire. The Lord also thundered in the heavens and the Most High uttered his voice, hailstones and coals of fire. And he sent out his arrows and scattered them: he flashed forth lightnings and routed them. Then the channels of the sea were seen, and the foundations of the world were laid bare at your rebuke O Lord, at the blast of the breath of your nostrils. He reached from on high, he took me, he drew me out of many waters. He delivered me from my strong enemy and from those who hated me: for they were too mighty for me. They came upon me in the day of my calamity: but the Lord was my stay. He brought me into a broad place: he delivered me because he delighted in me.'

David recalls the seriousness of his situation – v. 3-4 when he felt that his life was in grave danger. In this distressing situation, he called upon the Lord to help him – v. 5. He has a vivid imagination inspired by the Holy Spirit and as he looks back, his description of the Lord is in majestic, powerful terms in comparison to his helplessness. From one perspective Psalm 18 is a complex, striking and an unusual literary composition with some archaic language. The theme of God's theophany (the manifestation of God) – v. 7-15 has been given cosmic dimensions achieved by the use of language which is rooted in the Near Eastern mythology, but which has been transformed to express the Lord's deliverance. The Lord's divine response is depicted in language reminiscent of the Sinai theophany, that was a way of expressing God's preparation for warfare in the early Hebrew poetic tradition on behalf of his servant the king.[8] From another perspective, Psalm 18 is a personal expression of David's confidence in the Lord and his faith in him. But this psalm is not so much about David. It is more about God's covenant faithfulness to his anointed king and his commitment and love to him and to Israel. At the same time, it can also be interpreted as pointing to a future descendent of David as the messiah. But even if David was not the author, we can still imagine him speaking through the psalm as it accurately reflects his relationship with the Lord.

In Psalm 18, David thanks the Lord for continually keeping him safe as the king and rescuing him from his enemies. It is a psalm forged on the tested anvil of experience. In this, David glorifies God by declaring his love for the Lord and also testifying to his salvation. This is a carefully composed psalm and is resplendent with metaphors that mirror God's glory. M. Wilcock points out, 'The Hebrew word for love is used nowhere else in the OT quite as it is here. The psalmist bursts out at once with his affection, even his passion, for his beloved Lord. A flood of metaphors follows, showing something of what this God means to him.'[9] Goldingay is more cool in his interpretation, and says the term *raham* does not suggest intimacy so much as commitment.[10] But David does not indulge himself in elaborating on his love and commitment. His song of thanksgiving focuses on the Lord's glory – his character that describes his saving action – v. 1-3. Later in the psalm, he exalts the Lord when he says, 'Who is God, but the Lord? And who is a rock, except our God – the God who girded me with strength and made my way safe' – v. 31-32. After this, he further elucidates at length how the Lord helped him against his enemies and strengthened him in battle.

At the same time, Psalm 18 is an insight into David's faith in the Lord. On many occasions, he prayed to the Lord for help against his enemies and we can discern that the Holy Spirit spoke to him about the Lord's protection, by showing him images of God's glory that represented his help. While he was in the wilderness the Holy Spirit impressed on his heart that the Lord was: 'my strength' – 'my rock' – 'my fortress' – 'my deliverer' – 'my refuge' – my shield' – 'my horn' and my 'stronghold.' These images of God's glory reveal the Lord's protection and are associated in David's life with the wilderness, where he sought to escape and hide from his enemies.

David learned to tenaciously place his faith in the Lord and his character that was as solid as the granite rocks that helped shelter him from his enemies. Wilcock points out that the '*rock* in v. 2 was the cliff in the Desert of Moan, the second *rock* (a different word) was the crags of the Wild Goats in the desert of en Gedi, the *fortress* and the *stronghold* were the caves of Adullam. All of which are located in Israel's southern wilderness.'[11]

In v. 1-3 the repeated emphasis on 'my' is a reminder of the close personal relationship and intimacy David had with the Lord and his reliance on him, both of which are integral features of his psalms. In some of the psalms that have an underlying intimacy and personal knowledge of the Lord, his saving activity and character are portrayed by his authority and majestic power, that he exercises over heaven and earth and over the kings and rulers of the earth. We also find metaphors that capture the Lord's activity and character that appeal to and strengthen the imagination of faith. One of the themes that stands out in Psalm 18 is that the Lord comes down from the heavens to earth to help David and he manifests his power and presence as in v. 16-17: 'He reached from on high, he took me, he drew me out of many waters. He delivered me from my strong enemy and from those who hated me: for they were too mighty for me.' We also read in v. 33, the Lord made his feet like hinds feet and set him secure on the heights – implying he was out of reach of his enemies. In v. 38-49 we see David's enemies falling down at his feet and in v. 47 the Lord subdued peoples under him.

Although David was a hardened man of battle, he learned to be reliant on the Lord from a young age when he killed Goliath. He clearly knew that his victories as the king over Israel's enemies was not just down to his fighting ability or that of his men, it was because the Lord was with him. It was the Lord who gave him victory over his enemies. Psalm 18: 31-42 vividly describes how the Lord helped David. It was the Lord who strengthened and supported him. It was the Lord who made his feet like hind's feet. It was the Lord who trained his hands for war. It was the Lord who gave him the skill to use a bow, and it was the Lord who made his enemies sink under him. David had a profound trust in the Lord and he knew he was the God of his salvation as he learned to rely on him.

It is a reminder that the Christian life is one of continual dependence and trust in the Lord – 'Be strong in the Lord and in the strength of his might' – Eph. 6: 10. It is also a reminder that our enemy the evil one is invisible and he wages spiritual warfare against us so that we may fail and be defeated as Christians. Eph. 6: 12 reminds us that we 'are not fighting against flesh and blood, but against the principalities, against the powers, against the world rulers of this present darkness, against the spiritual hosts of wickedness in the heavenly places.' Just as David learned to rely on the power and strength of the Lord to be victorious, we too have to put on the whole armour of God to stand and be victorious over the evil one.

Psalm 18 vividly describes the Lord's glory – his character, goodness and salvation throughout David's life. At first glance, it may appear the Lord always rescued and saved him as soon as he asked for help, and that he was like a warrior riding on his heavenly chariot brandishing his power and sweeping his enemies from under his feet. But this is not the way it always turned out. On occasions, he had to wait a considerable time before the Lord's salvation was revealed in his life. The theme of David waiting for God to answer his prayer and save him from his enemies was not a new experience for him. For example, this is seen in Psalm 22 where David distinctly voices his concern that the Lord is ignoring his plea for help and he is virtually at the mercy of his enemies. The reality is that on many occasions, he prayed for help and the Lord did not answer him immediately, or as quickly as he wanted. We see this in Psalm 13: 1-2: 'How long O Lord? Will you forget me forever? How long will you hide your face from me? How long shall I bear pain in my soul and have sorrow in my heart all the day? How long shall my enemy be exalted over me?' We also see David waiting for help in Psalm 40, 62, 69 and in Psalm 86, when he states he had to wait patiently for the Lord to help him. During the times when he waited for the Lord to rescue him from his enemies, his faith was tested and refined, and he had to learn to be patient and trust the Lord to help him in his perfect timing. Psalm 18 reveals the Lord's glory, when in God's perfect timing David was delivered from the hands of all his enemies and from the hand of Saul.

In v. 4-5 David in effect declares that his life is threatened and in mortal danger. He is being assailed by powerful opposing forces that seek his life and he is in distress because he might be killed. Here he may be referring to a number of situations he found himself in, but it is presented as the one distinct issue he faced at times as the king. After voicing his distress to the Lord and making his plea for help we can readily imagine v. 6 moving naturally onto v. 16, when the Lord heard his cry and reached out from on high and rescued him. But inspired by the Holy Spirit David has had a glimpse into the heavenly places. He has been taken via the imagination of his faith into the throne room of the universe and seen that the Lord reigns in his Temple, where he is worshipped night and day without ceasing by the heavenly host. God is depicted as a heavenly warrior who has authority and power over the destructive forces of nature. This is the same power that bears down on David's enemies. What then is the significance of the heavenly manifestation of the Lord in v. 7-15? A. Weiser says:

> The particular features of the magnificent portrayal of the appearance of God coming down from heaven, strange as they may seem to us on account of their archaic imagery, serve the purpose of illustrating – and of veiling – the awful, majesty and might of God.[12]

He also points out that the archaic and almost mythical traits are related to the original theophany that took place at Sinai, rooting God's appearance with the ancient traditions of Israel's faith.[13] The account of the Lord's appearance brings to their remembrance in the imagination of their faith, God's presence with them here and now. The Lord who is in heaven, is also the God who is with them here on earth. This majestic powerful God who reigns in the heavenly places does not remain distant, but comes to help his people and in this instance his anointed king. Just as when we celebrate Holy Communion we do this in remembrance of Christ and are reminded of the significance of his death that we are included in now – so too the revelation of God linked to the theophany at Sinai, is experienced as an actual event in which God's people are also included. We may discern that the Lord is described in this manner because he was acting on behalf of his anointed king who represents Israel. Therefore, in helping his servant David, the Lord was also acting on behalf of Israel against her enemies. David's revelation of the theophany of the Lord put into a new perspective his saving activity on his behalf throughout his life. God, who was with him, was the same powerful God of the Exodus. He was also the God of his people Israel and would continue to be the same God to David's descendents forever. For Psalm 18 to be used in corporate worship was like a covenant renewal between the Lord and Israel and also an affirmation of their faith in the Lord.

The covenant faithfulness of God is mentioned in v. 20-30, when David interprets the Lord's deliverance, protection and saving activity on his behalf, because of his faithfulness in keeping God's commandments. This was the foundation on which the covenant relationship between the Lord and his people was based: and as the Lord rewarded obedience, this is why he was confident of receiving his help. Despite David's failure and sins against Uriah and Bathsheba, he knew he was forgiven. Despite this failure along with other failures during his life, although not so spectacular, he had been committed to the Lord since he was a young lad. His sins did not ultimately turn his heart away from the Lord to other foreign gods or idols. The reference to David's righteousness is seen as representative of his life.

From this perspective, David knew the Lord would be faithful in protecting him because of his faithfulness in being obedient. In his song of praise and thanksgiving, he wants to exalt the Lord not only when God's people celebrate in corporate worship. He also wants to exalt and praise him among the nations and he declares in v. 50 that 'the Lord will show his steadfast love to David and to his descendents forever.' His confidence is founded on God's promise to him that one of his descendents would always sit on the throne. The Lord's character and his promise to him are the basis for his confident faith in the Lord. We can reasonably say there is not only a close, intimate relationship portrayed in Psalm 18 between the David and the Lord. There is also a tenderness and an intense bond forged between them over the years.

PSALM 19
ECSTATIC PRAISE

In the previous psalm, David's imagination runs away with him as he embraces ancient images to describe the Lord's glory and his saving activity on his behalf. Whereas, in Psalm 19, the psalmist's creative imagination is more aesthetic and lyrical as he uses cosmic and heavenly metaphors to portray God's glory. The poetic character of the author is acknowledged by biblical commentators and also lovers of literature like C. S. Lewis who says: 'I take this to be the greatest poem in The Psalter and one of the greatest lyrics in the world.'[14] Here we find the most beautiful poetry alongside some of the most profound biblical theology. It must have made quite an impact in worship when it was originally sung to music.

At my wedding in 1985, Psalm 19 was the reading I chose, as it was a favourite of mine and because it contained the reference to the bridegroom, leaving his chamber with joy – a joy that is reflected in keeping the law of the Lord. While some biblical commentators think this psalm may originally have been composed of two separate halves v. 1-6 and 7-14, as a complete entity it is an extremely accomplished piece of literature. As a teenage shepherd, David would have spent countless days and nights with his flock when he gazed at and contemplated the beauty of the heavens, the sky and the stars. As a soldier when he spent periods in the wilderness fleeing from Saul, he also would have had looked at the heavens and the sky. Equally, he would have had time to reflect on God's word and his laws.

We can readily perceive that David has clearly thought at great length about both sections of this psalm and we can discern an underlying joy and delight that permeates his reflections. My feeling is that he captures something even more profound than joy and delight. He capturers something of the awe and wonder of God's glory through his creation and also captures the ecstatic nature of God's glory through his word and his laws. Ecstatic, because it is through these the Lord revealed himself to him. It was through keeping God's laws that David knew the Lord in a close personal relationship that thrilled his heart and his soul. 'For the poet the law is the point at which an encounter takes place with the living God who reveals himself in the law.'[15]

1-6 The heavens are telling the glory of God and the firmament proclaims his handiwork. Day to day pours forth speech and night to night declares knowledge. There is no speech, nor are there words: their voice is not heard, yet their voice goes out throughout all the earth and their voice to the end of the world. In them, he has set a tent for the sun which comes forth like a bridegroom leaving his chamber, and like a strong man runs its course with joy. Its rising is from the end of the heavens and its circuit to the end of them: and there is nothing hid from its heat.

In v. 1-4 there is a clear emphasis on the heavens and sky proclaiming – telling out aloud God's glory and his creative action. But as David has observed on innumerable occasions, it is silent speech that the observer can discern. Verses 2-4 are simple but sublime statements about the silent speech that day after day, and night after night, throughout the world proclaims God's glory. We may well allude to this as natural revelation as it is plainly there for all to see. The impact of v. 3 is quite stunning in its antithesis. The cosmos offers no spoken speech – but it stills says so much about God's glory. The heavens do not speak any words – but they conjure up phrases in our imagination about God's glory. Day and night have no audible voice – yet the sun, and the moon and the stars speak clearly and loudly about God's glory. We should take care not to miss the obvious declaration that God clearly speaks to us through his creation. His speech through creation may well be silent –

but the silence is audible enough for us to hear.

J. M. Boice points out that in the Hebrew text the phrase *'pours forth speech'* is so much stronger than the English translation. The image is literally one of a gushing spring that copiously pours forth the sweet, refreshing waters of revelation.[16] God's glory is abundantly and lavishly proclaimed by and through his creation. It is no exaggeration to say that there is not only an abundance, but a superabundance of silent speech that declares God's glory. As we gaze in our silent adoration at the heavens and the stars and admire their phenomenal beauty, or enjoy the warmth of the sun that gives us a sense of well being on a gloriously sunny day, we can imagine the joy ascribed to the sun by the psalmist because it also fills our hearts with joy.

7-10 The law of the Lord is perfect reviving the soul: the testimony of the Lord is sure making wise the simple: the precepts of the Lord are right rejoicing the heart. The commandment of the Lord is pure enlightening the eyes: the fear of the Lord is clean enduring forever: the ordinances of the Lord are true and righteous altogether. More to be desired are they than gold, even much fine gold: sweeter also than honey and the drippings of the honeycomb.

In v. 7-10 if we say David deliberately composed this psalm as an entity, it is reasonable to assume that he is making a comparison with the glory and joy of God revealed in creation, and the glory and joy of God revealed through the law. He has clearly thought deeply about God's law and has found great fulfillment in his relationship with the Lord by keeping it. So satisfying and sweet is his communion with the Lord that in v. 10 he likens this to fine gold and honey from the honeycomb. 'The abundance of the finest gold, the sweetest honey still dripping from the honeycomb, familiar symbols of ancient poetry, are brought into play to express divine and human happiness.'[17]They express great joy and delight in finding ultimate pleasure in the Lord through his commandments and his laws.

12-15 But who can discern his errors? Clear thou me from hidden faults. Keep back your servant also from presumptuous sins: let them not have dominion over me. Then I shall be blameless and innocent of great transgression. Let the words of my mouth and the meditation of my heart, be acceptable in your sight, O Lord my rock and my redeemer.

As David's meditation has reached this marvellous height in v. 11, the Holy Spirit brings to his attention the possibility of becoming arrogant and proud. It also raises the possibility of being so self-righteous that he may have been unaware of or blind to his hidden faults. 'The clarity that illuminates the human faculty of comprehension (v.12) still sustains the terminology of luminosity, for the idea of warning is phonetically close to that of 'being in the light.'[18]

Psalm 19 is an inspired and carefully composed piece that gladly expresses a delight in God, his glory and his law. To prevent himself from being too carried away with his joy and wonder and ecstatic feelings, David comes down to earth as the Holy Spirit reveals to him that while he wholeheartedly keeps God's law and word, he may become complacent or even proud. He has been made aware of the danger that faces deeply religious people – that of becoming self-righteous. In response, he prays the Lord would reveal any hidden or presumptuous sins he is unaware that he may repent of them and be blameless in God's eyes. So he composed a profound prayer in v. 15.

Although these are ancient words written by David who clearly found ecstatic delight in God's laws and in the Lord himself, they have a particular relevance to contemporary worship at the beginning of the 21st century. They act as a warning in case we are carried away with our celebratory worship and think how wonderful it is, that we inadvertently become blind to the faults we cannot see in our lives. The prayer in v. 15 contains a challenge and a corrective to this possibility. It is offered up in the context of sublime ecstasy with the Lord that we take care not fall under condemnation because of arrogance or pride. It is a reminder that the Lord by his grace draws us to himself and that through Christ we may know his fellowship and presence. It is a salutary warning not to become self-satisfied and proud spiritually.

Verses 12-15 are a prayer that the praise and worship we declare to the Lord with our lips may have integrity and be acceptable and pleasing to him. In our contemporary worship while it may not be intentional, there is a tendency to be too simplistic and almost naïve in our corporate confession. This is evident as confession is usually a nonevent, whose content generally has no depth or reality. Verse 15 in Psalm 19 stops us in our tracks and invites us to examine our hearts against any hidden faults or presumptuous sin in our lives. Similarly, in Psalm 139 when the Holy Spirit reveals to David sublime truths about the Lord that he is ecstatic about, he responds by praying in v. 24: 'Search me O God and know my heart. Try me and know my thoughts. And see if there be any wicked way in me, and lead me in the way everlasting.' Through Psalm 19, the Lord impresses and lays on our hearts the possibility of great joy and ecstatic communion with him. In turn, this involves learning to find great joy and delight in God's ways and his word, because they lead to an intimacy with him. An integral part of maintaining closeness in our walk with the Lord is to have an awareness of any faults or sins that surreptitiously infiltrate our lives and spoil this. It is not being a fundamentalist or an extreme religious fanatic to tell the Lord that we delight in his ways and his word because they enable us to rejoice in the Lord. But Psalm 19 invites us to walk with care and wisdom in our daily lives and to avoid the things which are displeasing to the Lord. That we may express our pleasure in the Lord and maintain an intimate walk with him.

PSALM 22
ABANDONED

It does seem surprising that David the successful warrior for whom defeat was a rare experience composed so many psalms that indicate a clear psychological weakness about his enemies. As J. Magonet observes, 'David is a man of extraordinary power and passion, self-confident and assured, suddenly experiencing his weakness, helplessness and dependency, beset by self-doubts.' He interprets the groaning of v. 2 as a 'roaring' from David's mouth. A roar of anger and bewilderment.'[19] Bewilderment, because the Lord appears to betrays David's trust in him.

In Psalm 22, David's faith is stretched and tested in a new way, and this clearly causes him considerable emotional and psychological distress. There is agony, unbearable tension, and urgency in its composition. Yet this psalm is holy ground, as it also speaks to us about the suffering of Christ on the cross. Inspired by the Holy Spirit David prophetically points to the suffering of Christ. We can approach this psalm in two ways. We can view it as a Complaint Psalm, a prayer for help that Christians down the centuries have made their own. Alternatively, it can be seen as a prayer from Christ's lips. The first 21 verses of the psalm are a prayer of complaint voicing acute suffering and asking the Lord for help. Whereas verses 22-31 are a testimony to the Lord's deliverance. Weiser says:

> The song first leads us down into the uttermost depths of suffering, a suffering which brought the worshipper to the brink of the grave and reduced him to utter despair. It then soars to the heights of a hymn of praise and thanksgiving sung in response to the answering of the prayer...The poet who composed the psalm has the gift of describing his sufferings in words which deeply move our hearts and in figurative language which grips our imagination. His lamentation is one of the most touching in The Psalter.[20]

James Mays highlights that in Psalm 22, 'The genre of lament is raised to such an extravagance and intensity of scope and dimension, that it appears to exhaust the possibilities of the typical and brings it to its ultimate statement. Just when the climate and tension of the lament is well-nigh unbearable, there is a shift to a stance in apparent contradiction to the preceding prayer. The prayer becomes a vow of testimony and praise in the midst of the great congregation. Powerful and exceptional as this psalm is in its particularity, it does not abandon the typical characteristics of the lament. Form and content are an inseparable unity. This is a text that has had a life of its own. The dimensions of suffering and deliverance described in Psalm 22 are unparalleled and it poses the central mystery of the lament. We are left to ponder the mystery by the silence of history on the question. These prayers with their great turning, their conversation of complaint to praise, are simply given us by the Scriptures – given us with their mystery.'[21]

It is reassuring to know that in Scripture the Lord shares his feelings for his people and the world. He is not a God who is detached but emotionally involved. Through The Psalms, the Lord invites us and indeed gives us permission to share our feelings with him. He doesn't expect us to hide or repress our emotions. Just as the Holy Spirit led David to share how he felt in Psalm 22 with the Lord, in this psalm the Lord also gives us a framework and a model of how to share our feelings with him. With the help of the Holy Spirit we can have an emotional intimacy with the Lord as we share the things on our heart and mind with him. Psalm 22 also speaks about David's fear of his enemies that play on his mind, as Saul and his soldiers have been pursuing him on and off now for a number of years to kill him. Understandably, every now and then, fear and panic grip his heart and greatly trouble his mind. Calvin saw how this psalm outruns any experience in David's life. 'From the tenor of the whole composition it appears that David does not here refer to one persecution, but comprehends all the persecutions he suffered under Saul.'[22]

The first two thirds of Psalm 22 is like a litany of personal disaster, which shows that David could not comprehend why his prayer is being ignored by God. But unknown to him, God had a greater purpose in not answering him immediately. Unknown to David this psalm was to have a deeply significant prophetic meaning for Christ, as he identified himself with it on the cross. At his crucifixion when Christ felt completely abandoned by his Father, he instinctively turned to this psalm to voice his sense of dereliction. Jesus' cry on the cross: *'Eloi, Eloi, lema sabachthani'* (Matt. 27: 46, Mark 15: 34) is a direct quote of Psalm 22: 1. Aramaic was the first language for most Jews living in Palestine and had been since the Babylonian exile. Many would also have spoken Greek, which was the language of the Greco-Roman empire and spoken by Gentiles and most of the Diaspora too, hence the gospels being written in Greek. Hebrew was generally the language of the Scriptures and not widely used for regular communication. So although it was a closely related language to Aramaic, many Jews would not understand Hebrew. A version of the OT was made in Aramaic called the Targum (from a root meaning to translate/paraphrase) to cater for them. This is the version that might be read in the synagogue and Jesus' quote is Aramaic, not Hebrew, and is not directly from the original psalm text. But there is also some evidence in Luke 4 that Jesus read from the Hebrew texts. J. Mays points out:

> Citing the first words of a text was in the tradition of the time a way of identifying with an entire passage. The very experience of the psalmist becomes a comm.-entary on Jesus' passion on the cross. In the intellectual world of Judaism, one of the most important ways of understanding the meaning of present experience was to make sense of the contemporary by perceiving and describing it in terms of an established tradition.'[23]

Therefore, Christians down the centuries have seen the special significance of this psalm in relation to Christ.

1-2 My God, my God, why have you forsaken me? Why are you so far from helping me, from the words of my groaning? O my God I cry by day but you do not answer, and at night but find no rest.

The theme of David waiting for God to answer his prayer and save him from his enemies was not a new experience for him, as this is also seen in other Psalms. In Psalm 13: 1-2, he says, 'How long O Lord? Will you forget me for ever? How long will you hide your face from me? How long shall I bear pain in my soul and have sorrow in my heart all the day? How long shall my enemy be exalted over me?' In Psalm 62: 1, 3, he says, 'For God alone my soul waits in silence: from him comes my salvation.' In Psalm 69: 1, 3, he says, 'Save me O God for the waters have come up to my neck. I am weary with my crying: my throat is parched. My eyes grow dim with waiting for my God.' In Psalm 86: 1, 3, he says, 'Incline your ear O Lord and answer me, for I am poor and needy. You are my God be gracious to me O Lord, for to you do I cry all the day.' In God's providence, David had to learn to call on him for help and deliverance from his enemies. He also had to learn to be patient and trust the Lord's perfect timing to answer his prayer. In Psalm 40: 1-2 David testifies to God saving him from his enemies when he says, 'I waited patiently for the Lord: he inclined to me and heard my cry. He drew me up from the desolate pit out of the miry bog.'

While David knows that on occasions, the Lord may not answer his prayer immediately, his tone in Psalm 22: 1-2, clearly states that the Lord is taking an unusually long time to answer him. He is perplexed and does not understand why the Lord is doing this. In God's silence, David feels that he has abandoned and forgotten him and betrayed his trust in the Lord. 'My God, my God' – is a reproach and makes his complaint an outright accusation. Goldingay says:

> The succeeding lines of the psalm will make clear that we should not infer the suppliant will be satisfied if this 'Why?' question were answered. The question is rhetorical and implies, 'You should not have abandoned me and I appeal to you to come back now.' Abandonment lies in failing to act on the suppliant's behalf.[24]

In v. 1-2 God is silent and has not answered David's prayer. He is now becoming desperate, as the Lord whom he knows intimately appears to have abandoned him. Emotionally and psychologically, he is feeling threatened and needs assurance that the Lord is going to help him. D. Tidball observes, 'In the moment when he needs God and seeks his comforting presence, fully expecting to receive it, he is faced with the total absence of God…God neither steps in to deliver him from his affliction nor seems even to hear his prayer. The God-forsakenness David feels is made worse by the massive tension between his belief and his experience. His theology tells him he ought not to be ignored by God at such a time as this. His experience tells him he is being deserted by God…The silence of God sometimes seems most unyielding precisely when we most urgently need him to speak to us.'[25]

The absence of God has been supplanted by the presence of David's enemies. God now seems distant and his enemies feel near. Why is the Lord absent? Why is he ignoring his prayer for help? Why isn't he answering him? Perhaps there is sin in his life that has not been confessed? As he doesn't mention this anywhere in the psalm, we can rule this out. We can perceive that the Lord is teaching David to trust him on a deeper level, despite how he feels. He is taking him to a new level of trust, even though the Lord is silent. The Lord is also teaching him to view how he feels in the light of his character and to remember the Lord's faithfulness, his steadfast love and past deliverance. While David's feelings are real, they may be misleading and way off beam about the silence of God.

3-5 Yet you are holy enthroned on the praises of Israel. In you our fathers trusted: they trusted and you delivered them. To you they cried and were saved, in you they trusted and were not disappointed.

Why does David focus on the Lord's character and how does this help him? He recalls that God is reigning, enthroned on the praises of Israel. This is a reminder that the Lord is sovereign and in control of his life. He remembers the Lord's past faithfulness in answering his peoples' prayers when they trusted him and were not disappointed. Three times in v. 3-5, David reminds the Lord of his trustworthiness in the past, to question his silence and to prompt him into action.

6-8 But I am a worm and no man, scorned by men and despised by people. All who see me mock at me, they make mouths at me, they wag their heads. He committed his cause to the Lord, let him deliver him, let him rescue him, for he delights in him.

David began this psalm by sharing how he feels with the Lord, because he appears to have abandoned him and is not answering his prayer. Then he focuses on God's trustworthiness in the past. Now he shares with the Lord how he feels because of his enemies. His self-esteem has been assaulted and he has no confidence in himself. His imagination is running wild and getting things out of perspective, as he imagines what people are saying about him. He feels scorned and despised. He feels humiliated and insignificant. He feels his enemies are laughing at him and ridiculing him. They taunt him and imply that God is not going to help and rescue him, and this only adds to his agony of mind.

9-11 Yet you are the one who took me from my mother's womb: you kept me safe upon my mother's breasts. Upon you I was cast from my birth and since my mother bore me you have been my God. Be not far from me for trouble is near and there is none to help.

After sharing for a second time how he feels with the Lord, David again focuses on God's character. He casts his mind back to when he was young to describe a fond tenderness in his relationship with him. He reminds the Lord of his past protection and how he relied on him and he mentions his earliest experience of trust in the Lord from a young age. This is in sharp contrast to now feeling abandoned by him. The Lord's absence instead of his familiar presence has left him feeling acutely vulnerable. Reading in between the lines David may be saying: 'Why are you acting so out of character Lord?'

12-21 Many bulls encompass me, strong bulls of Bashan surround me, they open wide their mouths at me like a ravening and roaring lion. I am poured out like water and all my bones are out of joint, my heart is like wax, it is melted within my breast: my strength is dried up like a potsherd and my tongue cleaves to my jaws: thou dost lay me in the jaws of death. Dogs are round about me, a company of evildoers encircle me: they have pierced my hands and feet, I can count all my

> bones – they stare and gloat over me: they divide my garments among them and for my raiment they cast lots. But thou O Lord be not far off. O thou my help hasten to my aid. Deliver my soul from the sword, my life from the power of the dog. Save me from the mouth of the lion, my afflicted soul from the horns of the wild oxen.

David uses vivid animal images to describe the impact his enemies are having on him. D. Tidball says, 'Using metaphors from the animal kingdom he feels surrounded by bloodthirsty, baying beasts that will not be satisfied with anything less than his total destruction inflicted in the most terrifying way. He feels surrounded by the bulls of Bashan who were well known for their size and strength. He feels mauled by lions mercilessly tearing the flesh of their prey. He feels hemmed in by dogs snarling, growling and ready to pounce and destroy their prey. 'The words' writes P. Craigie, 'evoke the abject terror of one who is powerless, but surrounded, with no avenue of escape.'[26]

In v. 12-21 there is an atmosphere of mounting tension. David is now panicking as he imagines what his enemies might do if they capture him. A frightening scenario that emotionally and psychologically overwhelms him. He is feeling desperate and exhausted as he imagines being pinned to the ground and tortured by them. He visualises a terrifying scene as they gloat over him as a prisoner. His anxiety escalates, as he fears for his life when he says, 'Thou dost lay me in the dust of death.' This suggests the Lord allowed this to happen. An alarming prospect when David thought about the Lord's past protection.

As the Lord has been silent and deaf to his request for help and as David feels abandoned by him, he vividly describes the situation so the Lord will be moved to help him. The prospect of what might happen to him has reached the stage where he feels desperate. His prayer for help invites the Lord to, 'be not far off' – 'hasten to my aid' – 'deliver my soul' – 'save me from the mouth of the lion.' Tidball captures David's acute dilemma his faith has been trying to make sense of.

> Battling with the dominant, haunting melody of trouble is the irrepressible music of trust. Terrified though he is at the mystery of God's desertion of him, he does not allow himself to lapse into unbelief. His 'restlessly searching mind'...brings the reality of his suffering into contact with another reality – the reality of his covenant God.[27]

David's enemies were his Achilles heel, and his psychological weakness, similar to although not the same as Paul's weakness and thorn in the flesh. This can be probably be traced back to Saul's jealousy when he twice tried to kill David with a spear – 1 Sam. 18: 11, 19: 10, and the years afterwards when Saul pursued him to kill him. In around 35 of David's psalms, his enemies are the subject of his prayers for help. A brief look at some of these psalms enables us to see the extent of his psychological fear concerning his enemies. Psalm 31: 11-13: 'I am a reproach among all my enemies but especially among my neighbours, and am repulsive to my acquaintances: those who see me outside flee from me. I am forgotten like a dead man out of mind: I am like a broken vessel. For I hear the slander of many: fear is on every side while they take counsel against me, they scheme to take away my life.' Psalm 55: 2-6: 'I am overcome by trouble. I am distraught by the noise of the enemy because of the oppression of the wicked. For they bring trouble upon me and in anger they cherish enmity against me. My heart is in anguish within me, the terrors of death have fallen upon me. Fear and trembling come upon me and horror overwhelms me. And I say, 'O that I had wings like a dove. I would fly away and be at rest.' Psalm 69: 1-4, 'Save me O God. For the waters have come up to my neck. I sink in deep mire where there is no foothold. I have come into deep waters and the flood sweeps over me. I am weary with my crying: my throat is parched. My eyes grow dim with waiting for my God. More in number than the hairs of my head are those who hate me without cause: mighty are those who would destroy me.'

22-31 I will tell of your name to my brethren, in the midst of the great congregation I will praise you: you who fear the Lord praise him. All you sons of Jacob glorify him, and stand in awe of him all of you sons of Israel. For he has not despised or abhorred the affliction of the afflicted, and he has not hidden his face from him, but he has heard when he cried to him. From you comes my praise in the great congregation: my vows I will pay before those who fear him. The afflicted shall eat and be satisfied. Those who seek him shall praise the Lord. May your hearts live for ever. All the ends of the earth shall remember and turn to the Lord: and all the families of the nations shall worship before him. For dominion belongs to the Lord and he rules over the nations. Yes to him shall all the proud of the earth bow down: before him shall bow all who go down to the dust and he who cannot keep himself alive. Posterity shall serve him: men shall tell of the Lord to the coming generation and proclaim his deliverance to a people yet unborn that he has done this.

Verses 22-31 mark a turning point, not only in Psalm 22, but also in how David feels. In hindsight, he can see that the Lord is faithful and trustworthy, even when he is silent. Even when the Lord is not answering his prayer in the way he anticipated, expected or wanted. The danger he was in is now past and resolved although we are not told how. This is frustrating because his sense of desperation was palpable and we do not know if he was getting paranoid and exaggerating. The Lord has answered his prayer but we do not know if he has rescued him from his enemies, or merely resolved how he was feeling because of them. Either way, having been rescued David's heart is full of praise. Weiser says:

> The darkness which filled the worshipper's soul has vanished and rejoicing with great joy, he begins to sing a song of thanksgiving. He has become assured his prayer has been answered and that God has helped him…Having been delivered by God the psalmist is

> so fully conscious of his happiness which has been brought about by the re-establishment of his communion with God, that even the fact that he is now able to give thanks to God is accepted by him as a gift from God's hands. As a visible sign of his gratitude he will pay a votive offering in the midst of the godly ones and invite the poor to a meal so that they may share his happiness.[28]

David wrote Psalm 22 when he was feeling abandoned by the Lord and he felt isolated as an individual. But he ends it by placing himself firmly in the worshipping community of God's people. We have a striking shift of scene, as he wants to testify to the Lord's deliverance in the midst of the great congregation. Presumably, to fulfill a vow he made to the Lord as he called on him to answer his prayer. In the closing verses of Psalm 22 David is so grateful and relieved for being rescued from his enemies that he is now bursting with thanksgiving. He is elated and wants to testify to God's goodness. His audience is now not only the great assembly of God's people, but nations and generations not yet born. 'With an elegant sense of style, David describes a community of worship in which Israelites are complemented by Gentiles, the poor by the rich and the dead by the yet unborn. Distinctive in this psalm is the way David sees in his own rescue a glimpse in the way God delivers others, beginning with Israel's faithful and poor but finally including everyone.'[29]

As we reflect on this extraordinary psalm, we are struck by the fact that after the Lord has answered his prayer, David does not question the reason why, or wonder why the Lord has deliberately delayed his answer. Seeing that he quite vocally expressed his dismay at the Lord's timing in answering his prayer, we may well express some surprise that there is no theological reflection on his part as to why the Lord did this. It almost seems as if he is in the Lord's hands for him to do as he wishes, without the Lord explaining his action to him. Moreover, right at the beginning of Psalm 22, David does not understand why the Lord is ignoring his prayer, nor why he is not answering him. So too, at the end of it, he is no nearer to understanding why this happened.

We can see a parallel in Christ's experience on the cross, when he cried out 'My God, My God, why have you forsaken me?' Christ had not expected to be abandoned by his Father, and at that moment, he may not have understood God's purpose for this. But just as God had a far greater purpose in mind for not answering David immediately, his prophetic psalm in a remarkably accurate way describes Christ suffering on the cross, to which Christ alluded – so too God had a far greater purpose in abandoning Christ on the cross that involved our salvation. And it may be that at certain times in our lives, we too might never comprehend why the Lord chose to delay answering our prayers, nor understand what this accomplished.

PSALM 22
THE CRUCIFIXION

Before he was crucified, Jesus was scourged – whipped. Having seen Mel Gibson's 'The Passion of The Christ,' one cannot be certain how accurate the scene where Jesus is scourged is. In the film, this involved being beaten with canes until he could no longer stand. Then when Jesus did stand up he was beaten even more brutally using leather whips, with flails with barbs on the ends that tore out the victim's flesh. This scene lasted a long time and it seemed very unlikely anyone could have survived this double beating that was truly violent and horrific. What also stood out was the brutality and cruelty of the soldiers who scourged Jesus. One can imagine the victim being completely exhausted by the scourging and it would have been no surprise if they lost consciousness or died, if it was as brutal as Mel Gibson's portrayal. This is a reminder from Matt. 27: 26 that Jesus was scourged before he was crucified. He was also subject to a fair amount of violence by the soldiers who spat at him and hit him with their fists. Jesus also had a plaited crown of thorns placed on his head – Matt. 27: 29. These events alone must have caused acute violent physical suffering for Jesus and weakened him considerably too. Arguably, in Mel Gibson's film, the most brutal scene is the scourging and Jesus carrying his cross to Golgotha.

Death by crucifixion usually came slowly and involved nailing and tying the wrists by rope to the crossbeam, as nails on their own could not support the body weight of a victim. The nails–iron spikes were 5-7 inches long. Exposure, disease, hunger, shock and exhaustion were the immediate causes of death. The cramped position of the body caused fearful tortures and ultimately paralysis. As a result, the victims were likely to drift in and out of consciousness. Before the nailing, a mixture of vinegar, gall, and myrrh was offered to alleviate some of the suffering. Wooden planks were usually fastened to the vertical stake as a footrest or seat, allowing the victim to rest his weight and lift himself up for a breath. This prolonged the suffering and delayed death for up to three days. Unsupported, the victim would hang from his nail-pierced wrists severely restricting breathing and circulation. This excruciating ordeal led to exhaustion, suffocation, brain death, and heart failure. As a result, the victim could not push up to breathe and would quickly suffocate. At times mercy was shown by breaking the victim's legs causing death to come quickly. This indicates the crosses were probably fairly close to ground level. Crucifixion was one of the most horrific and violent methods of capitol punishment. Victims were usually beaten and tortured, and then forced to carry their own cross to the crucifixion site.

David wrote Psalm 22 about 1000 years before Christ and it is remarkably accurate about his suffering on the cross. The title of Psalm 22 'The Hind of the Dawn,' has particular significance for Christ. It is of interest to note that the ancient synagogue took this title as a name for the Shekinah *(glory of God).* And as a symbol of the dawning redemption, applied it to the morning sacrifice. According to the traditional definition, it refers to the 'early light preceding the dawn of the morning, whose rays are likened to the horns of a hind.' In Mosaic law, Christ as the sinless sacrifice is symbolised most prominently by the lamb slain and offered on the altar. But in the poetical books, Christ is compared to the Hind of the Dawn, that is generally seen in the morning tripping along in the forest glades licking the dew. It is one of the most beautiful creatures, but it is also one of the most defenseless. It has many natural enemies and its only means of survival are a keen sense of smell and speed in flight. This is the beautiful figure used of our Lord in Psalm 22 that mentions a number of animals that are enemies of the 'Hind of the Dawn.'[30] It is also possible that David used the image of the hind as an expression of hope, that help would arrive early in the morning when prayer is offered.[31]

Psalm 22 is a description of an execution particularly of a crucifixion. Crucifixion was only practiced many centuries after David, so it is a picture of the suffering of Christ on the cross. Therefore, it is prophetic and entirely Messianic. This is undoubtedly a psalm Jesus thought about as he hung upon the cross. Especially during the great darkness that came over the land at noon which lasted until three o'clock. This was the time each day when the lamb was brought into the Temple. 'Behold the lamb of God who takes away the sin of the world – John 1: 29. God allowed Jesus who was sinless to experience sin and know what it was like to be a sinner cut off from God – 'Christ became sin who knew no sin' – 2 Cor. 5: 21.

1-2 My God, my God, why have you forsaken me? Why are you so far from helping me, from the words of my groaning? O my God, I cry by day, but you do not answer and at night but find no rest.

At his crucifixion when Christ felt completely abandoned by his Father, he instinctively turned to this psalm to voice his sense of dereliction. Jesus' cry on the cross: *'Eloi, Eloi, lema sabachthani'* (Matt. 27: 46, Mark 15: 34) is a direct quote of Psalm 22: 1. (Aramaic was the first language for most Jews living in Palestine and had been since the Babylonian exile. Many would also have spoken Greek which was the language of the Greco-Roman empire and spoken by Gentiles and most of the Diaspora too, hence the gospels being written in Greek). Mays points out that, 'Citing the first words of a text was in the tradition of the time a way of identifying with an entire passage. The very experience of the psalmist becomes a commentary on Jesus' passion on the cross. In the intellectual world of Judaism, one of the most important ways of understanding the meaning of present experience was to make sense of the contemporary, by perceiving and describing it in terms of an established tradition.'[32] Therefore, Christians down the centuries have seen the special significance of this psalm in relation to Christ.

Towards the end of the period of darkness shortly before he died Jesus said 'I am thirsty' – John 19: 28 and was given wine vinegar on a sponge, almost certainly a quote from Psalm 69: 21. At the end of the period of darkness, Jesus called out, 'It is finished' – John 19: 30, a quote from the last verse of Psalm 22. In our text that verse reads, 'he has done it' referring to God as the subject. But there is no object for the verb in Hebrew and it can equally well translated: 'It is finished.'[33] Bruner says, 'As there was a unique fellowship with God in his life and preaching, so in Christ's death there was a unique abandonment by God.'[34]

Amos 8: 9a-10b reads, 'And on that day' says the Lord God, 'I will make the sun go down at noon and darken the earth in broad daylight. I will make it like the mourning for an only son.' This darkness can be seen to be symbolic portraying God's mourning and suffering at Christ's crucifixion too. As Bruner says, 'The most portentous thing ever to happen is happening now.'[35] The language of darkness is symbolic of the darkness that passes over the face of God and also in the heavenly places and symbolises a cosmic sadness as its Creator dies. The darkness can also represent the wrath of God as Christ the 'lamb of God' – John 1: 35, takes away the sin of the world. Darkness can also point in the narrative to the activity of the evil one against Jesus. The darkness was the time when Jesus was arrested – Luke 22: 53. It can also symbolise the activity of the powers of darkness against Jesus on the cross. But the darkness gives way to light, and the victory of God over the principalities and powers that God disarmed and made a public example of, by triumphing over them in Christ on the cross – Colossians 1: 15.

Jurgen Moltmann says, 'The Son suffers and dies on the cross. The Father suffers with him…The Christ event on the cross is a God event. And conversely, the God event takes place on the cross of the risen Christ. Here God has not just acted externally in his unattainable glory and eternity. Here he has acted in himself and gone on to suffering himself… Christology must take seriously the fact that God himself really enters into the suffering of his Son, and in so doing is and remains completely God.'[36] Jesus has undeniably suffered on the cross. But God his Father has also suffered, as he abandoned his Son who became an offering-sacrifice for the sin of the world. A rupture occurred in their relationship for the first and last time. God feels the pain of separation from Jesus in a profound way too as his Son suffers not only emotionally and physically, but also spiritually as he experiences sin in his life. In some measure, the Father shares in Jesus' suffering. For God and Christ had been inseparable before time and history, as Jesus had always been in the bosom of the Father – John 1: 18. Their divine union and communion was ruptured on the cross. It was heart breaking.

From Psalm 22: 1-2, we can imagine that on the cross Christ prayed to be saved by God and that he cried out in a loud voice. In v. 2 the literal Hebrew translation for cry is 'roaring.' This implies an emotional, physical agony, loudly imploring God in excruciating pain to help and save him. Instead of being strengthened and comforted by God's presence, Christ felt his father's absence. Verse 1 poignantly captures Christ's sense of dereliction when he felt completely abandoned by his Father. On the cross, a rupture occurred between God and Christ, as he was abandoned by the Father and separated from him. Christ was cut off from his relationship with the Father for the first time. As he quoted, Psalm 22: 1 and asked 'Why?' – perhaps it was the shock of separation he had not anticipated. For Jesus who had been in the 'bosom of the Father' before time and history, this was unprecedentedly traumatic. Perhaps he was expecting God to intervene on the cross and save him. Perhaps it was during these last three hours on the cross, that Jesus fully grasped his death was essential for the forgiveness of sins and the reason for his abandonment.

The first two thirds of Psalm 22 is like a litany of personal disaster which shows that David could not comprehend why his prayer is being ignored by God. But unknown to him, God had a greater purpose in not answering him immediately. Unknown to David his psalm was to have a deeply significant prophetic meaning for Christ, as he identified himself with it on the cross. Christians down the centuries have also seen the special significance of this psalm in relation to Christ. For Christ to feel abandoned and forsaken by God involved despair, utter desolation and doubt, despair as he felt alone, betrayed and frightened. In that fully human moment he may well have doubted that what was happening to him was God's will.[37] Donald Coggan, a former Archbishop of Canterbury, captures the essence of v. 1 that he describes as: 'The agony of doubt.'

> Now at the end of Jesus' ministry when doubt and darkness assailed him with a force he had never known before, his mind reverted to Scripture – and in that Scripture he found words which seemed to express his need…Jesus was carrying a load the like of which none of us will ever be called upon to bear. 'He carried our sins in his own person on the tree' – 1 Peter 2: 24. It was a crushing load that blotted out for Jesus the consciousness of the presence of the God who had meant more to him all his life than anyone or anything else. A sense of sheer, stark dereliction swept over him. If the cross is the place where God's disgust with sin and his burning love for human-kind meet in terrible expression: if God in Christ is there clearing up the mess made by a rebel race, can we wonder that there is a mystery? We can dare to look – and adore.[38]

F. D. Bruner points out, 'It is significant that Jesus does not call out 'My Father.' His abandonment has raised a doubt about God himself. This is the deepest darkness of all. Jesus is not only surrounded by outward darkness (Matt. 27: 45), he does not inwardly feel God's presence at all…Jesus' lifeline had been cut. He dies here before he dies. This is Jesus' descent into hell. We should simply stand back in silence before this awful verb (abandoned) and wonder what it means.

Death is the ultimate abandonment for Christ who had always existed. Jesus, who represents all men, feels himself deserted by God and he allows himself to experience annihilation, this total suffering.[39] Bruner also says:

> The God who is felt not to be there is addressed by Jesus – 'You!' There is something wonderful in that… The God whose presence Jesus does not experience, Jesus invokes. The Cry of Dereliction looks like a cry of despair at first, like a temporary loss of faith, as if Jesus and God were no longer close. Yet Jesus right here, better than perhaps anywhere else, teaches us exactly what faith at its deepest level is: it is believing God even when we do not feel him.[40]

6-9 But I am a worm and no man, scorned by men and despised by people. All who see me mock at me, they make mouths at me, they wag their heads. He committed his cause to the Lord let him deliver him: let him rescue him, for he delights in him.

As we remember from Matthew's Gospel the taunts of those who saw the crucifixion of Jesus – Matt. 27: 29-44, we see how closely it resembles Psalm 22: 6-8. 'And those who passed by derided Jesus, wagging their heads and saying, 'You who would destroy the temple and build it in three days, save yourself! If you are the Son of God come down from the cross.' So also, the chief priests with the scribes and elders mocked him saying, 'He saved others: he cannot save himself. He is the king of Israel let him come down now from the cross and we will believe in him. He trusts in God: let God deliver him, if he desires for he said, 'I am the Son of God.' And the robbers who were crucified with Jesus also reviled him in the same way.' The physical agony and torture of the cross was exacerbated by the contemptuous and cruel taunts that ridiculed Jesus. Their taunts raised issues of great significance: 'If you are the Son of God?' – 'He trusts in God let him deliver him, for he delights in him.' 'If you are the Son of God?' is no accidental comment. It is the identical taunt that the devil tempted Jesus with in the wilderness before his public ministry began. 'If' raises an element of doubt on the cross about Jesus' identify, that is undoubtedly greater at the end of his ministry. 'If God delights in him' also raises another element of doubt. Was God displeased with Jesus? Did he not delight in him?

> But the sharpest sting comes in the last clause, 'If he likes him.'...If Yahweh does delight in the suppliant then deliverance will follow. But he can no longer have conviction about that, having been abandoned by Yahweh. The mockers' sarcastic affirmation, implying that Yahweh does not like him, corresponds to the suppliant's fear.[41]

At his crucifixion, Jesus was abandoned by all of his disciples, except his mother, her sister Mary Magdalene and John. 'Jesus was humiliated, less than human, and of no significance compared to that of a worm. The bystanders at his crucifixion would have seen him in this light. But there is another interpretation of the Hebrew *tolaath* – worm. This appears 31 times in the Old Testament and is often translated 'scarlet' or 'crimson.' The word applies especially to the coccus from which the scarlet dye of the Tabernacle was obtained by its death. The word is used in Isaiah 1: 18 for the colour of sin – 'though your sins are like scarlet they shall be white as snow' says the Lord.' The tola of the orient is a little worm that feeds on certain cactus. These are beaten until the tola fall into a basin, and then they crush the little insects and the blood is the brilliant crimson dye that makes bright Mexican garments. In Palestine and Syria, they use the tola in the same way and it makes the beautiful permanent scarlet dye of the orient. Solomon is said to have clothed the maidens of Israel in scarlet. Daniel was to be clothed in scarlet by Belshazzar. The word 'scarlet' is literally 'the splendour of the worm.' Now, the Lord Jesus Christ says, 'I am a worm. I am the tola.' He had to be crushed to death that you and I might be clothed in glory. The glorious garments of our salvation come from his shed blood, suffering and death.'[42]

In Matthew Gospel three groups of people mock and scoff at Jesus, taunting and ridiculing him. A reminder of Isaiah 53: 3: 'He was despised and rejected by men, a man of sorrows and acquainted with grief.' While it is speculative I believe we can imagine on the cross Jesus would also have remembered the suffering servant described so vividly in Isaiah 53, with whom he would have indentified himself during his ministry and crucifixion. This may have helped Jesus to make sense that what was happening on the cross was God's will.

12-13 Many bulls encompass me, strong bulls of Bashan surround me: they open wide their mouths at me, like a ravening and roaring lion.

Jesus was likely to be aware of the terrifying animal imagery David used to describe his enemies. These can stand for the powerful opposition of the chief priests and scribes, and to Annas and Caiphas the high priests responsible for his arrest and trial, and Pilate who condemned him to death. The animal imagery represents a frightening picture of predatory behaviour towards Jesus. He was surrounded by a pack of vicious evildoers. 'These animal metaphors symbolise vicious threats to life. The conventional pair of the lion and bull represents the epitome of power.'[43] The lion, bull and dogs, represent an image of powerful beasts ready to pounce and finish off and kill their prey.

14-18 I am poured out like water and all my bones are out of joint, my heart is like wax, it is melted within my breast: my strength is dried up like a potsherd and my tongue cleaves to my jaws: thou dost lay me in the jaws of death. Dogs are round about me, a company of evildoers encircle me: they have pierced my hands and feet, I can count all my bones – they stare and gloat over me: they divide my garments among them, and for my raiment they cast lots.

Verses 14-15 portray a terrifying account of the feeling of desperation Jesus felt at his crucifixion. His life is ebbing away. He is literally physically being torn apart on the cross.

This paints a picture of extreme physical distress and emotional fragmentation and the awareness by Jesus that he is dying. 'The bones of his hands, arms, shoulders and pelvis are out of joint. Visualise the suffering this would cause. The profuse perspiration caused intense suffering: the action of the heart was affected. His strength was exhausted and extreme thirst took place. His hands and feet were pierced.'[44] These verses also describe extreme emotional, psychological and spiritual trauma, as Jesus feels overwhelmed by what is happening to him. His heart like wax melted away – is he also dying of a broken heart as his relationship with God is being ruptured? He is becoming aware that his life is ebbing away and that God is 'laying him in the dust of death.' Jesus is as good as dead. His bodily parts are failing. He is desolate as he is aware that God is allowing him to die.

This presents us with an unfathomable mystery. For while we can understand Christ died for sinners, there is an element of mystery, as God who can save him is not doing so. In Christ God was reconciling the world to himself – 2 Cor. 5: 19 – but on the cross God is holding back from saving Jesus. The reality is that on the cross Jesus felt as brittle as a potsherd, so brittle that he could crumble – fall apart. In reality, Jesus was defenseless against the 'dogs' that surrounded him. A term used for human agents of evil. The scavengers who will benefit from his death gloated over his predicament as they cast lots for his garments – Matt. 27: 33. 'I can count all my bones' – implies Jesus' bones were so out of joint and protruding and he was aware of his body being distorted. Jesus is overwhelmed by what is happening to him. If there was a time for Jesus' faith in God to fail him, it was now. Abandoned, helpless, isolated and ridiculed, Jesus' body was broken and distorted by his physical suffering and inner spiritual torment – this is holy ground to reflect on in holy adoration.

19-21 But thou O Lord be not far off. O thou my help hasten to my aid. Deliver my soul from the sword, my darling from the power of the dog. Save me from the mouth of the lion, my afflicted soul from the horns of the wild oxen. You have heard me.

Although Jesus only uttered the first and last verses of Psalm 22 on the cross, he would have been familiar with this psalm, aware that it contained a prayer for deliverance from death and his enemies – and aware that God had heard the psalmist. During his crucifixion, we can imagine Jesus was praying in his spirit for his deliverance. 'My darling' in v. 20 can be translated in a number of ways. 'Solitary one' – 'dear one' – 'beloved one'[45] or 'my only-one' that emphasises his dignity and deity as the only begotten Son of God.[46] The horns of the wild ox represented the altar of sacrifice that had four horns one at each corner. On this altar, animals were sacrificed. Christ was the perfect sacrifice for sins and his prayer was to be saved after he had borne our sins on this altar.[47] 'You have heard me' is a cry of triumph, not despair. It marks the moment at which the period of darkness passes, and Jesus having suffered a true alienation from the Father as punishment for our sins, becomes aware again of God's presence.[48]

22-31 I will tell of your name to my brethren, in the midst of the great congregation I will praise you. You who fear the Lord praise him. All you sons of Jacob glorify him, and stand in awe of him all of you sons of Israel. For he has not despised or abhorred the affliction of the afflicted, and he has not hidden his face from him, but he has heard when he cried to him. From you comes my praise in the great congregation: my vows I will pay before those who fear him. The afflicted shall eat and be satisfied: those who seek him shall praise the Lord. May your hearts live for ever. All the ends of the earth shall remember and turn to the Lord, and all the families of the nations shall worship before him. For dominion belongs to the Lord and he rules over the nations. Yes to him shall all the proud of the earth bow down: before him shall bow all who go down to the dust, and he who cannot keep himself alive. Posterity shall serve him, men shall tell of the Lord to the coming generation, and proclaim his deliverance to a people yet unborn that he has done this.'

While David praised the Lord for his deliverance we can see that these verses as a messianic prophecy pointing to Christ take on a new meaning. Not only are we completely speechless at the dramatic reversal of fortune in v. 22, we are equally stunned by the ecstatic nature of v. 22-31 that describes it – but also points to Jesus' resurrection. These verses bear witness that Jesus was assured his Father heard him and his atonement was accepted, and untold generations of people in the future would be saved and become his brothers and sisters.

Hebrews 2: 11-12 sees Jesus as the one whom Psalm 22: 22 is speaking about: 'For it was fitting that he for whom and by whom all things exist, in bringing many sons to glory should make the pioneer of their salvation perfect through suffering. For he who sanctifies, and those who are sanctified have all one origin. This is why Jesus is not ashamed to call them brethren saying: 'I will proclaim your name to my brethren, in the midst of the congregation I will praise you.' In v. 22-31 Jesus testifies to God's salvation to an ever-widening circle of people. In v. 22 it is to 'my brethren' – the Jewish nation, and this had a partial fulfillment when Jesus appeared to the disciples after his resurrection. In v. 25 it is to 'the great assembly or congregation' – this is to the Early Church and includes the Gentiles. In v. 27 it is to all 'the ends of the earth' and 'all the families of the nations' – that is to the Christians throughout the earth and all the nations. In v. 30 it is to 'the coming generation' and in v. 31 it is to 'a people yet unborn.' This final ambitious witness to a group of people highlights the universal proclamation of the truth of the Gospel down the centuries. What is striking about this reference to this ever increasing circle of people is that in turn each group is exhorted to praise or worship the Lord for the salvation he has secured, through the death and resurrection of Christ.

PSALM 23
PROVISION

Clearly, and indisputably, Psalm 23 must rank as one of the best known and best loved psalms. Not only because it voices in a very personal way a confidence and trust in the Lord, but because of the poetic beauty and imagery that powerfully touch the imagination of faith, that in turn make it a memorable psalm. At first glance, the sentiments of the psalm roll of the tongue with an almost naïve confidence and youthful abandon, that almost suggests a carefree existence. However, behind the sentiments of Psalm 23 is a profound faith in the Lord, with powerful allusions to his protection and provision. This psalm may well roll off our tongue with relative ease, yet only once we have explored its imagery can we fully appreciate its magnificent poetic power. A power that transmits faith, as we comprehend on a deeper level the truths of Psalm 23.

None of the biblical commentators I referred to mention what a striking contrast there is between the previous Psalm, and Psalm 23. In Psalm 22, David's faith is stretched and tested to the limit, as he struggles to comprehend why the Lord is not responding to his prayer to rescue him from his enemies. The Lord allows David's faith to go to places that emotionally, psychologically and spiritually he had never been to before. He has experienced a sense of abandonment and faced in his imagination the prospect of death at the hands of his enemies. For Psalm 23 to follow with David's tranquil tones, appears to present a world far removed from the sense of abandonment in Psalm 22 – and is almost out of place as the succeeding psalm.

The opening metaphor of Psalm 23, 'The Lord is my shepherd' sets the tone for a psalm composed in a metaphorical style. This metaphor is also the underlying theme that controls the imagery of the psalm. To appreciate the significance of the shepherd as a metaphor for the Lord, it is necessary to be aware of what this meant for David. In his culture, a shepherd was an integral feature of life and a common sight, although his work was of a very low rank. The shepherd had to live with the sheep twenty-four hours a day to fulfill the task of caring for them. He protected his flock from predators and provided for them by leading them to suitable pastures. He was responsible for the sheep and accountable for their welfare. As David had been a shepherd, being the youngest in his family he knew first hand what he was talking about, when he spoke of the Lord as 'my shepherd.' Mays informs us, 'In the ancient Near East the role and title of shepherd were used for leaders as a designation of their relation to the people in their charge. As a title 'shepherd' came to have specific royal connotations. God and kings were called the shepherd of their people and both are described with rod and shepherd's crook-staff as a sign of office. In narrative, song and prophecy, the Lord is called the shepherd of Israel, his flock (Gen. 49: 24, Psalm 28: 9, 74: 1, 95: 7, 100: 3, Jer. 31. 10, Micah 7: 14)...To say, 'The Lord is my shepherd,' invokes all the richness of this theological and political background as well as the pastoral.'[49]

P. C. Craigie points out, 'The metaphor of shepherd is pregnant with meaning and is not a random picture. So it goes beyond the horizon of David's experience and draws on the ancient resources of the Hebrew tradition. Therefore, his use of the metaphor is linked to the broader concept of the Lord, who had been the shepherd of his people over many generations. This metaphor is rich with meaning and significance, as it is associated with the Exodus from Egypt and the Hebrews' time in the wilderness, when God provided for and protected his people. Whether it is explicit or a subtle allusion, David's confidence and trust in the Lord as shepherd, is linked to his saving activity in the history of his people that was the basis of their covenant faith.'[50]

1-3 The Lord is my shepherd I shall not want: he makes me to lie down in green pastures. He leads me beside still waters: he restores my soul. He leads me in paths of righteousness for his name's sake.

The use of shepherd as an image of God sovereign over the people of Israel in a first person singular confession is unparalleled. It is the focus of the shepherd's care on one person that gives the psalm such intimate force.[48] The Lord is 'my shepherd' introduces the distinctive feature of Psalm 23. So it is not surprising that Christians down the centuries have identified Jesus, as the 'good shepherd' in John 10, who laid down his life for the sheep – as this reinforces the personal emphasis of the Lord, is 'my shepherd.' But what exactly gave David the assurance to say in such a personal way, 'my God' in Psalm 22 and 'my shepherd' in Psalm 23? What is it that enabled him to have confidence in his relationship with the Lord? We should take care to note that these two references to the Lord by David were not quaint or sentimental images. In Psalm 22: 9-10, in effect he speaks of knowing the Lord from a very young age. And in Psalm 23 we can imagine that David as a young shepherd boy experienced God's care as his shepherd. When he says in v. 3, 'He leads me in paths of righteousness' – this gives us the clue for his confidence in calling God 'my shepherd.' David knew the Lord as a young man because he kept his commandments and walked in his ways. Therefore, he had an assurance of the Lord's care and protection in his life. For Christians to call the Lord 'my shepherd,' demands they too walk in the Lord's commandments.

The green pastures and still waters of v. 2 can refer to the provision of food, water and protection, for the sheep by their shepherd. But the main emphasis of v. 2-6 can be seen as an exposition of v. 1, that states because 'the Lord is my shepherd I shall lack nothing.' The allusion in v. 1-3 of the Lord's provision is that spiritually he feeds, nurtures and sustains his people. A reminder of Jesus saying, 'I am the bread of life' – in John 7. The poetic language of these verses presents an idyllic picture of provision for the Christian. Green pastures, suggests an abundance of spiritual sustenance. Still waters, is an image of tranquility. He restores my soul is an allusion to spiritual renewal. To be led by the Lord in paths of righteousness refers to the Lord's guidance and is an image of spiritual nourishment. But this guidance is not solely for the benefit of the individual. It is for the glory of God as he shows himself to be faithful because of his name's sake.

As we absorb the blessings of the rest of Psalm 23, we may be lulled into a false sense of security that the Christian life is a carefree existence without any concerns, because of the abundant provision of the Lord as a shepherd for his people. We only have to read Psalm 22 to know that this is a false conclusion or interpretation. Psalm 23 appears to represent a quite different world where such struggles of faith are alien to the psalmist's experience. How then can we reconcile these two psalms? Psalm 22 represents the struggles and trials of faith that Christians invariably will go through, whatever they may turn out to be. Through them, the faith of God's people is refined and stretched so that they learn to trust the Lord in a deeper manner. But Psalm 23 represents God's provision and protection for his people, in the overall context of their lives. And despite facing difficulties, despite encountering the valley of the shadow of death, God's people can be confident they will overcome them, because the Lord is 'my shepherd.' The truth in both Psalm 22 and 23 is the personal knowledge the Lord is with the believer to nurture and protect him, whatever difficulties he may encounter. 'My God, my God' in Psalm 22 and 'The Lord is my shepherd' in Psalm 23, both speak of the distinctive personal involvement of the Lord with the believer, as he puts his faith and trust in the Lord. But Psalm 22 warns us there will be times when emotionally and psychologically our faith is severely tested. When this happens, it is a challenge to be obedient and trust the Lord, so that we experience his provision and protection that Psalm 23 so idyllically portrays.

4 Even though I walk through the valley of the shadow of death, I fear no evil, for you are with me: your rod and your staff comfort me.

Although the image of shepherd dominates Psalm 23, we can find three images in it. The first is that of the shepherd and the sheep – v. 1-3. The second is that of the Lord as companion and the traveller – v. 4, and the third is the Lord as the host and the guest – v. 5-6.[49] Verse 4 clearly shows why Psalm 23 is used regularly at funeral services, because of its reference to death and the comforting truth of God's nearness at this time. We can perceive that David's experience as a shepherd enables him to use this analogy for the Lord's presence and protection, in times of danger quite possibly from his enemies mentioned in v. 5. Verse 4 is a reference to the seasonal passage from the lowlands where sheep spend the winter, through the valleys to the high pastures where they go in the summer. The valleys are places of rich pasture and water but they are also places of danger. Wild animals may lurk there and sudden floods and storms may occur. Since the sun does not shine in the valley it is a place of shadows.[50] For the Christian the valley can represent difficulties and trials and a reminder that life is not always tranquil spiritually, something we clearly see in Psalm 22. Spending time in the valley can make us apprehensive and afraid. But the truth that David shares is that the Lord is his companion and his presence is with him, therefore he is not afraid of any danger. The comfort of the shepherd's rod and staff refers to the Lord's protection, as the rod-club fended off wild beasts and the staff-crook guided and controlled the sheep.

5-6 You prepare a table before me in the presence of my enemies: you anoint my head with oil, my cup overflows Surely goodness and mercy shall follow me all the days of my life, and I shall dwell in the house of the Lord for ever.

Through the imagination of his faith, the Lord has given David a picture about his generous provision. The mention of a banquet in v. 5 may have an association with a sacrificial meal in the house of God to celebrate God's goodness. Or it may be a reminder of the Passover when the Hebrews ate in haste a meal before their deliverance. Or it may even allude to the Lord's provision for his people when they wandered in the wilderness. For Christians it may even be a reminder of the Lord's Supper. Moreover, for the Lord to prepare a meal and act as host is a reminder of close fellowship with him.

Psalm 23 overflows with a clear confidence in the Lord's protection, provision, and presence. At some particular time, David has been prompted by the Holy Spirit to reflect on these things – why we do not know, but throughout the psalm, there is an accumulative confidence expressed in the Lord. From this perspective, Psalm 23 can be seen as one of thanksgiving and praise to the Lord, because of his faithfulness in caring, providing for, and protecting David, and also for his presence accompanying him. Thanksgiving that has its climax in v. 5-6.

As David has reflected on his life and the Lord in v. 5-6, he then focuses on the future with a confident expectation of the Lord's provision once again. As he thinks about his enemies who on occasions are a real threat to his life, he dismisses them with ease. They pose no concern for him. Instead, he ecstatically visualises God preparing a banquet for him, at which he gives thanks and celebrates God's goodness. Verses 1-4 speak of God's abundant provision for him in a number of ways. Now v. 5-6 speak of the superabundance of the Lord's provision for the future. As he reflected on these things, David is overwhelmed by God's faithfulness and goodness. Even in the midst of possible danger due to his enemies, the Lord has anointed him with the oil of gladness. Using the analogy of a banquet, the Lord's provision as his host, has overflowed like a cup of wine filled to excess. David's confidence is compounded in v. 6, when he anticipates that the Lord's goodness and mercy shall be with him throughout his life. A. Weiser says:

> At this very point, his delight in God reaches its climax and throws him into raptures. The experience of the hour which he spent in the house of God in the direct presence of the Lord symbolically transcends the barriers of time and space. He will dwell with God to the end of the days and not only as his guest, but indeed as a member of his household, that is, in a most intimate and unbroken fellowship with God… The hallowed atmosphere of worship is and remains a holy experience, whereby the heart feels exalted and becomes more strongly conscious of the nearness of God…[54]

PSALM 42
LONGING FOR GOD

Psalms 42-43 are considered by biblical scholars to have originally been one psalm. Psalm 42 is one of many collected by or for the director of music. It is a psalm by one of the sons of Korah that are grouped together as subsections of Books 2 and 3 of The Psalms. The Sons of Korah originated from the family of Levi and from Levi's son Kohath came Moses and his brother Aaron, (and through him the hereditary priesthood) and their relative Korah, who rebelled against their leadership in Numbers 16 during the journey from Egypt to Canaan.

Although Korah and his family died at least one of his sons survived, and later generations of the family were installed as worship leaders in Jerusalem by David. The Sons of Korah seem to have formed a guild of musicians, who composed or edited another collection most of which is in book 2 of The Psalms. The 1st Korah Collection along with the 2nd Davidic Collection and the Asaph Collection (the whole of Book 2) and the larger part of Book 3 form what is known as the 'Elohistic Psalter.' These 42 psalms regularly address their prayers and praises to Elohim (God) rather than to Yahweh (the Lord)[55] – but, in the 1st Book of Psalms 1-41, the name Lord is used.

One of the best clues to the setting of Psalms 42-43 is the taunt, 'Where is your God?' 'The question is a formulaic motif, used to characterise the situation in which those who trust in the Lord are put to shame in the presence of others, because of some trouble that calls their faith into question.'[56] In these two psalms the enemies of God's people are clearly the antagonist. They may have been composed in the post-exilic period when God's people were at the mercy of a foreign nation. While they are considered to be a lament, the depth of grief and longing they express on behalf of the community, is haunting and overwhelming. They express an inconsolable depression and a relentless mourning because of the ongoing situation they have found themselves in, as there is no apparent solution to alleviate their emotional and psychological suffering. In this context the passionate desire they express for God from the depths of their heart and soul, speaks of a longing for intimacy with God that is almost unparalleled in its intensity, because of the loss and pain it springs from.

1-5 As a hart longs for flowing streams, so longs my soul for you O God. My soul thirsts for God, for the living God. When shall I come and behold the face of God? My tears have been my food day and night, while men say to me continually, 'Where is your God?' These things I remember as I pour out my soul: how I went with the throng and led them in procession to the house of God, with glad shouts and songs of thanksgiving, a multitude keeping festival. Why are you cast down O my soul, and why are you so disquieted within me? Hope in God, for I shall again praise him, my help and my God.

The Sons of Korah describe the peoples' plight using a simile from nature about the deer in a dry landscape longing for a drink, to powerfully convey their spiritual thirst for God. Because of the circumstances of their unbearable grief and loss, they have become consumed with a longing for God. Especially, for an encounter with God conveyed as beholding the face of God in his Temple in Jerusalem. Ironically, the people who longed for a refreshing drink from the well of God, have tasted instead the bitter water of their tears.[57]

Verses 1-5 are composed in a reflective mood, with the psalmist speaking to himself and expressing his longing for God. But they also enable God's people to begin to voice how they feel deep within their spirits by pouring out their soul. Yet this process of beginning to express their feelings and then focusing on God has to continue until a resolution is reached. Because the reality in v. 6-8, is the people are particularly depressed and despondent. They have reached a very low point and while v. 1-5 offer a brief glimpse of hope they are still overwhelmed by their feelings. Now the psalmist enables the people to not only express how they feel, but to focus on God.

6-8 My soul is cast down within me, therefore I remember you from the land of Jordan and of Hermon from Mount Mizar. Deep calls to deep at the thunder of your cataracts: all your waves and your billows have gone over me. By day, the Lord commands his steadfast love, and at night his song is with me, a prayer to the God of my life.

'Initially v. 6-7, offer another expression of pain that goes behind and beyond the one in v. 1-2.'[58] The metaphors that mention the land of Jordan and Mount Hermon and Mount Mizar, only serve to reinforce the reality that the people are far from Jerusalem where they want to be and where God is.

> A reference to Mt. Hermon and the Jordan headwaters could link with the imagery of v. 7. The streams that come together to form the Jordan pass through several waterfalls and cascades of crashing waters...The 'sound' of the worshipping crowd and the prospect of 'passing' on into the Temple is here replaced, by the 'sound' of the crashing waters that are 'passing' over the suppliant...The poet who desperately seeks water finds it, but it is not life-giving water it is destructive.[59]

As we work our way through Psalm 42, we can perceive this is an outstanding literary composition by the Sons of Korah on behalf of God's people. They not only express how the people feel, but also come up with a solution when the situation seemed insoluble. They express the peoples' longing for God along with their grief, and also nostalgically look back and remember when they were in Jerusalem, in the procession of a festival celebration that took place in the Temple. Having created this sharp contrast they then ingeniously introduce a ray of hope for the people, when they write v. 6 as a refrain for them. To get the people to say out aloud in v. 6, 'Why are you so depressed?' appears to be strange psychology, because they know very well why. But this is followed by them saying: 'Hope in God for I shall again praise him, my help and my God.' In effect, the people focus on the present situation, then look back at the past, and then introduce hope for the future. This is an innovative dialogue of faith with the Lord and themselves, to renew their faith and hope in the Lord that one day they shall again praise him.

The strategy of the psalmist to look back to remember familiar landscapes is not yet successful. 'It is only the springs of chaos and despair which are released in his mind. Now the motif of water is reversed (v. 2-3). He longed for water in thirst, but was thinking of the waters of the ocean and those of the river, it is their waves and waterfalls that dominate his mind like one chaotic deep calling to another. He had longed for the waters of refreshment, but somehow in the effort to remember God he had unleashed the primeval waters of chaos, which seemed to depict so powerfully his terrible situation.'[60] But the psalmist is not speaking personally, he is speaking on behalf of God's people and voicing their acute distress. All the images of water reinforce that it is God who has been like a thunderous cataract cascading down on them. In effect, they have been submerged in the waves and billows of God, metaphors that signify what his hand has allowed to happen to them. The strategy of remembering God in familiar land has resulted in a further outpouring of their feelings. But the psalmist also recalls that in their homeland there was an assurance of God's steadfast love with his people during the day and at night, as a song of praise and thanksgiving was offered up.

9-11 I say to God my rock, 'Why have you forgotten me? Why am I mourning because of the oppression of the enemy?' As with a deadly wound in my body my adversaries taunt me, while they continually say, 'Where is your God?' Why are you cast down O my soul, and why are you so disquieted within me? Hope in God, for I shall again praise him, my help and my God.

As the beginning of Psalm 42, the people express to God the longing of their heart's desire for communion and fellowship with him, and for an intimate encounter with the face of God. As the psalm progresses they remember the wonderfully happy memories of celebrating in the Temple, and experiencing the nearness of God in their homeland. At the same time, they have expressed their feelings to God about their situation. Now in v. 9 they bluntly address God and ask him why has he forgotten and neglected them, and in effect, why he has not answered their prayers. They cannot understand why God is allowing their enemies to continually oppress them and taunt them with the words: 'Where is your God?' They are deeply depressed and mourning because of this, as God is not listening to them.

In v. 9 they address God as their rock to remind him of the intimate relationship in protecting his people. As you read in between the lines of Psalm 42, when God's people tell Him their enemies keep saying, 'Where is your God?' – one cannot help but feel, this is what God's people were also beginning to echo in their hearts. Having spoken to God and confronted him with his absence and neglect, once again the people speak to themselves. By addressing God in this personal way they are seeking to rouse him into action, as they proclaim the liturgical refrain: 'Hope in God, for I shall again praise him, my help and my God.' Not only is this refrain directed at God but also to themselves to stir up their confidence and faith, and their hope in God – although there is no resolution to their problem by the end of the psalm.

PSALM 43
HOPE IN GOD

1-2 Vindicate me O God and defend my cause against an ungodly people: from deceitful and unjust men deliver me. For you are the God in whom I take refuge, why have you cast me off? Why go I mourning because of the oppression of the enemy?

In Psalm 42 God's people were turned in on themselves, because of their deep depression as they addressed God and also themselves. But having expressed their profound feelings to God, their hearts have been released from this introverted posture. Now in Psalm 43 they can reach out beyond their subjective feelings. The transition in this psalm is marked by a different atmosphere in the mood of the people. In comparison with the depressing tone of Psalm 42, this psalm is positive and uplifting. P. C. Craigie says, 'The lament of the two preceding sections of Psalm 42 is now converted into a prayer and the form of the transition is striking. In the lament sections, the psalmist is introverted, dwelling on memory and trying to summon it to his aid: for practical purpose, he is talking to himself. But now in this section of the psalm the internal dialogue of lament is turned into an external dialogue with God. And the change from introvertive reflection to external plea, is the beginning of real progress for the psalmist.'[61]

'Psalm 43 provides it *(Psalm 42)* with resolution, in the sense that here the suppliant speaks with conviction, as if having won the battle with the questioning inner person expressed in the refrain…Resolution in the form of deliverance has not yet come, but the suppliant can live with things better. There was no actual plea in Psalm 42 (despite v. 8-9): here v. 1

launches straight into plea. But the plea concerns not the suppliant's longing to be able to get back to Jerusalem to see God, nor the scornful questions, nor God's own abandonment: instead the plea concerns the enemy who makes that return both desirable and impossible, the one who reviles or provides the reason for the reviling and is the evidence of God's abandonment. Solve this problem and all others will be solved. The plea works with a legal framework suggesting God seated in the court in the heavens: that is the nature of a 'plea.' We know from 42:9 that the suppliant feels in the right over against the enemy.'[62]

Weiser eloquently describes the transition in the peoples' hearts and minds that has occurred in Psalm 43 although he only refers to the individual. 'The struggle of his soul against the doubts by which he had been seized, has enabled the worshipper to reach the stage where he is able to pass victoriously through the darkness of his suffering, until he has risen to the sure knowledge that his prayer has been granted.'[63]

3-4 O send out your light and your truth, let them lead me, let them bring me to your holy hill and to your dwelling. Then I will go to the altar of God, to God, my exceeding joy, and I will praise you with the lyre, O God, my God.

Verses 1-2 indicate a newfound confidence in God to defend and deliver his people from their enemies. In anticipation of God's salvation, his people can now see with the imagination of faith a real possibility of returning to Jerusalem and worshipping God in the Temple. Because of the darkness of their soul due to their enemies, the people now astutely pray for God's light and truth to lead them out of this darkness and to the Temple in Jerusalem. The taunt of, 'Where is your God?' was a deceitful claim of their enemies that oppressed them and sent them into a deep depression. The truth of God's love and faithfulness and deliverance is the light that will dispel the deceit of this darkness. They will not only be set free in their hearts and minds, but also be set free to come to the altar of God – to be with God their exceeding joy. The communion, fellowship, and intimacy with God they fervently desired in Psalm 42, but which seemed so elusive, is now becoming in the imagination of faith, a tangible reality before their very eyes.

5 Why are you so cast down, O my soul, and why are you so disquieted within me? Hope in God, for I shall again praise him, my help and my God.

In their newfound confidence and faith in God that he has heard their prayer and will at some time in the future enable them to return to Jerusalem, it seems somewhat surprising that Psalm 43 should end on the refrain that was dominant in Psalm 42. But perhaps it is not surprising, as in this context of assurance of answered prayer, this refrain no longer has any hold on them as they have been released from it. Now that they have been set free from their deep depression that the first half of this refrain expressed, they can embrace with confidence the hope that the second half of this refrain expresses, but which was not yet a tangible reality in Psalm 42.

'What touches our hearts here, is not only the high artistic quality of the psalm inherent in the life-like, and deeply felt portrayal of the struggle which took place in the psalmist's soul *(and the peoples' soul):* the way in which here man's longing for God is shown to be a power which sustains him through fear and torment, doubt and temptation, till he overcomes them by faith and by his waiting for God, is even today still able to bring comfort and help to troubled souls…'[64] Here, we do well to remember that it is the Lord who takes the initiative to draw us to himself that we might experience that communion, fellowship and intimacy with him, either on our own or with others in the context of corporate worship. Psalms 42-43 teach us that there will be occasions of great difficulty, oppression, or serious trouble, when we experience deep depression, but we can trust the Lord that he will save us from our circumstances so that they do not overwhelm us.

PSALM 51
RESTORATION

Assuming that David wrote Psalm 51, this is a profoundly

moving account of the confession of his sins, and how he finally faced up to them as he bared his soul. It is such a sobering psalm it can reduce us to silence, as this is holy ground. Whenever I read Psalm 51 it is always with a tangible sense of sadness, and a profound sense of remorse permeates it. This is no half-hearted measure at saying 'sorry' or an attempt to deal superficially with sin. David not only violated his relationship with the Lord, but also despised the Lord (2 Sam 11: 27b) and displeased him (2 Sam. 12.13). But it was the Lord who took the initiative through Nathan to bring David to a place of repentance, to forgive and restore his relationship with him. 'As a whole the psalm is a prayer of unrelieved intensity and eloquence.'[65] 'Here with inflexible earnestness the uttermost depths of sin is grasped and the way is shown that leads to forgiveness and true communion with God.'[66]

Psalm 51 incorporates archaic metaphorical language that may seem alien. Equally, we may feel our sins have never been in the league that David committed, so we do not identify with his prayer of confession. But we should take care to be mindful of the fact that the Lord inspired the composition of Psalm 51 by his Holy Spirit. This psalm can help us to confess and repent of our sins especially when serious sins have been committed. Brueggemann touches upon this when he says, 'Real sin is a violation of relationship with God…On the face of it most sin is played out in the social arena. It is sin against the neighbour as this was. But here the psalmist sees that sin is a *theological* problem – not moral, ethical, social or psychological. The problem is that sin violates God. This does not mean that others are also not hurt. But the righting of the wrong concerns the 'goodness' of God and none other. In the flat world of modernity, this psalm affirms to us a forgotten reality. Our skewed lives finally must deal with God.'[67]

While we may view Psalm 51 from an individual interpretation Broyles points out, 'It does show remarkable affinity to several prophetic passages around the time of and after Judah's exile. 'Holy Spirit' in v. 11 only occurs in Isaiah 63:10-11 and the mention of a broken/contrite heart/spirit in v. 17, as an attribute pleasing God occurs only in Psalm 34:18, Isaiah 57:

15 and 66:2. Similarly, Isaiah 63:7–64, 12 is a prayer of penitence and reflects an exceptional intimacy with God. It too confesses the dilemma of human sin that no human effort can save one from. In its downward spiral only God can – Isaiah 63:16-17, 64:5-9. The main petition section of Psalm 51:7-12 is remarkably unique in The Psalter, but strongly paralleled by the promises of a new covenant found in exilic prophecies, in Ezek. 36: 24-32, Jer. 24: 7, 31: 31-34.'[68]

Mays also thinks, that there are features in Psalm 51 that suggest it was composed during or after the exile and was used in Israel as a general penitential prayer. 'In its present form its language and thought are connected with that of Jeremiah, Ezekiel and Isaiah 40-66. It reads like an anticipation of, or response to the promises of a new heart and spirit in Jer. 24:7, 31:33, 32:39-40 and Ezek. 36:25ff. Interpreted in this context some of the prayer's difficult points will make better theological sense, and v. 18-19 form an appropriate conclusion rather than a contradictory addition.'[69] We may use Psalm 51 in corporate worship or individually as a prayer of penitence.

Psalm 51 can be a wonderful healing liturgy for the person who knows they have committed serious sins. Especially, if they have lived with the guilt for some time, and long to find forgiveness and peace. Psalm 51 stands in stark contrast to contemporary worship where confession tends to be over quickly and lacks biblical content and reality. Equally, when a confession is used that someone has composed this can also lack substance. Having a corporate confession without any Scriptural introduction, and time to reflect on what we are coming to confess to the Lord, does not help people to deal with their sins. As we live in a culture where the notion of sin is weak, it may well be timely to use the Penitential Psalms on which to base our models of confession. General or superficial confessions can result in our not being forgiven and thoroughly cleansed from our sins, because we have not thoroughly confessed them. Here it is interesting to be aware of what S. Mowinckel says about the Penitential Psalms.

> It is part of old Israelite mentality and of the way of feeling and thinking in the psalms, that the poet will try to give as strong expression as possible in the confession of sins…there can be no doubt at all that in the psalms, we do find evidences of a really deep and spiritualised consciousness of sin.[70]

As I have been studying Psalm 51 I have been struck by the importance of *'confessing and naming'* our sins before God in worship. Goldingay highlights this aspect from Psalm 32. He points out that to keep quiet is not a mark of OT piety, and gives the impression and raises the suspicion that a person is concealing something. He says, 'If the worshipper covered over wrongdoing instead of acknowledging it, then Yhwh would not cover it over. Because the worshipper did not cover it over or stopped doing so, Yhwh has done so – Psalm 32: 5.'[71]

Similarly, Mays also emphasises that confession of sin must be said to God as secret remorse or intimations of guilt are not confession. He believes that such silence must be broken in God's presence and also when we have wronged someone. Because silence can negatively affect relationships and reflect stubborn pride or the fear of being found out. Confession of sin to God is also confession of faith in God. He also points out that confession of sin must be made with the integrity that Psalm 32: 1 refers to by the phrase: 'in whose spirit there is no deceit.' Because, although God is not deceived, the sinner may deceive himself and others too.[72]

There is a great deal of repetition and parallelism in Psalm 51. For example in v. 1-2 abundance/abundantly: v. 1, 9 wipe away: v. 2, 7 wash: v. 1, 3, 13 rebellion(s)rebels: v. 2, 5, 9 waywardness/ wayward acts.[73] 'The word for sin comes 12 times in v. 1-9 and twice in v. 10-12. God is named once in v. 1-9 and 6 times in v. 10-19. Sin gives way to God with confession, and sin gives way to God's presence. The poet literally and literarily is emptied of sin and filled with grace.'[74]

1-2 Have mercy on me O God, according to your steadfast love: according to your abundant mercy, blot out my transgressions. Wash me thoroughly from my iniquity, and cleanse me from my sin.

David's sins are so serious that he realises that even as the king he has no basis on which to make a plea for forgiveness. In v. 1 he can only approach the Lord and throw himself on his mercy, his steadfast love and his unfailing compassion. His appeal is to the nature of God revealed in Exodus 33: 12-23. Weiser says, 'The worshipper stretches out his hand towards God and implores him to have mercy on him.'[75] He knows that he is guilty and completely undeserving due to the seriousness of his sins against the Lord, and because he himself showed no mercy whatsoever to Uriah. David's only hope now totally rests on God. This is not an intellectual exercise in theology, or a spiritual transaction to balance the books in his favour. All the evidence clearly and conclusively shows that he is guilty of the most serious sins against the Lord. His appeal for mercy to the Lord can only come from a real sense of remorse and a genuinely contrite heart. In v. 1, therefore, he eloquently and truthfully pleads for forgiveness, 'blot out my transgressions.' This is a request for the Lord to remove and wipe out his sins against him so they no longer appear before the Lord. In v. 2 he goes a step further as his request is to be thoroughly washed from his iniquity and cleansed from his sins. Their impact has seeped deep into his soul and like a lead weight rest upon his spirit. He feels defiled by the invisible stain of his sins and washing as an outward sacramental sign signifies removing them. Goldingay says, 'The third verb *tahar* refers more intrinsically to a sacramental cleansing, that makes something defiled into something pure.'[76]

3-5 For I know my transgressions and my sin is ever before me. Against you, you only have I sinned and done that which is evil in your sight, so you are justified in your sentence and blameless in your judgment. Behold I was brought forth in iniquity, and in sin did my mother conceive me.

In v. 3-5 we now discern in David's confession, a profound self-awareness about the serious nature of his sins and their impact on the Lord – 'Against you, you only have I sinned and done that which is evil in your sight.' Having lived in denial for around a year about what he had done he has now come to his senses. As he does so, these verses show an acute awareness of his sins when he identifies them as evil. They indicate the first step to true penitence is a clear recognition of one's own sins.[77] David not only admits his sins, he also acknowledges they are against the Lord and accepts that God's judgment in his life is right. While no mention is made in Psalm 51 of his sins against Bathsheba and also against Uriah, we perceive that in retrospect he was referring to these. After all Uriah was dead and he had clearly committed adultery, two undeniable facts. Yet he had 'blotted out' of his mind that these sins were also against the Lord. Now he acknowledges what he had refused to face. Namely, his sins were also against the Lord, as he had violently broken his commandments and his relationship with the Lord. David's self-awareness of his actions now embraces something he had never before considered – the realisation he was born with a sinful nature. This was a profound shock to him compounded by the shocking facts he had slept with Bathsheba and murdered her husband. It would not be surprising if in retrospect he felt as if he was living out some nightmare from which he could not escape. After all, he was David the king, a man after God's own heart. How could he have done these things?

6-9 Behold, you desire truth in the inward being, therefore teach me wisdom in my secret heart. Purge me with hyssop and I shall be clean, wash me and I shall be whiter than snow. Fill me with joy and gladness: let the bones which you have broken rejoice. Hide your face from my sins and blot out all my iniquities.

David's awareness has been illuminated by the Holy Spirit as he confesses his sins that shed light on what the solution is. He knows that he needs the comprehensive work of God to rescue him from his situation. In v. 6, 'You desire truth in the inward being' indicates at some stage he must have convinced himself that to sleep with Bathsheba was acceptable. What was clearly wrong presented itself to David's imagination as right, rather than sinful. In looking back, he can clearly see that he had deceived himself. What he concluded was true, had indeed turned out to be false. What he considered had been right, had conclusively proved to be sinful. God desired integrity from David as the basis of his confession and repentance. He had to be honest with himself and truthful with God. There is no room for denial before the Lord if we long to claim his forgiveness. 'God is concerned for truthfulness and insight in the way people talk and behave behind closed doors.'[78] In hindsight David's sins had been calamitously foolish so his request in v. 6 is, 'therefore teach me wisdom in my secret heart.' Wisdom that acknowledges 'the fear of the Lord.'

In v. 6-9 David reveals that his sins have left an indelible stain on his soul. Here, he repeats his request in v. 1-2 for cleansing – 'purge me and I shall be clean' – 'wash me, and I shall be whiter than snow' – 'hide your face from my sins and blot out my iniquities.' Radical sins require radical removal. Sins that he knows he cannot eradicate himself. Hyssop was a small ordinary plant and because of its shape, it was used as a small brush for the sacramental sprinkling of blood or water. David heart's had been contaminated by his sins, and to refer to hyssop was asking the Lord for the symbolic sacramental rite of sprinkling, to cleanse and wash him, and to blot out and remove his sins.

In v. 7-9 his petition asks the Lord, 'to purge' – 'wash' – 'hide and blot out.' Bruggemann says this about David's request for cleansing. 'In v. 7-9 we are dealing mainly with cultic language with words already used in v. 1-2. The speaker is apparently ready to undergo ritual washing physically to remove the stain and shame of sins. This is indeed going public with the acknowledged burden. In v. 8 as in Psalm 32: 3-4 it is as though some physical problem has arisen out of the guilt so that healing restores the whole person. Note that in v. 6 there is a request for wisdom and here a petition for restoration of bones. The two motifs are brought together in Proverbs 3: 8: 'Wisdom will be healing to your flesh and refreshment (medicine) to your bones. Psalm 51 suggests that a great deal of work needs to be done in our understanding of the effect of sin in our lives and what it does to our bodies.'[79]

In v. 9 David says to the Lord, 'let the bones which you have broken rejoice.' It is possible that there are Christians who may not recognise the hand of the Lord convicting them physically. We like David should not be too surprised that when the Lord convicts us of our sins, there is heaviness in our spirit or we may feel physically oppressed or weighed down. Psalm 32: 3-4 acts as a commentary on v. 10: 'When I declared not my sin, my body wasted away through my groaning all the day long. For day and night your hand was heavy upon me: my strength was dried up as by the heat of summer.' God is not out to make us feel physically oppressed or ill at ease for the sake of it. But he may use these means to convict us that we are not facing up to sin in our lives as this spoils our relationship with him. His heavy hand of conviction with its physical repercussions is intended to identify our sin so that we may repent of it. And we should not be too surprised when the Lord takes the initiative in this way. In v. 9 David tenaciously appeals to the Lord, 'Fill me with joy and gladness, and the let the bones which you have broken rejoice.' This indicates that he has been through a very unhappy period in his life. It points to an absence of joy and gladness in his relationship with the Lord, and that he has probably been depressed for some time.

10-11 Create in me a clean heart O God, and renew a right spirit within me. Cast me not away form your presence and take not your Holy Spirit from me. Restore to me the joy of your salvation, and uphold me with a willing spirit.

Verse 10 marks a dramatic point of transition in David's prayer of confession. He is well aware that while the Lord will cleanse and forgive him, and pardon and blot out his sins, he is still in need of inner spiritual renewal on a profound level. Having used metaphors for ceremonial outward cleansing in his appeal to the Lord, he now expresses his desire for inner purity and the transformation of his heart. His sins can be dealt with, but the condition of his heart requires restoration.

'Create (bara) is a rare verb, suggesting the sovereign power God exercises in doing something seemingly impossible...In effect the suppliant is asking God to do a transformative work in the inner person, that deals not only with the stain that results from past wrongdoing, but also with the dynamics that will continue to produce wrongdoing.'[80] Here Boice sees that David's appeal is for the Lord to 'create a clean heart' is a startling one.[81] This indicates that this was not a matter of wiping the slate clean, like using a cloth to wipe a table clean. His sins had contaminated him to the extent that he needed God to create a new heart and a new spirit in him. Something that is much more radical than just being forgiven for some superficial sin. 'Because of the inclination to sin that has caused the brokenness, this creative work needs to issue in a heart that is pure and stays pure…The verb 'make a new' – *hadas* often means repair or restore and that would fit with the idea that the suppliant's spirit is broken…In keeping with the parallelism then, v. 10b asks God totally to transform and not merely to repair something old.'[82] 'Spirit' thus restates 'heart' but goes beyond it, because 'spirit' draws attention to the dynamism of the inner springs of a person's being. A dynamism that reflects the fact God is spirit and is the one who breathes spirit into the person. Paradoxically, perhaps the suppliant then asks, that this spirit God creates should be a 'steadfast' one: it should combine stability with dynamism. A steadfast spirit will lack the weakness the psalm has implied, the susceptibility to rebelliousness, waywardness and failure. It will be firm and reliable, determined and committed, prepared and set to go God's way.[83]

As the Holy Spirit impressed on David the necessity of the Lord creating a clean heart and a new spirit within him, Goldingay has very perceptively and profoundly put his finger on the issue of the confession of sin and the need for spiritual renewal, that is integral to maintain our walk with the Lord. Confession as has already been pointed out in contemporary worship often tends to be a very superficial act. We compose lightweight prayers of confession that in practice are virtually worthless in their impact, because they do not deal with our sin or the condition of our heart or spirit. They do not acknowledge to the Lord, to ourselves or to others, that we are in need of so much more radical transformation in our lives for lasting spiritual renewal. Confession of sin has to be accompanied by a request for the Lord to renew our hearts and our spirits. Otherwise, we may well find that patterns of sin that repeat themselves are not broken. Ezekiel 36:26-27 also highlights that it is the work of God to give his people a new heart and a new spirit in order to be able to keep God's commandments.

Now that David has come to confess his sins and repent of them, he has become aware that he may justly receive the Lord's punishment for what he has done. So serious were his sins, that the Lord's judgment may have taken his Holy Spirit from him and barred him from his presence. The example of what happened to Saul was a warning to him about this possibility. God's presence and his Holy Spirit that were the two most precious things in his life could potentially be lost permanently. He may have continued to enjoy God's blessing to some extent, but he did not want to lose the closeness of his relationship with the Lord he had known throughout his life. And he did not want to lose the anointed power of the Holy Spirit in his rule as the king. He earnestly prays to have God's presence and the Holy Spirit, as he does not take it for granted that they will automatically be restored to him.

'Restore to me the joy of your salvation' indicates that during the recent past when David was living with the consequences of his sin, he was acutely aware that he had lost the joy of his salvation in his relationship with the Lord. His sin had not brought him any lasting joy or pleasure. He only reaped the opposite. He would have found that he could not rejoice in the Lord or praise him during this time, and he could not pray to him or enjoy his presence. He knew that only if the Lord was gracious and merciful could these things be restored to him. 'The fact that the psalmist prays for so many things in v. 7-12 indicates how many things he knew he had lost when he plunged into sin.'[84] 'Uphold me with a willing spirit' might mean David knows he needs the Lord's help in the future to stand firm and upright. But there is some ambiguity about this and it might be interpreted that he needs to be strengthened by the Lord to have a willing spirit to walk in his ways.

Whichever it is, this highlights David is keenly aware that he is susceptible to sin, in a way that he previously thought he was impervious to.

Brueggemann with penetrating insight sees more than meets the eye in these verses concerning the issue of 'spirit.' He says, 'If we assume this Psalm is linked to David, he received the wind/spirit in 1 Sam. 16 which enabled him to rule as king eventually. The tradition recognises that due to the seriousness of his sins he has lost the power of Yahweh authorising him to rule. The wind to govern is gladly given by Yahweh – Isaiah 11.2 – but it is never possessed. It is always held in trust. Sin can destroy God's royal mandate for David and for us. Such utterly alien sin can leave us powerless and without authority for living our lives. That much the psalmist knows. He places himself utterly at the disposal of Yahweh and asks for a re-issue of gifts that make a regal life possible. This act of deep repentance assumes a posture in which the gift of power for governance might be given.'[85]

13-14 Then I will teach transgressors your ways and sinners shall return to you. Deliver me from blood-guiltiness O God, the God of my salvation, and my tongue will sing aloud of your deliverance.

At first glance v. 13-14 seem out of place and do not naturally follow, or tie in with the train of thought up to this point. But in the psalms, there are occasions after the psalmist has made his petition to the Lord when he senses this has been answered and his response is to testify to this. Biblical commentators indicate that David has an obligation to witness to the community at worship about his deliverance, so that anyone who has sinned is encouraged to return to the Lord and praise him. To be delivered from blood-guiltiness may be a reference to David's sins and retribution for them. Goldingay points out, that the verb for bloodguilt, suggests the idea of being rescued from having one's own blood being shed. One might be killed as an act of retribution for having shed blood.[86]

15-17 O Lord open my lips and my mouth shall declare your praise. For you have no delight in sacrifice: were I to give a burnt offering you would not be pleased. The sacrifice acceptable to God is a broken spirit: a broken and contrite heart O God, you will not despise.

Weiser succinctly sums up David's train of thought in v. 15. 'How completely the worshipper considers himself dependent on God in everything, is evident from the fact that even the praise of God in the midst of the congregation becomes for him a gift from God, for which he now asks.'[87] David knows that due to his sinfulness he is not able to praise the Lord in and of himself. He is reliant on God to enable him to praise Him. He has clearly perceived that to offer sacrifices in corporate worship is not God's primary delight. What the Lord is looking for is the condition of the worshipper's heart. He is looking for a humble heart and a penitent spirit, not a rebellious or a stubborn heart, or a proud or unrepentant spirit.

PSALM 69
MAN OF SORROWS

The superscription of Psalm 69 is according *'to the Lilies.'* The lilies are traditionally linked with springtime and Passover season and they luxuriate in the valleys and grow among thorns. Nothing can be in higher contrast than the beautiful velvety softness of the lily and the thorns. The lily speaks of the purity of our Lord. On the cross, they put a crown of thorns on his head and in contrast, we have the lily with its perfect form, spotless purity, vivid colour, fragrant odour. Psalm 69 is associated with the lily of the valley.[88]

If David is the author of Psalm 69, it is difficult to identify the historical situation it refers to and some biblical commentators feel we cannot identify who wrote it. As we shall see, there are similarities between Psalm 22 and Psalm 69. Mays believes that Psalm 69 clearly belongs to the exilic/post-exilic period (see v 35-36), and comes from circles who in the hardships of those times persisted in 'waiting for God' and were treated with scorn. Jeremiah has often been identified with Psalm 69 as he suffered reproach from his own people. He was also zealous for God's house (Jer. 7) and was literally thrown into deep mire at the bottom of a cistern (Jer. 38).[89] Equally, Goldingay suggests the circumstances and attitudes in Psalm 69 also recall those of Jeremiah who was literally in danger of sinking in the mud in a cistern, and who pleaded for action against his persecutors, as Nehemiah did.[90]

Psalm 69 can be divided primarily into two categories: plea in v. 1, v. 6, v. 13-18 and v. 22-29, protest in v. 7-12 and v. 19-21, with a concluding confession of trust in v 30-36. Verses 7-12 portray David's commitment to the Lord and indicate his enemies are from within his own community. Verse 6 also suggests that to some extent he also represents others in the community. Vivid metaphors in Psalm 69 describe the acute danger he found himself in. Verse 2 and 13 mention *'sinking in the mire'* – v. 2 and 14 *'deep water'* – v. 2 and 15 *'let not the flood sweep over me, or the deep swallow me up, or the pit close its mouth over me.'* The distressing image of being overwhelmed by water, sinking in the mire, swallowed up by the deep or immersed in the pit – is one of being overwhelmingly close to death.

It is of interest to note, if David is the author of Psalm 69 we cannot identify the period or actual situation it refers to, as he never faced imminent death as this psalm portrays, although the same could be said about Psalm 22. Bearing in mind he was pursued by Saul and his son Absalom rebelled against him we cannot identify a time in David's life that v. 8-15 refer to. When did he become a stranger to his brethren and an alien to his mother's sons – v. 8? When did he ever become a byword and the talk of those who sat at the gate of the city – v. 11-12? Or when was he in such acute danger of facing death because of his enemies – v. 14-15? We also cannot identify a time when v. 20-28 refer to David. What was the occasion when insults broke his heart – v. 20? What was the occasion when he was given poison for food and vinegar to drink? Also, we are not aware that the curse of v. 22-28 ever happened to his enemies.

Along with Psalm 22 Psalm 69 is clearly a Messianic Psalm. Next to Psalm 22, it is the one most frequently quoted in the New Testament. In fact, seven of its verses are directly quoted, although other verses such as v. 5 do not relate to Christ. The psalmist states that he is a servant of the Lord – v. 17, 35. Moreover, that it is the Lord who has allowed him to be 'smitten' by his enemies – v. 26. This is almost an echo of Psalm 22: 14, 'Thou (Lord) dost lay me in the dust of death.' Weiser says:

> After Psalm 22, Psalm 69, is the most quoted in the New Testament and so was interpreted in a Messianic sense as referring to Christ. Although originally the individual statements were not meant to be understood as prophecies pointing to Jesus, this deeply moving testimony to human suffering nevertheless exhibits features which are so characteristic of suffering in general, that their relation to Christ who has borne the suffering of the whole world, automatically forces itself upon any serious consideration of the psalm.[91]

1-4 Save me O God, for the waters have come up to my neck. I sink in deep mire where there is no foothold: I have come into deep waters and the flood sweeps over me. I am weary with my crying, my throat is parched. My eyes grow dim with waiting for my God. More in number than the hairs of my head are those who hate me without cause: mighty are those who would destroy me, those who attack me with lies.

At the beginning of Psalm 69, there is a palpable sense of desperation because of unanswered prayer for deliverance from the psalmist's enemies. From v. 3 we get the impression he has been waiting for a long period of time for God to answer. But clearly, God has not listened. He has not answered his prayer and he is distraught. In this respect Psalm 69:1-3 is reminiscent of the start of Psalm 22. Also, Psalm 69:17 says, 'Hide not your face from your servant for I am in distress, make haste to answer me.' This is reminiscent of Psalm 22:19, 'But thou O Lord be not far off. O thou my help, hasten to my aid.' And as is the established pattern of a lament psalm and in Psalm 22, the psalmist goes into detail about his situation to prompt the Lord to answer his prayer. As he does so there is the temptation to think he is exaggerating the danger that he is in, because of his vivid images and metaphors. There may well be an element of imaginative hyperbole in this genre of lament and plea for help. As a result, it is difficult to know if his feelings about his enemies actually reflect the danger they pose to him. But Psalm 69: 19-21 indicates both may be real: ‘You know my reproach and my shame and dishonour: my foes are all known to you. Insults have broken my heart so that I am in despair. I looked for pity but there was none: and for comforters but found none. They gave me poison for food and for my thirst gave me vinegar to drink.’

Verses 1-4 focus on the suffering servant of God. ‘There could scarcely be a more unnerving image of what it was like for Christ to be forsaken by his Father. Psalm 22:1 gave Christ his words, these verses give a picture – a flood or worse a quicksand – mire...*(that threaten to overwhelm him).* If that kind of disorientation is your nightmare, Christ has been through it before you and for you. It is v. 4 that Christ actually quotes and that not on Good Friday, but on Maundy Thursday in the calm before the storm. To the disciples in the upper room he explains that he will go to the cross, because of those who *‘hate him without reason’*[92] – John 15: 25: ‘It is to fulfill the word that is written in their law, ‘They hated me without cause.’ Hebrews 5:7 can also be seen to reflect v. 1-4: ‘In the days of his flesh Jesus offered up prayers and supplications with loud cries and tears to him who was able to save him from death and he was heard for his godly fear.’

7-13 For it is for your sake that I have borne reproach, that shame has covered my face. I have become a stranger to my brethren, an alien to my mother’s sons. For zeal for your house has consumed me and the insults of those who insult you have fallen on me. When I humbled my soul with fasting, it became my reproach. When I made sackcloth my clothing, I became a byword to them. I am the talk of those who sit in the gate, and the drunkards made songs about me.

The reproach and shame of the psalmist, God's servant, is a distinctive feature and figures prominently in Psalm 69. The clear implication in v. 7 is that this happens to him because of God and on behalf of God. Reproach comes in v. 7, 10 and 19, while shame comes in v. 6, 7 and 19. We can identify Christ, God's suffering, sorrowful servant with the rejection, reproach, and shame in this psalm. This is also poignantly mentioned in Isaiah 53:3: 'He was despised and rejected by men: a man of sorrows and acquainted with grief: and as one from whom men hide their faces, he was despised and we esteemed him not.' Paul in Romans 15:3 also said of Christ: 'The reproaches of those who reproached you fell on me' – an echo of Psalm 69. Goldingay says, 'The shame affects the attitude of the suppliant's family. The line implies more than that. The family are horrified at what they see…They disown the suppliant like a family disowning someone who has committed a terrible crime…It is the closest family, the people with whom the suppliant lives, who have turned away.'[93]

From the New Testament we can readily identify Christ with v. 9: 'For zeal for your house has consumed me.' We see this in John 2 when Jesus drove out from the Temple those who were selling oxen, sheep and pigeons and the money-changers. As a commentary on this, we read in John 2:17: 'Jesus' disciples remembered that it was written: 'Zeal for your house will consume me.' M. E. Tate says: 'The nature of the speaker's zealous action is unfocused, but the context suggests deep concern about the behaviour of some in the community, whose actions are contrary to those appropriate for the 'house of God.'[94] Jer. Ch. 7 portrays God's zeal for his Temple, that was reflected in Jesus' action in John 2. God's own zeal found the worship of his people unacceptable. In Jer. Ch. 7 they had a false confidence in their worship expressed in the mantra 'the temple of the Lord.' Zeal indicates Jesus cared passionately for the glory of God concerning the Temple and its worship and what went on in its precincts. He had the courage to confront the compromises of these practices. We may well ask what it means to be zealous for the glory of God in our worship.

13-21 But as for me my prayer is to you O Lord. At an acceptable time O God, in the abundance of your steadfast love answer me. With your faithful help, rescue me from sinking in the mire: let me be delivered from my enemies and from the deep waters. Let not the flood sweep over me, or the deep swallow me up or the pit close its mouth over me. Answer me, O Lord, for your steadfast love is good: according to your abundant mercy turn to me. Hide not your face from your servant for I am in distress, make haste to answer me. Draw near to me, redeem me, set me free because of my enemies. You know my reproach and my shame and my dishonour: my foes are all known to you. Insults have broken my heart so that I am in despair. I looked for pity and there was none, and for comforters but I found none. They gave me poison for food, and for my thirst, they gave me vinegar to drink.

Psalm 69 reminds us that the Lament Psalms describe the psalmist's situation to the Lord by expressing his feelings using vivid metaphors. It is as if a liturgical drama unfolds to get God's attention, especially as he has not yet answered his prayer, and from the psalmist's perspective has not listened to him. After v. 13 we encounter a dramatic plea for deliverance, calling upon God's steadfast love, faithfulness, and abundant mercy to respond to him. There is also a note of urgency in his prayer, 'make haste to help me' – v. 17. His request also appeals to the Lord, 'Hide not your face from your servant.' It is as if he is establishing his right to have his prayer answered, especially as the Lord hiding his face inferred he was not with him or listening to his prayer. God hiding his face could mean his disapproval. We can also identify the request to be saved from the deep waters, the flood, and the pit, that all signify the prospect of being overwhelmed by death with Jesus and his agony in his prayer in the garden of Gethsemane, with Heb. 5:7: 'In the days of his flesh, Jesus offered up prayers and supplications, with loud cries and tears to him who was able to save him from death, and he was heard for his godly fear.'

In Psalm 69 the servant points out his suffering is clearly on behalf of the Lord – v. 7. In v. 19-21 he shares the extent of his suffering and tragedy as he recalls difficulty upon difficulty that increasingly worsens his humiliation that began in v. 7. In v. 20-22, 'Family solidarity essential for survival has given way to distrust and hostility. Therefore, the craving for human support, even traditional signs of sympathy, condolence, comfort, bread of pity, have not been extended to the one in sorrow and anxiety. Instead, social ties are broken: this is a cause for alarm and physical suffering. A vivid description of social ostracism is given in v. 6-9. Treacherous friends increase the pain by their calumny.'[95] From v. 7-21 we have seen that we can identify with Christ, the moving description of the sorrows and suffering of the servant in Isaiah 53:3.

The word reproach occurs six times in Psalm 69 and twice in v. 19-20. Jesus was mocked as a prophet before the Sanhedrin: 'And some began to spit upon him and to cover his face and to strike him saying to him, 'prophesy!' And the guards received him with blows' – Mark 14:65. Jesus was mocked by Pilate as a King and the Roman soldiers staged a mock coronation ceremony. 'And they clothed him in a purple robe and plaiting a crown of thorns they put it on him. And they began to salute him, 'Hail King of the Jews. And they struck his head with a reed, and spat upon him and knelt down in homage to him. And when they had mocked him, they stripped him of the purple cloak and put his own clothes on him. And they led him out to crucify him' – Mark 15:17-20.

On the cross Jesus was also mocked as the Saviour. 'And those who passed by derided him wagging their heads and saying: 'You who would destroy the temple and build it in three days, save yourself and come down from the cross!' So also the chief priests mocked him to one another with the scribes saying, 'He saved others: he cannot save himself. Let the Christ, the King of Israel, come down now from the cross that we may see and believe.' Those who were crucified with him also reviled him' – Mark 15:29-32. Here we see that prior to his crucifixion Mark's account poignantly portrays the mockery and scorn Jesus endured, for our sake and for his

Father's sake on the cross. Handel's Messiah takes up the theme of Psalm 69:20, 'Scorn has broken my heart.'

Psalm 69:21, 'for my thirst they gave me vinegar to drink' – is alluded to or quoted in each of the four Gospels, in Matt. 27: 34, 48; Mark 15:23, 36; Luke 23:36 and John 19:29. John's reference is the most precise because he says that Jesus was offered vinegar to drink – 'so that the Scripture would be fulfilled' – a reference to Psalm 69. 'Because of its relation to the pattern and the correspondence of the life of Jesus to it, Psalm 69 was used repeatedly in the New Testament for Christological and theological purposes. It furnished a context for reflection on Jesus' rejection by his own people – John 15: 25: on his motive in driving traders from the temple – John 3: 17: on the bitter treatment he was given instead of pity at the time of his death – John 19 and of the meaning of his suffering – Rom. 15:3…Even the harsh prayer against the persecutors in v. 22-28…Paul found here a clue to the hardening of those in Israel who rejected Jesus – Rom. 11:9-10. For the prophet of Revelation it pointed to the eschatological outpouring of wrath, against the foes of the coming kingdom of God – Rev. 16.1.

> Psalm 69 cannot be read directly as the prayer of Jesus, or as an intentional prophecy of his suffering. But it does provide a reflection on the passion of one who bore reproach, for the sake of his God and by the way he bore it…'[96]

Verses 22-28 are indeed difficult to interpret. In the context of the Old Testament, we know the psalmist in the Imprecatory Psalms that refer to his enemies, calls on God for vengeance, retribution and even on occasions as in Psalm 69 for their destruction. In effect, it is asking for suitable punishment in return – 'For they persecute him whom you have smitten, and him whom you have wounded, they still afflict more' – v. 26. There is intensity in the request for retributive justice on ones enemies in the psalm that increases as v. 22-28 unfold. This begins with a request for their table fellowship to become a snare and for family and friends to turn against them – v. 22. The psalmist then asks for serious illness – physical affliction to come upon them permanently – v. 23. He compounds this with a request for God's wrath and anger to overwhelm them – v. 24. His request escalates to their camp, presumably their accomplices and household, being desolate and devastated, wiped out – v. 25. These horrific requests are truly terrifying in v. 27-28: 'Add to them punishment upon punishment: may they have no acquittal from you. Let them be blotted out of the book of the living: let them not be enrolled among the righteous.' 'It is to the comfort of all right thinking people that determined destructive evil, should in the end meet its match and be itself destroyed. This is why so many of the psalms rejoice in God's coming judgment.'[97] Konrad Schaefer comments on v 22-28:

> The curse amounts to a request for the extinction of the family, an empty home – v. 25. A strong personal faith ascribes everything that happens to God's knowledge, plan and power, even the suffering which has incited this enemy assault – v. 26. The force of the anathema demands the adversary be ex-communicated from the community of the devout – v. 27-28. Retributive justice is passionately invoked.[98]

The logic of the severe punishment presumably is to match the extreme persecution his enemies inflicted upon him that almost resulted in his death. This may well be based on Exodus 21:24: 'eye for eye, tooth for tooth.' To pray in this way was not controversial for the psalmist as God had destroyed Israel's enemies in the past. In effect, the psalmist was calling on God to be the one who executed his judgment on them. What stares us in the face and startles us is how to reconcile these verses with Jesus' words, 'love your enemies and pray for those who hate you' – Matt. 5:43-45. 'Alexander Maclaren handles the seemingly incompatibility of Psalm 69 with this text when he says: 'It is impossible to bring such utterances into harmony with the teachings of Jesus and the attempt to vindicate them ignores plain facts and does violence to plain words. Better far to let them stand as a monument of the earlier stage of God's progressive revelation and discern clearly the advance which Christian ethics has made on them.'[99] It is also possible to perceive a prophetic dimension to them that the psalmist never envisaged, when we see God's wrath poured out in the book of Revelation, as for example in Ch. 16-17.

29-36 But I am afflicted and in pain: let your salvation O God set me on high. I will praise the name of God with a song, I will magnify him with thanksgiving. This will please the Lord more than an ox or a bull with horns and hoofs. Let the oppressed see it and be glad, you who seek God let your hearts revive. For the Lord hears the needy and does not despise his own that are in bonds. Let heaven and earth praise him, the seas and everything that moves in it. For God will save Zion and rebuild the cities of Judah and his servants shall dwell there and possess it. The children of his servants shall inherit it and those who love his name shall dwell in it.

As in Psalm 22, the last section of Psalm 69 also assumes a transition has taken place. God has heard the psalmist's prayer and rescued him from his enemies, although we are not told how this happened. We must assume v. 29 has taken place and salvation has come and the psalmist has been set on high – lifted up from the swirling waters of death that threatened him. As in Psalm 22, the ending of Psalm 69 bursts forth into praise, and if David is the author v. 33 is likely to have been the last line – because the rebuilding of the cities of Judah came from a later age than his. Verse 33 also reassures the reader that God does indeed hear the prayer of those in desperate need.

As in Psalm 22, the ending of Psalm 69 is ecstatic in its praise of God. 'In the end the poet will invite 'the seas and everything that moves in them to praise' – v. 34 – how complete the rescue! Threatening waters have been tamed. The complaint is concluded with the hope for Zion, the cities of Judah and the present and future generations of the devout – v. 35-36. Along with Psalm 22 this psalm is frequently quoted in the gospels in relation to Christ's suffering.'[100] In these verses, we find a cosmic and an international call to praise the Lord, not unlike that of the last lines in Psalm 22. 'The sufferer with his sorrow gives way to a song of praise. The singer in v. 29 prays, 'Let your salvation, O God, set me up on high!' The answer to the prayer is the resurrection and ascension. The Lord is the only one of the sons of men, to sing on both sides of the sea of death.'[101]

PSALM 95
WORSHIP

Psalms 93-100 can be classified together as a group. Most of them explicitly praise the Lord as king and all of them celebrate his rule and authority. Psalm 95 is a canticle known as *The Venite* in the liturgy of the Church of England. Having preached on this psalm in the past, what particularly struck me about it this time, is how it anticipates that God's people may come and have a wonderfully joyful celebration worshipping him – but may leave without responding to the Lord speaking to them. A reminder of the danger of celebratory worship.

GET READY TO PRAISE

1-5 O come let us sing to the Lord, let us make a joyful noise to the rock of our salvation. Let us come into his presence with thanksgiving and into his courts with praise: let us make a joyful noise to him with songs of praise. For the Lord is a great God and a great king above all gods. In his hand are the depths of the earth: the heights of the mountains are his also. The sea is his for he made it, for his hands formed dry land.

This psalm is an invitation to join in a procession of praise into God's presence and to rejoice in the Lord along the way. The worshippers are exhorted to joyfully declare the truths in v. 3-5 about the Lord. The atmosphere is exuberant and uplifting as God is the object of their praise. We can imagine the worship leader encouraging God's people to spontaneously shout out praise to the Lord because he is the rock of their salvation. Salvation at the Exodus from Egypt and from Israel's enemies, and salvation for New Testament believers through Christ's death on the cross are why we worship God.

In this psalm, the Lord teaches us that we should come into his presence and praise him with thanksgiving for who he is and what he has done for us. Here the worship leader reminds the congregation of two great truths about the Lord: 'He is a great God and a great king above all gods.' He is the living God and all others are idols. A truth that God's people would relate to in the OT that speaks to us about the Lord's reign and rule. God's greatness is described in terms of having the world in his hands because in the first place his hands formed the world. These verses speak to us about God's greatness as our Creator and as we look at the splendour and magnificence of creation, we can readily see God's greatness. Clearly, God is a great God and has the world in his hands.

GET READY TO WORSHIP

6-7a O come, let us worship and bow down, let us kneel before the Lord, our Maker. For he is our God and we are the people of his pasture and the sheep of his hand.

The worship leader now senses that it is time to move from exuberantly praising the Lord to worshipping him. We have a transition as he calls for the rejoicing and singing to be replaced by a calmer, quieter atmosphere. Silence and stillness comes over the congregation as they bow and kneel before Lord. 'The Hebrew text uses the verbs in direct sequence to one another so that the text literally reads, 'Come, let us prostrate ourselves, let us bow down, let us kneel.'[102]

The action of praise gives way to intimate worship, as God's presence has been manifest amongst them. The mood is now one of humility and reverence as the truths begin to sink into peoples' hearts that the Lord is their God and Maker. God who is the Creator is also the God who cares for his people and who sustains them like a shepherd who cares for his sheep. The objective truths about the Lord as God who reigns, give way to the more personal truths that the Lord is in a covenant relationship with his people. In the quietness of their hearts, there is adoration as they worship the Lord in his manifest presence. Praise was not just to make them feel better. It was the prelude to encountering the Lord and his presence.

GET READY TO OBEY

7b-11 O that today you would hearken to his voice. Harden not your hearts as at Meribah, as on the day at Massah in the wilderness, when your fathers tested me and put me to the proof though they had seen my work. For forty years I loathed that generation and said: 'They are a people who err in their hearts for they do not regard my ways.' Therefore, I swore in my anger that they should not enter my rest.

The initial reaction to the change in content and tone in these verses jars. Goldingay suggests that the people have been exhorted to praise the Lord and worship him in an overtly celebratory manner and then they have been set up.[103] Set up to be severely chastised in the following verses. Yet in the context it is not out of place, as during their quiet adoration, the Lord has deliberately challenged them with a warning about his severe judgment if they are disobedient, harden their hearts and do not listen to the voice of the Lord. Their praise and worship leads to a warning about possible punishment.

There is such an abrupt and unexpected transition after v. 7a, that one or two biblical commentators think Psalm 95 ends here. If that is the case, it resembles Psalm 100 as a complete entity. Bearing in mind the possible setting of this psalm in a procession of joyful celebration it is not out of the question that v. 7b-11 are a warning that the Lord requires we listen to his voice in the context of our worship. This is a reminder that obedience is an integral aspect of worshipping the Lord. Heb.3: 7-15 quotes Psalm 95 four times, as a warning not to become complacent and harden our hearts by ignoring the voice and word of the Lord. Psalm 95 can be seen as more aesthetically appealing if it ends at v. 7a in which case it parallels Psalm 100. But Kidner sees the latter part of Psalm 95 as appropriate.

> Annually at the Feast of Tabernacles, Israel in holiday mood remembered the wilderness…and was doubtless tempted to romanticise it as an idyllic age. What God remembered and reminded her of in Psalm 95, was her ingratitude and unbelief and his anger and disgust. It was a 'cold douche of realism.'[104]

FOOTNOTES

PREFACE

1. D. Jobling 1 Samuel Liturgical Press 1998 69
2. W. Brueggemann 1 & 2 Samuel JKnox 1988 108
3. D. Jobling ibid 3, 18, 19-20
4. P. Borgman David, Saul & God Oxford U. Press 2008 9

CHAPTER ONE

1. T. Cartledge 1 & 2 Samuel Smyth & Helwys 2001 19
2. F. B. Meyer Great Men Of God In The Bible Marshall & Pickering 1990 260
3. J. Godingay Men Behaving Badly Paternoster 2001 16-17
4. R. Alter The David Story Norton & Co. 2000 xv-xvi
5. J. Goldingay ibid 313-314
6. W. Bruegemann ibid 1-2
7. P. Borgman ibid 195
8. R. Alter ibid xviii
9. Ibid 16, 1
10. P. Borgman ibid 9
11. C. Swindoll David A Man Of Passion & Destiny Word 1997 4
12. P. Borgman ibid 8
13. Ibid 41
14. J. Alter ibid 4
15. P. Borgman ibid 45-46
16. Ibid xxi
17. R. J. Fontaine, J. Wojcik Purdue U. Press 1980 99-100
18. Ibid 102
19. C. Morrison 2 Samuel Liturgical Press 2013 64
20. D. Jobling ibid 98-99
21. Ibid 99
22. S. Bar God's First King Cascade Books 2013 xiv
23. E. Bock King & Prophets – Saul, etc Floris Books 2006 43-47
24. P. Long The Reign & Rejection Of King Saul Scholars Press 1989 202-203

25. Ibid 203
26. Ibid 41
27. B. Green King Saul's Asking Liturgical Press 2003 xviii
28. Ibid xix
29. Ibid 406
30. C. Morrison ibid 14
31. Ibid 15
32. D. Firth 1 & 2 Samuel IVP 2009 42
33. Ibid 43-45
34. Ibid 44-45
35. C. Morrison ibid 7-8
36. T. Tsumura 1 Samuel Eerdmans 2007 68
37. Daniel New David Internet
38. Manners, Customs Of Bible Lands Internet
39. B. Webb Judges Eerdmans 2012 13
40. Ibid 14-15
41. B. Webb ibid 14-15
42. T. Tsumura Ibid 35-36
43. Ibid 36-37
44. Ibid 37
45. P. Borgman ibid 4
46. Ibid 11
47. C. Morrison ibid 11
48. Ibid 9

CHAPTER TWO

1. D. Firth ibid 109
2. T. Tsumura ibid 242
3. Ibid 249
4. T. Cartledge ibid 112
5. T. Tsumura ibid 249
6. W. Brueggemann ibid 61
7. Ibid 63
8. D. Firth ibid 116
9. Ibid 116
10. Ibid 116
11. W. Brueggeman 66
12. B. Green ibid 38

13. J. Goldingay Ibid 73
14. W. Brueggeman 171
15. T. Tsumura ibid 264
16. Ibid 265
17. T. Cartledge ibid 123
18. P. Long ibid 1989 202
19. P. Borgman ibid 19
20. P. Long ibid 200
21. Ibid 240
22. W. Brueggemann ibid 72
23. D. Firth ibid 123
24. T. Tsumura ibid 278
25. J. Goldingay ibid 76
26. J. Woodhouse 1 Samuel Crossway 2008 164
27. T. Tsumura ibid 277
28. P. Borggman ibid 20
29. Ibid 21
30. T. Cartledge ibid 128
31. M. Evans Samuel IVP 2004 68
32. W. Brueggemann ibid 74
33. T. Tsumura ibid 285
34. D. Firth ibid 126
35. W. Brueggemann ibid 75
36. M. Evans ibid 62, 68
37. Ibid 68
38. T. Cartledge ibid 139
39. W. Brueggemann ibid 75
40. D. Firth ibid 127
41. J. Woodhouse ibid 184
42. T. Cartledge ibid 142
43. W. Brueggemann ibid 81
44. R. Alter ibid 58
45. S. Bar ibid 19, 21
46. D. Firth ibid 134
47. W. Brueggemann ibid 80
48. T. Tsumura ibid 299
49. T. Cartledge ibid 143-4
50. T. Tsumura ibid 300

51. J. Woodhouse ibid 188
52. W. Brueggemann ibid 82
53. M. Evans ibid 75
54. D. Firth ibid 139
55. W. Brueggemann ibid 85
56. Ibid 85
57. T. Tsumura ibid 313
58. M. Evans 78
59. W. Brueggemann ibid 89
60. Ibid 92
61. Ibid 93
62. Ibid 93
63. Ibid 95
64. J. Woodhouse ibid 221
65. Ibid 221

CHAPTER THREE

1. W. Brueggemann ibid 98
2. Ibid 101
3. M. Evans ibid 88
4. T. Tsumura ibid 331
5. B. Green ibid 46
6. T. Tsumura ibid 352
7. G. Vreeland The Darker Side Of Samuel, Saul & David Xulon Press 2007 139-140
8. P. Long ibid 87
9. T. Tsumura ibid 346
10. D. Edelman King Saul in the Historiography of Judah Library of Hebrew Bible/Old Testament Studies 2009 320
11. D. Gunn The Fate Of King Saul JSOT Press 1984 37-38
12. P. Long ibid 90-91
13. W. Brueggemann ibid 100
14. Ibid 100-101
15. D. Edelman ibid 79-80
16. M. Evans ibid 50
17. D. Gunn Ibid 30
18. Ibid 128
19. Ibid 129

20. Ibid 115-116
21. W. Bruegemann ibid 102
22. B. Green ibid 48
23. Ibid 49-50
24. H. Hertzberg SCM Press 1964 127
25. Ibid 112
26. P. Long ibid 108
27. Ibid 110
28. H. Hertzberg ibid 112
29. P. Long ibid 111
30. T. Tsumura ibid 366
31. Ibid 369
32. T. Cartledge ibid 185
33. W. Brueggemann ibid 105
34. P. Long ibid 172
35. Ibid 129
36. D. Edelman ibid 96
37. P. Long ibid 129-130
38. T. Cartledge ibid 192
39. W. Brueggemann ibid 109-110
40. P. Long ibid 135-136
41. Ibid 136
42. T. Tsumura ibid 395-396
43. P. Long ibid 87
44. D. Vreeland ibid 162
45. J. Woodhouse ibid 264
46. Ibid 264
47. B. Green ibid 55
48. T. Tsumura ibid 396
49. D. Firth ibid 174
50. J. Woodhouse ibid 268
51. P. Borgman ibid 30
52. J. Woodhouse ibid 264
53. W. Brueggemann ibid 113
54. Ibid 108
55. D. Gunn ibid 47
56. Ibid 56
57. Ibid 55

58. Ibid 54
59. T. Tsumura ibid 405
60. D. Vreeland ibid 164
61. P. Borgman ibid 28-29
62. D. Jobling ibid 87

CHAPTER FOUR

1. S. Bar ibid 46
2. Ibid 47
3. Ibid 46
4. T. Tsumura ibid 412
5. Ibid 412
6. J. Woodhouse ibid 283
7. H. Hertzberg ibid 137
8. W. Brueggemann ibid 121
9. Ibid 123
10. R. Alter ibid 96
11. W. Brueggemann ibid 122
12. D. Firth ibid 185
13. B. Green ibid 62, 65
14. D. Firth ibid 186
15. Ibid 187
16. G. Vreeland ibid 183-184
17. D. Edelman ibid 117
18. D. Miller internet
19. T. Tsumura ibid 427
20. Ibid 428
21. D. Firth ibid 187
22. W. Brueggemann ibid 125
23. J. Woodhouse ibid 295
24. W. Brueggemann ibid 125
25. S. Bar ibid 93
26. T. Tusmura ibid 429
27. J. Woodhouse ibid 295
28. D. Edelman ibid 119
29. D. Firth ibid 188
30. T. Tsumura ibid 430
31. D. Edelman ibid 120

32. W. Brueggeman ibid 125
33. B. Green ibid 65
34. D. Gunn ibid 78-9
35. W. Brueggeman ibid 126
36. D. Edelman ibid 122
37. P. Borgman ibid 41
38. W. Brueggemann ibid 127
39. J. Woodhouse ibid 437
40. M. Evans ibid 109
41. T. Tsumura ibid 445
42. B. Green ibid 66
43. D. Firth ibid 196
44. H. Hertzberg ibid 150
45. W. Brueggemann ibid 129
46. J. Woodhouse ibid 320
47. W. Brueggemann ibid 129
48. H. Hertzberg ibid 151
49. B. Green ibid 67
50. W. Brueggemann ibid 130
51. Ibid 132
52. D. Firth ibid 200
53. R. Pinsky The Life Of David Schocken Books 2005 18
54. D. Gunn ibid 79
55. P. Borgman ibid 46
56. Ibid 47
57. S. Bar ibid 57
58. T. Cartledge ibid 228
59. J. Goldingay ibid 139
60. H. Hertzberg ibid 154
61. Ibid 155
62. T. Tsumura ibid 473
63. R. J. Fontaine, J. Wojcik ibid 99-100
64. Ibid 102
65. D. Firth ibid 208
66. T. Tsumura ibid 471
67. Ibid 471
68. D. Edelman ibid 137
69. T. Tsumura ibid 477

70. S. Bar ibid 55
71. P. Borgman ibid 62
72. W. Brueggeman ibid 137-138
73. H. Hertzberg ibid 158
74. S. Bar ibid 56
75. R. Pinksy ibid 27
76. T. Cartledge ibid 233
77. D. Firth ibid 216
78. R. Alter ibid 118
79. T. Cartledge ibid 235
80. W. Brueggemann ibid 125
81. Ibid 144
82. T. Tsumura ibid 495, 497
83. B. Green ibid 75
84. W. Brueggemann ibid 145
85. D. Edelman ibid 152

CHAPTER FIVE

1. T. Tsumura ibid 501
2. W. Brueggemann ibid 147
3. B. Green ibid 79
4. H. Hertzberg ibid 172
5. W. Brueggemann ibid 146
6. H. Hertzberg ibid 172
7. W. Brueggemann ibid 148
8. T. Tsumura ibid 508
9. Ibid 508
10. W. Brueggemann ibid 148
11. Ibid 149
12. T. Cartledge ibid 241
13. D. Edelman ibid 159
14. D. Firth ibid 227
15. Ibid 227
16. W. Brueggemannn ibid 151
17. Ibid 151
18. T. Tsumura ibid 519-520
19. W. Brueggemann ibid 153
20. Ibid 152

21. D. Firth ibid 229
22. Ibid 229
23. T. Tsumura ibid 529
24. W. Brueggemann 155
25. D. Firth ibid 241
26. B. Green ibid 84
27. T. Tsumura ibid 542
28. D. Firth ibid 243
29. W. Brueggemann ibid 158
30. T. Tusmura ibid 547
31. Ibid 549
32. T. Tsumura ibid 562
33. Ibid 562
34. H. Hertzberg ibid 200
35. W. Bureggemann ibid 175
36. H. Hertzberg ibid 197
36. D. Edelman ibid 197
37. Ibid 200, 202
38. Ibid 203
39. D. Firth ibid 267
40. W. Brueggemann ibid 176
41. D. Firth ibid 268
42. T. Tsumura ibid 593
43. W. Brueggemann ibid 182,186
44. D. Firth ibid 283
45. D. Edelman ibid 232
46. D. Firth ibid 284
47. W. Brueggemann ibid 190
48. D. Firth ibid 286
49. W. Brueggemann ibid 191
50. Ibid 195
51. Ibid 196
52. Ibid 196
53. M. Evans ibid 155-156
54. W. Brueggemann ibid 199
55. T. Tsumura ibid 638
56. W. Brueggemann ibid 203
57. Ibid 204

58. Ibid 207
59. D. Firth ibid 314
60. B. Green ibid 114
61. W. Brueggemann ibid 208-209
62. Ibid 209
63. H. Hertzberg ibid 234

CHAPTER SIX

1. D. Firth ibid 323
2. W. Brueggemann ibid 212-213
3. Ibid 214-216
4. W. Brueggemann ibid 239-240
5. Ibid 247-248
6. Ibid 249
7. D. Firth ibid 376
8. W. Brueggemann 249-250
9. Ibid 250
10. T. Cartledge ibid 439-440
11. Ibid 442
12. D. Firth ibid 378
13. Ibid 381
14. W. Brueggemann ibid 254
15. D. Firth ibid 384
16. C. Morrison ibid 97
17. D. Firth ibid 387
18. M. Evans ibid 195
19. W. Brueggemann ibid 256-258
20. Ibid 259
21. D. Firth ibid 385
22. W. Brueggemann Ibid 259
23. Ibid 254
24. D. Firth ibid 385
25. Ibid 390
26. W. Brueggemann ibid 260
27. G. Knoppers 1 Chronicles 10-20 Anchor 2004 771, 778
28. A. Hill 1 & 2 Chronicles Zondervan 2003 299
29. G. Knoppers 1 Chronicles ibid 783
30. A. Hill ibid 299

31. Ibid 300
32. Ibid 322
33. G. Knoppers ibid 785-787
34. Ibid 961
35. Ibid 940
36. A. Hill ibid 329
37. R. Klein 1 Chronicles Fortress Press 2006 539
38. M. Selman 1 Chronicles IVP 1994 259
39. W. Brueggemann ibid 272
40. Ibid 273
41. Ibid 272
42. Ibid 275
43. F. B. Meyer ibid 329
44. C. Maria Martini David Sinner & Believer St Paul 1997 44
45. A. W. Pink The Life of David Baker 1991 17-18
46. Ibid 22
47. C. Swindoll ibid 188
48. Ibid 97
49. W. Brueggemann ibid 271-272
50. A. Weiser Psalms John Knox 1962 284
51. W. Bruegemann ibid 280
52. C. Morrison ibid 152
53. M. Evans ibid 220-221
54. P. Borgman ibid 126
55. C. Morrison ibid 172
56. H. Hertzberg ibid 324
57. C Morrison ibid 166
58. Ibid 165-166
59. D. Firth ibid 446
60. P. Borgman ibid 130-131
61. W. Bruegemann ibid 304-305
62. Ibid 318
63. C. Morrison ibid 237
64. Ibid 241
65. W. Brueggemann ibid 323
66. C. Morrison Ibid 249
67. W. Brueggemann ibid 323-325
68. P. Leithart 1 & 2 Kings SCM Press 2016 2006

69. M. Cogan 1 Kings Doubleday 2001 164-165
70. W. Bruegemann 1 & 2 Kings Smyth & Helwys 2000 20
71. R. Nelson JKnox 1987 16
72. M. Cogan ibid 164
73. J. Olley 1 & 2 Kings IVP 2011 42
74. L. Wray Beal 1 & 2 Kings IVP 2014 68
75. W. Brueggemann ibid 15
76. Ibid 20
77. R. Nelson ibid 21-23
78. R. Nelson ibid 28
79. W. Brueggeman ibid 26-27
80. R. Nelson ibid 29

CHAPTER SEVEN

1. W. Brueggemann The Psalms & The Life Of Faith Fortress Press 1995 68
2. T. Clark In Towards A Theological & Practical Understanding of The Psalms Crossroad Online Journal Vol 2 2010 7 quotes T. Longman 111 How to Read The Psalms IVP 1988 13, 53
3. T. Clark ibid 7
4. P. C. Craigie Psalms 1-50 Word 1983 172
5. J. Goldingay Psalms Vol 1 Baker 2006 254-255
6. M. Wilcock Psalms 1-72 IVP 2001 61
7. P. C. Craigie ibid 173
8. Ibid 173
9. M. Wilcock ibid 61
10. J. Goldingay ibid 257
11. M. Wilcock ibid 62
12. A. Weiser OT Library 1962 190
13. Ibid 189
14. J. M. Boice Psalms 1-41 Baker 1994 161
15. A. Weiser ibid 202
16. J. M. Boice ibid 163
17. S. Terrien The Psalms Eerdmans 2003 213
18. Ibid 213
19. J. Magonet A Rabbi Reads The Psalms SCM 1998 64
20. A. Weiser ibid 219

21. J. Mays Preaching & Teaching The Psalms JKnox 2006 109-110, 114
22. J. L. Mays Psalms JKnox 2011 107
23. Ibid 105-106
24. J. Goldingay ibid 325-326
25. D. Tidball The Cross IVP 2003 86-87
26. Ibid 88
27. Ibid 89
28. A. Weiser ibid 224-225
29. R. M. Kidd With One Voice Baker 2005 75
30. T. Wilson The Messianic Psalms Loiseaux Brothers 1978 59-60
31. J. Goldingay Psalms Vol 1 ibid 324
32. J. Mays Preaching & Teaching The Psalms ibid 105-106
33. J. M. Boice Psalms Vol 1 ibid 193
34. F. D. Bruner Matthew 13-28 Eerdmans 1990 747
35. Ibid 745
36. J. Moltmann The Crucified God SCM 1974 203, 205-206
37. J. Mattison The Seven Words Of Christ Augsburg 1992
38. D. Coggan The Voice From The Cross Triangle 1993 36,
39. F. D. Bruner ibid 749
40. Ibid 749-750
41. J. Goldingay ibid 330
42. T. Wilson ibid 63-64
43. K. Schaefer Psalms Liturgical Press 2001 54
44. O. E. Phillips ibid 74
45. T. Wilson ibid 64
46. O. E. Phillips Exploring The Messianic Psalms Hebrew Jewish Christian Fellowship 1967 75
47. O. E. Phillips ibid 76
48. J. M. Boice ibid 196
49. J. Mays Psalms ibid 116-117
50. P. C. Craigie ibid 205-206
51. J. Mays Psalms ibid 119
52. M. Wilcock ibid 86
53. J. M. Boice ibid 211
54. A. Weiser ibid 231

55. M. Wilcock ibid 151-152
56. J. Mays Psalms ibid 174
57. P. C. Craigie ibid 326
58. J. Goldingay Psalms Vol 2 42-89 Baker 2007 27
59. Ibid 27
60. P. C. Craigie ibid 327
61. Ibid 328
62. J. Goldingay Psalms Vol 2 ibid 30-31
63. A. Weiser ibid 351
64. Ibid 352
65. J. Mays Psalms ibid 198
66. A. Weiser ibid 401
67. W. Brueggemann The Message Of The Psalms ibid 99
68. C. Broyles The Psalms Hendrickson 2000 226-227
69. J. Mays Psalms ibid 199
70. S. Mowinckel The Psalms In Israel's Worship Eerdmans 2004 13-14
71. J. Goldingay Psalms Vol 2 ibid 455-456
72. J. Mays Psalms ibid 147
73. J. Goldingay Psalms Vol 2 ibid 124
74. Ibid 140
75. A. Weiser ibid 402
76. J. Goldingay Psalms Vol 2 ibid 127
77. A. Weiser ibid 403
78. J. Goldingay Psalms Vol 2 ibid 130
79. W. Brueggemann The Message Of The Psalms ibid 100
80. J. Goldingay Psalms Vol 2 ibid 133
81. J. M. Boice Psalms 42-106 Baker 1996 432
82. J. Goldingay Psalms Vol 2 ibid 133
83. Ibid 133
84. J. M. Boice Psalms 42-106 ibid 434
85. W. Brueggemann The Message of The Psalms ibid 101
86. J. Goldingay Psalms Vol 2 ibid 136
87. A Weiser ibid 409
88. T. Wilson ibid 71-72
89. J. L. Mays Psalms ibid 232
90. J. Goldingay Psalms Vol 2 ibid 338
91. A. Weiser ibid 493

92. M. Wilcox ibid 241
93. J. Goldingay Psalms Vol 2 ibid 343
94. M. E. Tate Psalms 51-100 Word 1990 196
95. E. S. Gerstenberger Psalms Part 2 Eerdmans 2001 49-50
96. J. L. Mays Psalms ibid 232-233
97. M. Wilcox ibid 243
98. K. Schaefer Psalms ibid 166-167
99. J. M. Boice Psalms 42-106 ibid 578-580
100. K. Schaefer ibid 167
101. T. Wilson ibid 77-78
102. J. M. Boice Psalms 42-106 ibid 778
103. J. Goldingay Psalms Vol 3 ibid 94
104. M. Wilcock Psalms 73-150 IVP 2001 9

BIBLIOGRAPHY

R. Alter The David Story Norton & Co. 2000

S. Bar God's First King Cascade Books 2013

E. Bock King & Prophets – Saul, etc Floris Books 2006

J. M. Boice Psalms 1-41 Montgomery 2005

J. M. Boice Psalms 42-106 Baker 1996

P. Borgman David, Saul & God Oxford U. Press 2008

C. Broyles The Psalms Hendrickson 2000

W. Brueggemann 1 & 2 Kings Smyth & Helwys 2000

W. Brueggemann The Psalms & The Life Of Faith Fortress Press 1995

W. Brueggemann The Message Of The Psalms Augsburg 1985

W. Brueggemann 1 & 2 Samuel John Knox 1988

F. D. Bruner Matthew 13-28 Eerdmans 1990

T. Cartledge 1 & 2 Samuel Smyth & Helwys 2001

T. Clark In Towards A Theological & Practical Understanding Of The Psalms Crossroad Online Journal Vol 2 2010 quotes T. Longman 111 How To Read The Psalms IVP 1988

M. Cogan 1 Kings Doubleday 2001

D. Coggan The Voice From The Cross Triangle 1993

P. C. Craigie The Psalms 1-50 Word 2010

D. Edelman King Saul in the Historiography of Judah in the Library of Hebrew Bible/Old Testament Studies 2009

M. Evans Samuel IVP 2004

D. Firth 1 & 2 Samuel IVP 2009

R. J. Fontaine, J. Wojcik The David Myth Purdue Uni. 1980

E. S. Gerstenberger Psalms Part 2 Eerdmans 2001

J. Godingay Men Behaving Badly Paternoster 2001

J. Goldingay Psalms Vol 1 1-41 Baker 2006

J. Goldingay Psalms Vol 2 42-89 Baker 2007

B. Green King Saul's Asking Liturgical Press 2003

D. Gunn The Fate Of King Saul JSOT Press 1984

H. Hertzberg SCM Press 1964

A. Hill 1 & 2 Chronicles Zondervan 2003

D. Jobling 1 Samuel Liturgical Press 1988

R. M. Kidd With One Voice Baker 2005

R. Klein 1 Chronicles Fortress Pres 2006

G. Knoppers 1 Chronicles 10-20 Anchor 2004

P. Leithart 1 & 2 Kings SCM Press 2016

P. Long The Reign & Rejection Of King Saul S. Press 1989

J. Magonet A Rabbi Reads The Psalms SCM 1998

Manners, Customs Of Bible Lands Internet

C. Maria Martini David Sinner & Believer St Paul 1997

J. Mattison The Seven Words Of Christ Augsburg 1992

J. Mays Preaching & Teaching The Psalms JKnox 2006

J. Mays Psalms JKnox 2011

F. B. Meyer Great Men In The Bible M. & Pickering 1990

D. Miller Internet

J. Moltmann The Crucified God SCM 1974

C. Morrison 2 Samuel Liturgical Press 2013

S. Mowinckel The Psalms In Israel's Worship Eerdmans 2004

R. Nelson 1 & 2 Kings JKnox 1987

D. New David Internet

J. Olley 1 & 2 Kings IVP 2011

O. E. Phillips Exploring The Messianic Psalms Hebrew Jewish Christian Fellowship 1967

A. W. Pink The Life of David Baker 1991

R. Pinsky The Life Of David Schocken Books 2005

K. Schaefer Psalms Liturgical Press 2001

M. Selman 1 Chronicles IVP 1994

C. Swindoll David A Man of Passion & Destiny Word 1997

M. E. Tate Psalms 51-100 Word 1990

S. Terrien The Psalms Eerdmans 2002

D. Tidball The Cross IVP 2003

T. Tsumura 1 Samuel Eerdmans 2007

G. Vreeland The Darker Side Of Samuel, Saul & David
Vol 1–2 Xulon Press 2007

B. Webb Judges Eerdmans 2012

A. Weiser The Psalms OT Library 1962

M. Wilcock Psalms 1-71 IVP 2001

M. Wilcock Psalms 73-150 IVP 2001

T. Wilson The Messianic Psalms Loiseaux Brothers 1978

J. Woodhouse 1 Samuel Crossway 2008

L. Wray Beal 1 & 2 Kings IVP 2014